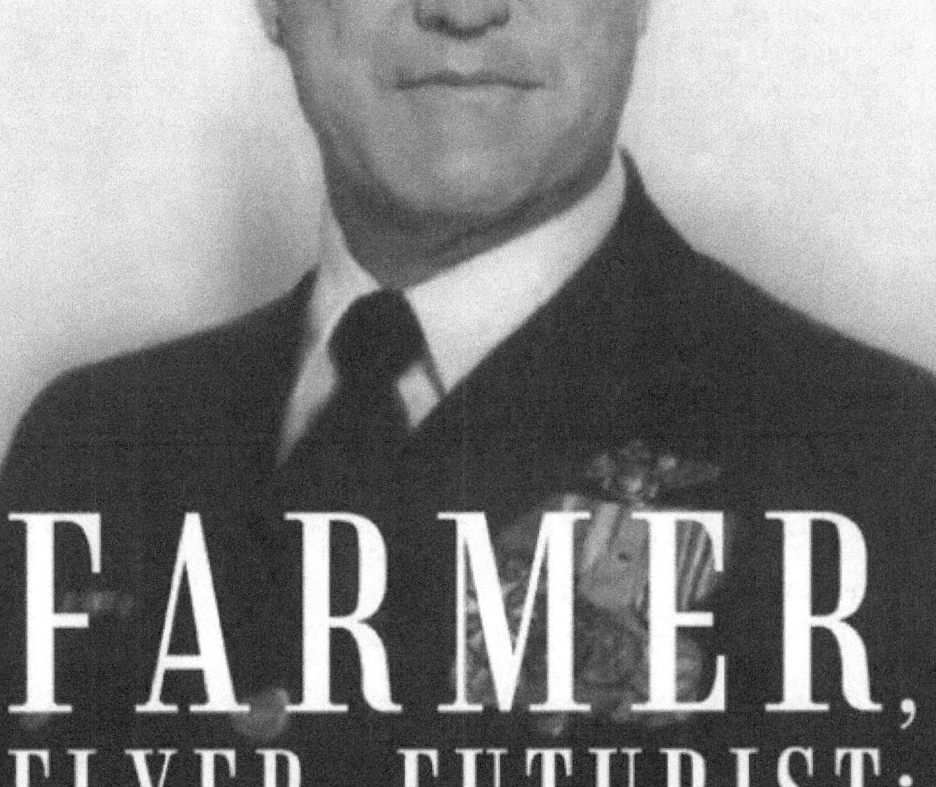

FARMER,
FLYER, FUTURIST:

The Memoirs of Admiral Owen Wesley Siler,
Commandant of the United States Coast Guard

OWEN WESLEY SILER
EDITED BY MARSHA SILER ANTISTA

WORKBOOK PRESS LLC
187 E Warm Springs Rd,
Suite B285, Las Vegas, NV 89119, USA

Website:	https://workbookpress.com/
Hotline:	1-888-818-4856
Email:	admin@workbookpress.com

Ordering Information:
Quantity sales. Special discounts are available on quantity purchases by corporations, associations, and others.
For details, contact the publisher at the address above.

Library of Congress Control Number:
ISBN-13:   978-1-957618-84-5 (Paperback Version)
             978-1-957618-85-2 (Digital Version)

REV. DATE: 01/03/2022

PREFACE

For two years, my father, Owen Wesley Siler, sat in his studio office above his garage in Savannah, Georgia, typing his memories on his word processor (before the days of computers).

I have taken the liberty of transcribing his memories into this manuscript. The vast majority of the text is from his original manuscript with minor edits from me.

Dad was a wonderful father and truly dedicated to the United States Coast Guard. He could be intimidating when he was angry (all of 6'4") but in general, he was thoughtful, kind, and insightful. He and my mother, Bette Lilian Walford Siler, were dedicated to the Coast Guard and were partners in their journey through life.

Owen Siler was called Wes by family members and Si by United States Coast Guard (USC) academy friends. Dad was never a farmer; his father, Walter Orlando Siler, had groves of fruit trees, livestock, and other ways to supplement his income for his family. Dad did help with many of these activities, thus, the farmer verbiage. Dad was a flyer and was able to see ways for the Coast Guard to lead the way for women and others to advance within the United States military services.

ACKNOWLEDGEMENTS

My thanks to Scott Price, USCG Chief Historia, for his assistance in gathering information for this book and thanks to Marlane Castellanos and Nessie Pruden Siler for their editing and feedback during the preparation of this manuscript.

Marsha Siler Antista

Tallahassee, Florida

May, 2019

Introduction by Owen W. Siler

I have no idea who will read this, if anyone. I would like my children to know a little more about my life, just because I think it may be interesting. It was to me. It has been a good life, and it is not something I particularly expected of myself or the environment in which I grew up. If this is boring, quit reading or throw it in the trash.

A New Direction to Life

The call came in the morning, I believe it was a Sunday, after my wife Bette and I had returned from a brief trip to Florida for a short vacation to visit our daughter Marsha, who was attending the University of Florida in Gainesville, to rest and relax at the beach. I was the Coast Guard district commander of the rivers district of the Coast Guard, the Second District, headquartered in St. Louis, Missouri.

I knew that the time had come, or was close, when a new Commandant of the Coast Guard was to be selected, but I had no concerns about it, because I was seven years junior to the officer who is in the position. It sounds like eight because my Academy class was 1944 while the Commandant's class of 1936, but our class was commissioned early due to the World War II shortening of the courses at the Academy.

I was actually commissioned in June 1943. Chet Bender, the Admiral in command of the Coast Guard, was on the phone, and told me he wanted me to come to Washington to be interviewed by the Secretary of Transportation regarding my being Chet's replacement.

I hung up the phone a little in shock. I told Betty what the subject was, and her response was "I'm not sure I want you to do that." Her meaning … to take the position, not just go to Washington. I thought about the others who might be in the running at the time, and replied, "I don't think that there is a chance that I would be selected. There are some very good officers who are available and I think I might be the most junior of any group asked to see Mr. Brinegar (the Secretary of Transportation). I really think that if it means anything, it might be that I would be considered sooner for one of the Area commands." Those two commands were in New York, which I knew little about, or in San Francisco, which I knew more about, having served in four of the districts that made up the area. That thought convinced Bette that at least I should go for the interview. The idea of living in the lovely quarters at Yerba Buena Island in the middle span of the San Francisco Bridge was too much to hold us back.

A few days later, I was on a plane headed for Washington. I planned to spend the evening with our son, Gregory and his then wife Holly, in one of the suburbs, and go to Coast Guard Headquarters the following morning. When I arrived in Washington, however, my bag did not. I made it a practice always to travel in uniform, and I had worn an older uniform and packed my newest and best looking suit of blues. Now I did not have that sharp uniform—only a wrinkled, sat out suit.

The evening was not as pleasant as it might have while I wondered whether or when my suitcase might catch up with me. I pressed some of the wrinkles out of my uniform, but it wasn't the one I had wanted to wear. I went to bed but didn't sleep until 2 A.M. when the bag was delivered by Eastern Airlines.

On my arrival at Coast Guard Headquarters, in the fresh uniform, where I knew the building well, having supervised the move into that location only a couple of years ago, I would visit with Chet Bender, the Vice Commandant, my good friend and former immediate supervisor, Tom Sargent, before going to see the Secretary of Transportation. They suggested some of the questions that either Mr. Brinegar or the Deputy Secretary, John Barnum might ask, but few were of much help when I actually met with first with Mr. Barnum and Secretary Brinegar later in the day.

Some of the things they did ask, and some they did not, rather surprised me. I really wasn't prepared to think as the commandant at that point. I remember well the question, "What characteristics would you be looking for in a vice commandant?" My answer was "The same as you would look for in a commandant. The two must work as a team and the vice commandant must be the alter ego of the commandant. He must be able to fill in, in cases of illness, or any such problems. He must be able to work with the commandant and, therefore, should be very close personally to the commandant."

I believe they asked if I had any individual in mind, but again, I hadn't progressed that far in my thinking. I could only give abstract thoughts. They did not ask if I had any new programs that I wanted the Coast Guard to undertake, and if they had, I would not have suggested any completely new departures. I did state that I believe that a new commandant must carry on the level-headed approaches that were the style of the Coast Guard in the past.

I returned to St. Louis, not knowing any more about my future that I had before. I knew that my assignment to the Second District must be drawing to a close. I've been there for three years, and at least one of the captains who worked with me told me years later that he had thought that if I spent that long in the district, I must be at the end of my road in the Service. I still had duties to perform, however, and the next week I was ordered back to Washington to serve on a board to select captains for rear admiral. This was expected to last for a full week, and since we had both friends and family in the Washington area, I took Bette with me, and we stayed in Army quarters in Fort Myers.

It was either Tuesday or Wednesday of our deliberations, when a messenger came to the boardroom with a message for Ed Perry, who was commander of the USCG Eighth District, just down the river, for the lower part of the Mississippi and most of the Gulf of Mexico. He had been chief of staff when I departed Headquarters three years earlier. I had been his deputy when I was detached. The message was that the Secretary wanted to see him; I believe it was in the mid-afternoon. I felt certain that Ed had been one of the rear admirals who had been ordered in to be interviewed, and assumed that this notification was that he was to be the new commandant. I had mixed emotions, I felt that the pressure was off, that I would not make Bette have those questionable feelings, and I knew Ed had all the right qualities. Naturally, when I had been called in, I had hoped that I would be promoted but if it wasn't to be, so be it.

Then, an hour or so later, a messenger came to tell me that the Secretary wanted to see me at 5 P.M. We would have quit our deliberations by that time, so it created no problem, but I had to let Bette, over at Fort Myer, know that I wouldn't be coming back when we stopped our work for the day. So I called her and she told me that we were going to get together with Lieut. Gen. and Mrs. Fred Kornett, Chief of Ordnance for the Army, after I returned, but it would be in our quarters. I had known that the Kornetts when he was Chief of Aviation Systems for the Army, with his offices just a couple of blocks from mine. The Army provided me a lot of transportation in small army planes over the huge area of the Second Coast Guard District.

After we closed for the day, I went to the Commandant's office and told Chet that I was to go up at five, but almost immediately, a message came to that office from the Secretary that he would not be able to see me until six. I called Bette again, and twiddled my thumbs for an additional hour. At six, I went to the eighth floor, and was told that I was to be the commandant. I then told them, that I thought about it more, and the person who should be vice commandant was Ed Perry. He'd been two years ahead of me at the Academy, and I had known him and his wife since those days. He had an excellent reputation for being an officer who made the right decisions, and I couldn't think of anyone with whom I could work any better. The Secretary and the Deputy agreed with my selection, and I went on to my business with the board for the next few days.

I obviously told Bette of my selection, we told our children, but the official announcement would not come until the White House announced that the President Nixon had sent to the Senate Commerce Committee for confirmation of the nomination of Rear Admiral Owen W. Siler to be Commandant. You just never knew how long the White House would take! There were two other persons who knew about the nomination that same night. We couldn't keep our lips buttoned completely with the Kornetts that night. Soon an Army general and his wife knew I was the nominee before I told anyone else in the

Coast Guard.

The next day I sought a quiet place and time to tell Ed Perry that I'd been told that I would be the new commandant and that I would like him to be my vice commandant. He replied that if this action was suggested was being directed by the Secretary, he wanted nothing to do with it. I replied, "No, you're my choice." He immediately agreed to be the vice commandant. This is noteworthy, because, as I stated before, he was two years ahead of me at the Academy.

When I made my first cruise as a cadet, I served as the cadet officer of the deck and the watch in port. I was doing the work of a seaman of the watch. I'd not worked directly with him as an officer, until he was a rear admiral. He became the chief of staff shortly before I put on my stripes as a rear admiral and left Headquarters. I was his deputy at that time. It was probably harder for his wife to accept the fact that Ed was to be junior to me. In fact, several years later, she admitted it to Bette. However, it was an unusual situation for the Coast Guard. I had jumped over something like 23 senior officers to move into the position and certainly some of them resented it.

Ed and I conferred next on where we would locate some of the other flag officers of the Coast Guard, and who should serve as the two vice admirals in the Areas. We had no problem with our decision, V. F. Rea in New York and J.J. McClelland in San Francisco. Our reasoning was that Bill had a great deal of Merchant Marine supervision and was proficient in relationships and New York was the location of the American Bureau of Shipping, and the corporate offices of several lines. Joe, on the other hand, although he had been Chief of Operations in New

York, was from Seattle, had served in several vessels on the West Coast, and seemed ideally suited for San Francisco. As Chief of Staff, we chose Ed Scheiderer, a very well-qualified admiral, who would have served very well anywhere, in all probability, but his forte was definitely administration.

A few weeks later, the announcement was made by the White House, and the pressure of saying to my friends and fellow workers in St. Louis that I didn't know who would be the next Commandant and that I had no idea what my next assignment would be, was over. I was ordered to Washington for a series of briefings on where the developments have proceeded in the years I had been out of Headquarters, and given some highly classified information on some activities that impacted on the Coast Guard.

This coincided with my appearance before the Senate Commerce Committee to have my confirmation hearing, along with the other promotions involved in this change of command of the Service. They were no difficult hearings, especially since Sen. Warren Magnuson of Washington was the chairman of the committee at that time, and he had noted that I was born in Seattle. He always liked to greet me with, "It's a pleasure to welcome my fellow Washingtonian to this hearing," and I never mentioned the fact I left for California at the age of six months.

Those couple of weeks in January, 1974 brought to me and Bette probably the biggest changes in our lives, and in the direction of our thinking, that could have been made. Neither of us had had that position is a definite goal in life. We were ambitious, and tried to do the right thing as it occurred to us, but this was an unthinkable, until now. We had to think it through again. Bette put it into words, as she said, "It would be work, but we will have fun, together."

MY EARLY LIFE

I was born in a snowy day in January, 1922, in Seattle, Washington, my parents told me. They took a photograph of the house at 3237 Thirtieth-Fifth Avenue South, and my mother could recite that address anytime we asked her to until the time of her death. She gave it in a singsong effect, and I was always amused at how she said it. I was born at home, so now I have the address on my birth certificate. I guess Mother didn't like hospitals, or they were just too expensive when the doctors would make home deliveries, because I know that my sister was born at home, and I would guess my brothers were as well.

I was the second child born in our family. Walter Orlando, Junior had been born in Atascadero, California nearly two years earlier. My father had been in the accounting department for Atascadero Colony, when he observed the illegal processes being utilized to sell the land of the Colony, and he left to go to Seattle to teach in a business college. The head of the company promoting the Atascadero Colony later served time in prison for using the mails to defraud.

As I stated earlier, we left Seattle when I was approximately six months old, to seek the warmer climes of California again. This time it was another business college in Los Angeles, but on the way south, my parents stopped in Santa Maria, California, where my father applied for a position in the business department of the local high school. We moved north from Los Angeles to

Santa Maria in time for the next school year. I guess that was September 1922.

The first place we lived was on South Broadway, only a few doors from the high school. I'd forgotten that we lived there, until I returned to Santa Maria with Bette, to spend a little time with members of my high school class and make a mini-reunion in the summer of 1992. At that time, Katherine Preisker reminded me that we had once been neighbors, since she had lived in a mansion a few houses further south. (Her father was chairman of the County Board of Supervisors as long as I could remember.)

The first house I had any memory of was on South Pine Street. We were only a short distance from the Santa Maria Valley Railroad, and I remember Mother putting straight pins on the tracks, in order that they would be rolled into tiny knives or two could make scissors by the weight of a passing locomotive.

We lived there when a hernia that I had had for some time needed to be repaired. It been giving me trouble for some time. My parents had taken their two little boys to Missouri to visit in my father's old home at Weston, Missouri, perhaps on the way to Santa Maria from Los Angeles. Mother told me that the hernia had started to strangulate, and I must been screaming up a fit. We took the train to head for either St. Joseph or Kansas City, the nearest place with a fully equipped hospital, I don't know which. The herniated area eased, I stopped screaming and went to sleep, and we returned to Weston without the operation then.

I remember the people who knew who they were brought me gifts to keep me happy while I was in the hospital. I particularly remember a balloon in the shape of a rooster, which had a squeaker valve in the stem, and was supposed to sound like a chicken. When I came home from the hospital, it was in the backseat of the 1922 Dodge sedan we had at the time. The stretcher boards were used to carry me to the car and into the house were boards, I presume nailed together. I was only three when this took place. My younger brother was born while we lived here.

My father had been raised in his younger years on a large farm in Missouri, and he was convinced that the discipline of caring for the farm animals, and working the soil were beneficial to young people. To move in this direction, my parents rented two country homes, both with sufficient space to have orchards, and to raise some chickens and other farm animals.

First we rented a place very near where the Santa Maria Golf and Country Club was in later years. Then we moved about a mile closer to town, I don't know quite why. We remained in the latter home for several years. My older brother, Walt, was always known as ("Junior") in those days, and I and perhaps some neighborhood boys used to roll up our blue jeans, to the approximate length of football pants, and play football in among the trees in the orchard. When we were sweating from our exertions, and rolling in the cultivated soil between trees, we became walking dirt piles!

At one time here, the septic tank failed, and a new cesspool had to be excavated, near the house. The removed earth became a play area where my brothers and I dug roads, built mud houses, and spent hours developing the real estate in miniature. This activity led my parents to look for toy autos, trucks, and road equipment for gift material over many years. I had a cast iron cement mixer that was around the house, although it was a different house, even when I went off to the Coast Guard Academy years later.

The property here had an undeveloped area just to the north, along the highway. It was ideal for young boys to play Indian games. There were sand dunes covered with white wild bush lupin, and other brush which made great areas to pretend the Indians or "bad men" were hiding. Off to the east there was a field which was cultivated by a neighbor, Mr. Dale Porto. It had oats and beans in it during a part of the year. At other times it was just a big open space. The main highway running north and south along the California coast, Highway 101, was our front street.

To the south there was a more undeveloped area, then a shotgun range where the sharpshooters from the town practiced skeet, and then an "auto court" in a grove of eucalyptus trees. It was a good place for our family to grow up. We had a cow for a good part of the time we lived here, and either my brother or my mother would milk the cow. I would bring the cow in from the place where we had staked her to graze, however, and this led to an interesting incident.

The cow had been staked out early in the morning, before my father and we boys had to go to school. She had been there all day, enjoying the lush green grass at the edge of the field which was cultivated. I was sent out to bring the cow in to be milked, and went out, a distance of probably 1/8 to a quarter of a mile. When I arrived there, the cow was at the far end of the circle of grass available to her, and still was pulling up grass. I pulled up the steel rod holding her, and tugged on the chain. This brought no response at the other end.

I then flipped the chain, to give it a "standing wave." The wave reached Bossie's head, and she bobbed her head as she had to turn to look at me. Then she started running toward me, and I turned to run away as fast as I could toward home with the cow approaching rapidly. I shouted at the top of my lungs, "Mother! Mother!" since she was standing at the fence which bordered our property, and I hoped she would have some inspiration about what to do about a cow chasing her son. I dropped to a dispirited walk, however, when Bossie passed me still at a good speed, and headed for her enclosed pen, where she could have her first drink of water for the day! I always wished that someone had timed me for a short dash, say 50 yards or 100 yards. I believe I must set some kind of record for that distance.

My father always wanted to own his own property, and therefore he bought land near where we had lived and built a house in approximately 1932. Prices were right at this time, and labor was cheap. He bought eight acres along the same highway, but two acres farther south. Then he planted an orchard, berries, grapes, and contracted for construction of a house big enough for the family of six, with a few things that my parents thought of as luxuries at the time. The house had a basement under part of the house, and unheard of item in most houses in that part of California.

We had a fireplace as the only installed heating. It was all stucco on the exterior, and plaster wall throughout the inside. We had two bathrooms which was progress in those days. The garage was a separate structure, and it had plenty of space for storage of poultry and cow feed. My father acted as the contractor of the construction, and did some of the work on the house himself.

The only bad thing about this move was that my parents had considered buying the house we had previously lived in, instead of striking out in a new area, and then decided a new place was better. At the time we moved, oil was discovered on the property that we had previously lived on, and our neighbor, Mr. Dale Porto, the Italian farmer, was a rich man.

His daughters, who had once been not too popular, were now in great demand for dates because they would provide their own wheels, big Buicks or convertibles. Another neighbor, not too far away, who was the art teacher in the high school, had enough oil income that the family moved after few years to Santa Fe, New Mexico, to spend the rest of their days and just enjoying painting, and the good life. Our new location was put under an oil lease, but the field apparently didn't reach that far. We never received any income other than his few dollars for the lease.

I attended Orcutt Union Elementary School from the second grade to graduation, and my brothers and sister, five years younger, did also. I took part in some school plays, tried to perform in athletic events, not very well and did better academically. When I graduated from the eighth grade in 1934, Frank Wyckoff, who was at the time a school principal somewhere to the south, but had been a 100 yard dash man in three Olympics, was a speaker. I don't remember his message; it was enough to know that this man had been successful in his athletic career.

I, perhaps, had an easier time moving from elementary school to high school than some young people, because my father had an office where I could keep my things, and I could refer questions to his authority during the lunch period. Freshman year progressed without complications, except I was absent for nine days when I have mumps. I made the California Scholarship Federation both semesters, as I did all but one semester thereafter.

At the beginning the sophomore year, the class was told that we should elect a class president, and other officers. I was nominated for president, and the nominees were told to leave the gym, where we were assembled, in order for there to be voting. As we returned after the voting by raised hands, a group of boys started cheering, "Yeah Siler." I broke into a big smile, until the class advisor rushed over to tell us who had won the election, it wasn't me.

My older brother had become quite a swimmer at about this time. He was the third fastest ever (at that time) to swim the 100 yards in our city pool. I went out for swimming, thinking that I, too, could become a good swimmer. Unfortunately, I developed nasal problems with the constant exposure to the chlorinated water; just about that time, I discovered I wasn't too bad it at the backstroke. So I gave up swimming as my sport and spent quite a little time seeing doctors to stop the constant nosebleeds from the irritation. The following year, I went out for track, and tried to run the 880, and the high hurdles. I was on the traveling squad, but didn't ever place. In my senior year, I did place in a few meets, but not the big ones.

During my junior year, I discovered girls. I "hung around"

at lunch time at school with a group of young people who are thoroughly and completely nice kids. It was natural that we would pair up, when we would go to some activities, and I "went" with Marie Myers for several months. I eventually went to her senior prom with her at her invitation. I think she asked me to hurt the boy who she had turned to months before. I dated quite a few different girls at this period, but it was difficult for some time, because I was so young. I couldn't have a license to drive a car until I was 16, and I had my 16th birthday in January of my senior year. I had to look for someone else to drive us, and I lived four miles out in the country.

During the first semester of my senior year, there was an effort to revise the constitution that the student body was using, and then a series of meetings to ratify the constitution. The candidates who were running for president were used as presidents pro tem during these meetings. John Spears, a cheerleader in football season, and a good swimmer and diver on the swim team, was my main opposition at the time, but he was not well qualified as a presiding officer.

Besides that, I had quite a few posters around the corridors, made and posted by my campaign manager, Mitsui Mitani, who had already graduated from high school in Japan but was completing high school here. (I never knew what happened to him after World War II.) I won that without difficulty, and the last semester, I attended the Rotary Club of Santa Maria, as a junior member. We didn't have a lot of business that had to be taken care of by the student officers, but it was a way to find and use leaders.

During this time, I had become active in High-Y, a high

school activity associated with the YMCA, and was president of the club in my senior year. I had taken part in a series of plays, including <u>HMS</u> <u>Pinafore</u>, where I was Admiral Porter, KCB, the ruler of the King's Navee. I was also in the senior play, which was <u>The Nut Farm,</u> which was a farce. I was in the Boys' Glee Club and on Sundays, sang in the Methodist church choir, as one of the two basses, the other one being twice as big around as I. He looked as if he should be a bass.

My father always had a pickup truck for use around our eight acres of land. I learned to drive, first on the Model T that we had for many years, and then on the GMC that replaced it. After a few years of driving experience, I would take the truck, with a load of friends and classmates to the beach in the summertime. Even though California is warm, it would be quite cool, when the vehicle was moving along the highway, and the only way to keep warm was to be near someone in the back of the pickup. We went to Pismo Beach, Oceano, Avila, and Casmalia. There were usually one or more vehicles but the back of the truck was always popular.

I decided during my senior year that I wanted to go to Annapolis or the Coast Guard Academy, after I discovered it, or as a much lower priority California Maritime Academy. I decided that the Coast Guard was for me, after examining the missions, and was going to try for that, but I was too young, until I waited another year. You had to be 17 as of April 1 of the year you wanted to enter. I went to junior college at home, to wait the year, and to take classes that I believed could help me. I took analytical geometry and calculus, more English, and more Spanish. Then in June I would take the exam.

My father had never wanted us boys to play football, even though he had as a youth. I went out in junior college, without asking my parents, and was in the game before my father realized it. He always sold the tickets to those games, so he saw the second half of the games, and the PA system announced that I was being sent into the game. He couldn't miss the fact that I was playing, and I rode home after the game with him. There were some long silences on that ride.

We won that game, but I injured my wrist and never had it treated, because I didn't want to admit I'd been hurt doing something he didn't want me to do. I earned my letter that year, playing in most of our games as a tackle, and then in the spring, I improved enough in track that I was lettered there as well. I was president of my freshman class in junior college, and president of the College-Y.

When it came time to take the exam for the Coast Guard Academy, there were four parts to consider. We had the first morning on mathematics. There were usually 10 questions and there were some options which had to be answered to make the 10. The afternoon was spent on English, and the next day was an aptitude exam, and a personal interview. I went to Los Angeles to take the exam, and spent the day before the exam at the library of the University of Southern California, where Walt was a junior.

I knew no one, so I had no distractions as I went through the math books again. I began to realize that I have forgotten much of the material that I had wished I had been on top of. Walt helped me in the evening before the exam, but the time was short. The result of the exam reached me in the latter part of July, when I was employed at the county fair as a go-fer for the manager of the fair. I had failed, a 54 in math, so they didn't correct my English. I received a C on my interview, and I remembered it well. I was interviewed by a senior officer; I believe he was the most senior officer in the Los Angeles section of the San Francisco District at the time. He looked up at me over his pinch-nez glasses and asked, "What makes you think you want to be a Coast Guard officer?" I wasn't sure at that moment that I did. It must've come through to him that way too.

I went back to junior college rethinking what I wanted to do with my life. I thought I would be interested in foreign trade, and both the University of California and UCLA had such majors. I knew that I could transfer to those schools as a junior if I had enough credits from my school, and had the right subjects. I needed economics, Spanish or some foreign language, to show that I could handle the work and I shifted from the math I had been working on, to Mathematical Theory or Finance. I took some accounting (from my father), but only the second semester, when I tried to do an entire year's work. I nearly did it too.

I played football again in the second year, and I believe that I played in every game, in a variety of positions. In those days, you played both offense and defense, and so usually the center on offense played linebacker on defense. I rather like that position. I competed in track, and still have a ribbon from the Cal Poly Royal Relays, where I took a place in the high hurdles. I was business manager of the junior college student body, and I took part several plays. At one time we went to the Pasadena Playhouse to compete in a one-act play competition. We didn't place. Even with these activities, I remained a member of Alpha Gamma Sigma, the honor scholarship organization.

In the spring of that year, a Coast Guard officer, Lieutenant D.T. Adams, came to our school, where both the high school and junior college were on the same campus. He explained to the counselors that he was looking for people who might qualify and were interested in attending the Coast Guard Academy. The counselors, sent for me, and I spent quite some time with lieutenant. He was impressed by the fact that I have been an honor student all the way through high school, was still keeping that record, had been student body president, and especially that I played two years of college football. At that time the Academy had lost every game in the previous session of football. He put me in touch with a math instructor at the Academy, and he, Lieutenant Commander W.R. Richards, coached me by mail. The principles were those that I'd known before, but cannot recall when I took the exam last June.

I took the entrance exam again in June, not holding any great hopes this time. But I had some organized notes to review this time, and it served me well. I left the math exam, sure that I had had nine of the 10 questions thoroughly correct, and perhaps some credit for the 10th. The English exam called for, among other things, a 500 word essay on what Shakespearean character you liked best and why? One of the plays I had been in the past year was Twelfth Night, and I even know some of the lines still. I chose Sir Toby Belch, not my role but one I had often been on stage with, and I must've done well. When it came to the personal interview, this time I was interviewed by an ensign, who was in uniform, who stood as I approached, and introduced himself, "I'm Ensign Shoemaker," with a big grin. I passed the exam this time with 90 in math, 89 in English, and a good grade in adaptability. I ranked as 12th in the country, and entered the Academy in July as number eight in the class.

My efforts to become a Coast Guard cadet were not over yet, however. I had to take the physical exam, again in Los Angeles, when told to report. Since the past year I had not been notified of the results until July, a classmate of mine and I decided that we would take a vacation in Mexico. I'd studied many parts of Mexico in my Spanish classes, and he wanted to visit his old home in Colorado, so we tried to put together some plans. My father then decided he would like to visit his relatives in Missouri, so we put the plans all together, and we drove off, shortly after the end of the school year, in June. We camped in campgrounds, in parks, or simply by the side of the road at times. We sent spent one night beside the lake at Lake Mead, saw the Painted Desert, camped out at Tamazunchale on the way to Mexico City, and took a cabin in the city.

We did a great deal of sightseeing, and exhausted poor Dad. The last day in the vicinity of Mexico City, Ira, my friend and I went to go to Xochimilco for the day, a bullfight later, and then to the Sanborn's, the American restaurant for dinner. Unfortunately, I lost my dinner in the gutter just as soon as I left the café. We headed back the next day, and every time we stopped for "Gasolmex," the Mexican gasoline, I searched for the bathroom-- I had the "touristas."

When we arrived in San Antonio, Texas, we had arranged to pick up mail. My mother had a letter there waiting to let me know that I had been given a tentative appointment to the Academy, and was supposed to report to the Public Health

Offices in the Los Angeles Federal Building that day. She had arranged for a one-week delay, but I needed to get to Los Angeles. Today they would've had me report to a Texas military base, and it would've been simple. My father was convinced that it would be easier to go from Dallas, where we were headed next anyway, then to try to cross the country from San Antonio so we headed on. When we arrived there, he found that the train had a 12-hour layover in El Paso and did not make much better time than the Greyhound bus, and the trains were much more expensive. So, I boarded the Greyhound the next morning.

From Dallas to Los Angeles, every time the bus driver announced a five-minute rest stop, I led the procession to the restrooms. Often it was a useless trip but the urge pressed me on. When I arrived in Los Angeles, I was generally recovered, but I hadn't had much of an appetite for anything. I spent the night with Walt, my brother, who was lifeguarding for the county at the time, and was renting a small apartment for the summer. In the morning, he gave me instructions about which buses to take, where I should transfer, and sent me on my way. I took the first bus with no trouble but at the transfer point, I waited and waited, and grew impatient. I could see the Federal Building, so I walked up the slight incline to the building, about four to six blocks away. I expected that I would have a considerable wait before my exam, so I didn't think about arriving fresh and ready for anything.

When I walked into the Public Health Office, I told them, "I'm Owen Siler and I'm here for the Coast Guard Academy physical." The doctor replied, "Oh yes, we've been expecting you. Come over here and strip to the waist." He quickly took my pulse and said "What have you been doing lately?" I told him I had returned from Mexico, ridden the bus from Dallas, and walked from the transfer point for the bus. He said, "Lie down here for a couple minutes." After that, my pulse, blood pressure and all of their tests were normal, and I received my formal appointment a few days later with a reporting date at the Academy of July 17, 1940.

The Academy

To arrive at the Coast Guard Academy in New London, Connecticut on July 17, 1940, took some planning. I was in a small town in California, with the choice of bus or train to travel across the country. My parents did inquiries for me, and we purchased tickets for the Union Pacific Challenger, a low-fare train from San Francisco/Oakland. First, of course, I had to get to San Francisco, and this required traveling on the Southern Pacific Railroad from either the whistle stop in Guadalupe, or driving to San Luis Obispo, 30 miles north.

Then, you took a ferry from the San Francisco ferry building to the actual train departure in Oakland, then the train spent about three days to arrive in Chicago. There you changed stations, and took the Pennsylvania Railroad, or the New York Central to New York. We chose the Pennsylvania, but there was a train station change again in New York to take New York New Haven and Hartford to New London.

Since I had to change stations, at least, in both San Francisco and New York, and in this year of 1940, there were the Golden Gate International Exposition and the New York World's Fair. I didn't go directly from station to station in either the cities. I spent only one day at each of the two big shows, but I did at least get the flavor. I had been to the San Francisco Exhibition in the previous year, so I didn't feel I was missing anything, even what if it was a hurried visit.

I arrived in New London on the evening of July 16, and spent that first night at the Mohican Hotel. The next morning, bright and early, I took a cab to the Academy and reported in.

There were a great many details to be taken care of. We were issued equipment, clothing, books, paid our required deposit to cover these initial costs, assigned a room and a roommate, and much of the activities became a blur. My new roommate, Ralph Peterson, and I studied the cadet regulations which were on the study table, in a designated spot, and saw that it was covered, among many other items, how to make your bed. We stood with the regulations open, and made the bunks according to the instructions, we thought. Later in the day, a cadet who had failed one subject the previous year, but had taken the exam and was appointed again to our class, came into our room to ask, "Do you know how to make your bunk according to the regulations?" and "oh I see you don't." So we attended a "how to make your bunk session," and were properly indoctrinated.

During the summer, only the new class of fourth classmen were at the Academy, except for one first-class man who hadn't passed the physical to be an ensign. He had broken his arm shortly before graduation and needed some special therapy. He left with his ensign stripe on his sleeve before "Swab Summer" was over.

Once during the summer, the second classmen who were on a short coastal cruise on smaller cutters, stopped in New London, we saw the cadets who had used the rooms that we were in during the past year. They really impressed us with their military manner, and their knowledge of the systems around the area. Norm Horton, who had been in the room during the previous year, stopped in and asked, "Where are you from, Mister?" Ralph answered, "Manchester, Connecticut sir." and I replied, "Santa Maria, California, sir." Norm was from Arizona, but he must've known California, because he returned, "Oh yes, that's where the fog rolls in!" The fog does come up the Santa Maria Valley at times, when the hills hold it back further south, but I had never known it to be famous for that.

We went to classes during a large part of the day, reviewing mathematics to make sure that we were well grounded in the subjects we would have to pass in the next academic year. Part of the day we had military drill; introduction to the waterfront; rowing and sailing; tying knots and splicing line; and athletics, or just physical education. Naturally, it was football for me. There were some evenings, however, when the Coast Guard band, which had long been stationed at the Academy, gave evening concerts in the bandstand at the end of the parade ground. That was just in front of the cadet barracks, so it was just as easy to go out and listen, as to be distracted in your room. It was one of the only times when the cadets were allowed to be out of their rooms during study hour, and made it doubly pleasant to be outside.

There were a few of the new cadets who didn't like what they were confronted with when they arrived. One of the young men with whom I had taken the exam in Los Angeles, from Porterville, decided he couldn't be separated from his girlfriend for as long as it would take. We agreed not be married during the course, and four years was not acceptable for him and his girlfriend. He must've left after only two or three weeks. Some didn't pass the arrival physical, for some reasons, and a few others couldn't fathom the math we worked on. A few others worked their way through the swab summer, only to fail after one or more semesters at the regular pace.

One I remember, Avdevich, lasted only through the first semester in the football season before he failed too many subjects, and left. He later became an Army Air Corps pilot and was shot down in World War II. Hugh McColl, a quarterback on the team and a good passer, lasted longer, but his eyes were not good enough, and he left after perhaps a year. D. B. Kinnard, who never really wanted to be a Coast Guard officer, wanted to go to West Point. He failed one or more subjects after the first semester, was given re-exams, which he passed. During the next semester, he learned that he had a primary appointment to West Point, and he finished the year by failing six out of six subjects. He was an honor man at West Point, and retired as a brigadier general.

We sailed as well as rowed in the big whale boats that summer. Some of the sailing was not too expertly performed, but it was difficult to tell when those hulls. On one of the sailing outings, we had a pleasure boat come alongside the boat I was in, and we were all eyes for the girls in shorts on the yacht. We extended invitations to come to the band concerts, and some of them did, and we met again. I met the girl with whom I had a date for the first Academy dance that way. She lived in Groton, across the river, and getting her to and from the Academy was quite a task for the fourth classman, who could not drive in New London.

When the regular school term began, I had new roommates, two this time, because the enrollment of the school was increasing, and the entire fourth class lived with three to a room. Some of the third class were assigned three to a room as well, and we lived next door to a room with three. My new roommates were Bromley Blackshaw, a Californian and Barney Kolkhorst, from eastern Maryland. Brom had tried to enter the Academy the year before, as I had, but had spent one more year at UCLA, just as I did it at junior-college. We were a compatible group, and had fun at times enduring the heckling of the upperclassman next door. Across the hall were three more classmates, of whom only one was able to make it to graduation.

I could not say I was particularly successful in my football efforts that fall. I played tackle or end, and I actually played in only two home games. I injured my knees, and spent a great deal of time in the whirlpool baths in the gym, and some time on sick report, which was not too bad for a fourth classman. The upperclassman often then assigned "details" at the meals, and if it were not performed just as they desired, the fourth classman "swab" was the name used for them was required to sit in position at the table without a chair. With a sick report band around your arm, you could not be required to do that. The normal position for swabs at meals was sitting only on the four inches of the chair closest to the table, to make sure you sat ramrod straight.

Our everyday uniform was white sailor-type uniforms with a border around collars and hats in blue, to differentiate between the enlisted personnel and cadets. We also wore the tie of the enlisted personnel, with the difference between swabs and upper classmen being that the swab must keep the knot small, and upperclassman would make it large, sometimes all the way to the throat to cover the fact they didn't always wear the uniform

T-shirt. This knot was required to be above the tabletop, sitting straight, even if you didn't have a chair and you. I spent the night of last football game of the season and sick bay, because I had this huge swelling on my knee, and the doctor drained it, thinking I had water on the knee. It was blood and I simply had a large hematoma.

Following the football season came boxing, and at that time, boxing is both a major sport, and one that the cadets were very successful, not like football. We had an excellent coach, who'd been a successful boxer in the service when he was younger, Mickey McClernon. He was a chief warrant officer at this time. I'd never boxed before, but was so big, that I was a heavyweight, and had the box against the people who had the power to land tremendous blows. We would train with three minutes of activity, and then one minute of rest. In a match in collegiate circles, the rounds were only two minutes, and the extra minute of activity took us to better conditioning. We would hit the light bag for quick hands, the heavy bag working on strength of our blows, the weight machines, and skip rope.

Then we were rescheduled for boxing matches against someone of approximately the same weight and experience. I developed rather well, I guess, because I was scheduled often against the two regular heavyweights, the varsity light heavy weight, and once against the 165 pounder. These were often only one round for me, while the regular scheduled against a series of three opponents. The 165-weight man was a very sharp puncher, and seemed to have a particular sting to his blows. I don't remember his winning or losing a bout that year by either a knockout or TKO. I received two black eyes on alternate eyes every week all that season, except the time I boxed Frank Schmitz, the

165-pounder. He gave me one that lasted two weeks

At the end of the season, we had inter-company matches, and I "volunteered" to be the heavyweight for A Company. There weren't too many cadets of that size, and I was scheduled to defend the honor of our company. I had a bye in the first matches, and became the finalist the next day, and had to box John Day who was a third classman. I knew him rather well, from football, where he had shown me a few things, and we practiced against each other often. He had shoulders that looked like he had worked out on weights for years, and huge biceps. If he connected with a roundhouse blow, I knew I had had it! But the outcome, probably on boxing and not brawling, was that I was the winner, and the intramural champion.

Shortly after the beginning of the regular school year, to make sure that we knew cadets were properly prepared for social life of Coast Guard officers, we were informed that when there was a cadet formal dance, all cadets were invited, and would <u>attend</u>. The next step in our social education was to hold the tea dance with the new freshman from Connecticut College for Women which was across the street and up the hill about a half a mile.

My roommate, Brom Blackshaw, met a girl from Andover, Massachusetts, who he dated most of the school year. I met her friend, Barbara G____, from the same city, and I dated her for the rest of the year. Brom and I went to Boston on Easter to meet the two of them who came in from Andover. Neither of us continued after the first year with the girls, because Brom left the Academy after being chronically seasick on our first cruise, and the summer interval cooled things between Bobby and me.

When springtime arrived, there were things of continuing interest for cadets. One hundredth day was the time when the fourth class was given the opportunity to even things with the cadets who were one class ahead. We assumed the role of upperclassman, and the third class acted as fourth class swabs for the day. Of course, the roles were resumed as usual on the following day, so the punitive acts for error of their ways had to be considered rather carefully. Ring dances were only for the second and third classmen, because they received their Academy rings on that occasion.

The second class were given their large rings, which they wore as a symbol of their attendance and, hopefully, graduation from the institution, and the third classmen received miniature rings, which were often used as engagement rings in the future. Many of the dates who attended this dance expected or hoped to exchange rings with the second classmen received his large ring, he would (could) present the small one that he had from the previous year, to his date, as an engagement ring.

Since this event was only for the two classes, the first classmen, who were about to be commissioned, went about their own business, or pursued their own interests, which would be those of an officer in a few days. The fourth class was allowed some liberty off the Academy reservation.

However, the liberty ended before the dance was over, and it was traditional to do some evil pranks on the members of two classes who were at the dance. In one room, the mattress from the bunk of the beneficiary of the interest of the swab was lowered on a sheet out the window, to the limit of the sheet's length. One of the second classmen had locked his room to avoid pranks, but this was officially illegal. He rigged a string to the inside of the knob to be able to open the door on his return. This was discovered by persons unknown, and the door was opened. Once inside, Limburger cheese was rubbed over the radiator, and the steam turned on full, even though it was May and heat was unneeded. Then, the door was locked again, and the string removed! There wasn't much sleep in some parts of the barracks that night.

The most important part of the spring was preparing for the summer cruise, where a more true part of the education of a cadet takes place. The third class (just promoted from being swabs), would perform the duties of the seamen and lower petty officers on the ship, and the first class, just after graduation of the other class, would perform the duties of the officer of the deck or in port, the officer of the day. There were important classes in seamanship and general indoctrination which were important to our preparation to leave on our cruise.

At this time, the majority of the vessels of the Coast Guard were necessarily assigned to international neutrality patrols, and the assignment of a vessel to training duty all summer was a problem. However, the solution seemed to be a natural one. The Coast Guard, was at that time operating two vessels, one on each coast for the Maritime Service. The *American Seaman* was assigned to St. Petersburg, Florida, and the *American Sailor* was in Port Hueneme, California. The *Seamen* was our training vessel for the summer. The itinerary was to sail from New London to St. Thomas, Virgin Island; San Juan, Puerto Rico, to Havana, Cuba; to Moorhead City, North Carolina; Larchmont, New York; and back to New London. There may have been one more port after Larchmont, but we never got to it either, and I've forgotten.

On our trip to St. Thomas, some of the cadets who had never been to sea before were very seasick. I'd been to sea, fishing, but I was seasick for the first morning, as we went past Cape Hatteras. Brom, my roommate for the last year, was green he was so sick; and, he was sick any time we went to sea long enough for him to feel it. He left the Academy shortly after the cruise and became a submarine officer during the War. There, he stated he hoped he could stay below the effects of the sea.

In St. Thomas, rum was cheaper than soft drinks in 1941. The only alternative was to drink rum with your Coke, and so we did. It tasted like bad medicine to me, but we had to try it. We also had some time to visit the lovely beaches in St. Thomas, but it wasn't such a good port for us because we had no money to spend in the free port.

Next call was San Juan and there I was introduced by a classmate, Tom Cheatham, who was a Marine Corps junior, to a daughter of a Navy officer who helped us to see the area. She was quite a good diver and good-looking enough that one of my classmates, Art Pereira (who later changed his name to Perry) wrote to one of the class of 1941, who had just graduated and was assigned to a cutter in the area, about her. They were later married, and I was assigned with them many years later.

In Havana we did the usual sightseeing in a foreign port, and somehow a group of us were introduced to a recent graduate of the Cuban Naval Academy. His father had written a book and I had it my library for many years. It was <u>Lo Que Yo Vi en Europa</u>, or <u>What I Saw in Europe</u>. The young man had not yet received his commission, and was yet through with training.

He was waiting for a vacancy to occur, which he would fill, in order to become an ensign.

He had three sisters, none of whom spoke English as well as he did, but we arranged to take the girls, and a chaperone, to a nightclub the last evening in Havana. It was quite interesting trying to carry on any conversation. Between the girls and the cadets, we did manage to be out of the year should have no trouble finding the sight of the chaperone, an aunt, much of the time.

Our next port of call was Morehead City, North Carolina, where we were to use the Marine Corps rifle and pistol ranges. The installation is today Camp Lejeune, but we never heard that name in 1941. We spent several days firing the Springfield rifle, and several people made expert rankings. I did not! We spent the last day or perhaps two firing the 45 caliber pistol, which was standard issue for so long. Our time was cut short, however, and not many, if anyone, made expert with the pistol.

Our time was cut short because the cadet cruiser commander had received a message telling us that our ship, the *American Seaman*, was needed in Bermuda. We had the largest freshwater evaporators available to the US fleet, except for those on two huge aircraft carriers, the *Lexington* and the *Saratoga*. Both the ships were from the Pacific and could not proceed to Bermuda on short notice due to an acute water shortage. Bermuda's water is provided by rainfall, which is diverted, after rinsing off the road roofs, into cisterns.

There had been no rainfall to provide that water, and the alternative was to make water for them. We filled the ships' tanks with freshwater at the dock, and then sailed east, instead of north, to the yacht races and the social functions where our white uniforms would've been interesting in Larchmont.

Before we left Morehead City, it may have been our last night, but on Saturday evening, there was a dance at Atlantic Beach, a nearby beach community. That evening, after the evening meal, as was the practice of the local ice cream vendor, the ice cream truck arrived on the dock to sell ice cream in pint cartons to us. I finished dinner early, and was one of the first to buy my pint. I also was early to finish the pint. I bought another one, since I have always enjoyed my ice cream. Then my friend, Art Perry and I headed for the shore, and eventually for Atlantic Beach. But we were early, and had time to spare, so we stopped by the ice cream parlor we had found earlier.

That evening at the dance, we made the acquaintance of two local lovelies, and spent a great deal of time with them, until the intermission, when the band stopped playing for some period. At that time, they introduce us to their cousin, who brought them to the dance in his red Chevrolet convertible. Someone suggested that we go for a ride in the convertible, and we all climbed in. There had been some dew there at the beach after sunset, which did interesting things to Art's and my white uniforms where the red upholstery contacted the backs and seats of our whites. But, we didn't know that until later. We headed off, and real inspiration was a suggestion that we get some ice cream if the ice cream parlor was still open. I believe it was the first in my life that I really didn't want any more ice cream. Fortunately, the ice cream parlor was closed when we arrived. And so farewell to Morehead City and its beauties.

We arrived in Bermuda, we went to the dock in Hamilton

for two days at first, and we may have transferred some of our water. One of those days, I had duty on the ship, and I saw very little of the island, except one pink beach. We moved then to His Majesty's Dockyard and transferred the rest of the water.

Following that, we moved on to an anchorage where we stayed most of the next two weeks and meet water with our evaporators. The only breaks in the routine came with swimming call in the afternoons and movies on deck at night. The swimming parties were a mixed blessing, because there were so many jellyfish in the water, there was a very good chance you would itch for hours from hitting one. Of course, during this time, it was very hot below decks and at times we would try to sleep on the deck. We might fall asleep without trouble, but it rained almost every night. So much for that water shortage!

Toward the end of our time in Bermuda, we were running low on food and stores, and a destroyer about to return to Norfolk was ordered to come alongside and transfer any food not essential for its voyage to Norfolk to us. Someone in the working party on our ships saw the date written on a case of eggs we received, two years before we received them. On the rest of the cruise, the cooks always served eggs scrambled, regardless of what the menu said, and they always broke the eggs into a bowl before letting them hit the griddle. I couldn't eat eggs without ketchup for six months!

We headed back for New London, after our water-making episode, and docked at the City Pier. We were then transferred back to the Academy to pick up our suitcases and head home on leave. While we were at the Academy, we saw how strange and bewildered the new cadets seemed. One of the new class, who had been in our class, but had failed one or two classes, came to us, commenting on our soiled white uniforms, our suntans from being in the fresh air in Bermuda, and our butch haircuts, said, "You guys sure look old!" Thinking of the comparison with the new class, we thought we were, too.

My brother, Walt, had by now graduated from the University of Southern California, was employed by Western Air Express, the predecessor to Western Airlines. He was entitled to send passes to members of his family to permit them to fly without charge on Western, and with only the payment of the tax on certain other lines with which they had agreements. Northwest was one of those other lines.

So, I took the train to Chicago, and called Northwest. They gave me no encouragement until later that evening and I had the opportunity to see a stage show starring a very young Dinah Shore. That evening, I flew to Montana, and then took a train to Salt Lake, where I made connections to fly into Los Angeles on Western. I had a short pleasant visit with my parents, my younger brother, my sister, and most of the old friends who were still around, and then reversed my directions.

This time Walt told me which hotels gave Western personnel a discount, and after flying into Salt Lake City checked into the hotel as a Western Air man. There were only two flights a day to Montana from Salt Lake, and I made the flight the next morning. The pilot on the flight was the senior pilot on that leg of Western, and he loved the mountains. We flew in a Boeing plane, and went through the passes giving us a spectacular view of country not often seen. I was bumped by a paying passenger in West Yellowstone, however and spent a very long day in that very small town. I waited until it was definite about how full the evening flight was, and by that time, I had investigated alternatives.

I took the Karrst Stage to Bozeman, Montana, as that was the only possibility for me. The stage was actually a panel truck with two additional seats located just behind the driver and the normal second seat. In Helena, I boarded a Northwest flight, thinking I was on my way, but was bumped again in Fargo, North Dakota. There were several persons with passes, and we all were pacing the terminal in Fargo, hoping something would show up. It did! An executive of Northwest came through with his private Lockheed plane, and picked us all up to take us to Minneapolis, where the rest of the trip was easier, because of the number of flights. The train across the eastern part of the country was routine.

We started football practice immediately upon our return. The third day we scrimmage in full pads, and without limits on action. In the last play of the day, I was blocked from the side, and twisted my knee. We never x-rayed injuries in those days, orthoscopic surgery was unheard of. You simply healed or became a civilian. I stopped being an active football player and became a manager, assisting a player who had injured his knee earlier.

When boxing season arrived, I decided I might have better chances as a light heavyweight, since I was a light person for the heavyweight class. I spent the year at about 180 pounds, but I took quite a battering, and never had a chance to lose the additional pounds I would have to in order to make the weight for a light heavyweight bout. In the inter-class matches, I went back to heavyweight, since I was the defending champion.

Again I had a bye in the first round, since I was the defending champion. I was scheduled to meet the winner of the first match, Stratton. He had won, but looked awkward; I thought he was lucky to have beaten his opponent. I was looking for a good match, but I thought I could beat him. I came out of the corner, fully ready, so I thought, as he came roaring out, and swung from the floor. I couldn't block it or dodge it well enough, if at all, and I was on the canvas, after about 10 seconds of the match.

The referee was our intercollegiate champion, Mark McGarrity and he told me later that when he saw that I was taking the eight count, as the coaches had prepared us, if ever we were floored, he thought I was not hurt. I wasn't ready for Stratton's next onslaught, however, and he caught me again, and that was the match. I really didn't remember much of the rest of the night.

On December 7, it was approaching the end of the semester, since we usually were finished before the break at Christmas. Some courses required term papers, and Professor Hoag, teaching physics, wanted us to research the photographic process and write a paper about that. I was in the room of my friend, Art Perry in order to use his typewriter. It was a routine Sunday morning, and we had the room door closed, against regulations.

Since Sunday was a little noisier than usual, if one wanted to study, it was not uncommon for upperclassman to close the door, and the first class were the only ones who could assign the demerits, other than the commissioned officers, usually ignored the condition of the door. Fourth class men could never do this, but it was almost always the case for the first class.

It was doubly convenient that we had the door closed, because Art had a small portable radio, that was small enough to fit in the desk drawer, and it went off if the lid was closed. If the desk drawer was closed, the radio lid closed at the same time, and there were no sounds of a radio. Thus, if an officer, or a senior upperclassman, opened the door, we would spring to our feet, to attention, and the desk drawer was closed. We heard the news of the Pearl Harbor attack on the radio about as soon as anyone, because of our radio.

Shortly after the first announcement, as we wondered what this would mean to us, a first-class man, who lived nearby came down the hall, opening doors and inquiring, "Have you heard the news?" He had been engaged to his wife-to-be for some time, and had thought that they would have to wait to be married until May or June. Now he knew that his class would be commissioned soon (it was 8 days), and the marriage restriction would be gone.

When he saw and heard the radio in our room, he continued, "Oh I see you have," and closed the door. Art never received any demerits for the non-regulation radio but another first classman told him he had to get rid of it a few days later. He hid it for some time, and then brought it out again. It seemed like such a good idea to have that kind of a radio, but I bought a similar one later, and together we built rectifiers to replace the batteries, which became impossible to obtain as the war went on.

War brought changes to the Academy, and to our class, as well as our courses. The first class graduated on December 15, and we were now second classmen. There was no longer a fourth class, and the Academy continued in this way, until there was no graduating class of 1947, forcing the class of 1948 back to four years. But by this time, things that changed a great deal for me.

The Academy After the War Began

To the extent that was possible, the powers tried to give us the same education at the Academy as before the war. But they knew that there were only three years to do this now, and with the new first class, there was only a period of around five months to do all that would have been done in seventeen.

Many of the courses were simply canceled. In our case, they tried to expose us to as many of the subjects that we would've taken, but the courses were shortened. In the case of international economics, taught by a visiting professor from Yale, we had only two or three lectures, and I'm not sure if we really understood all we heard. Other courses were held in a shortened version during the summer of 1942.

I had been elected president my class in the fall of 1941, and while there weren't not many duties to perform, it was an honor. Now came the question of whether I was president for the year, or for the time as third classmen. I placed the question before the class, and was president for the second class year as well.

We had to hurry with the procurement of class rings, since we had so much less time to buy them. This is also shortened the time when we would have someone expecting to get the ring when large rings were put on our fingers. We worked on a ring design, trying to emphasize the year figure since it was a 44. We knew that we would graduate 1943 now, but we kept the designation of the class of 1944, as did the Naval Academy,

West Point, on the other hand, redesignated their classes, and I believe the original class of 1942 became the class of 1941-A.

We also had to choose a company to produce the rings, and buy them in time for the ring dances. When it came time for the ring dance, I was playing the field of available dates, and took a very nice girl from Connecticut College and she was from Connecticut, to that dance where she gave me my small ring. She never asked for it for her, but we were never on that level anyway. Her sister, years later, married a Coast Guard officer who is now a retired vice admiral.

We were given leave that summer before the cruise, instead of after, as was usually done. Transportation across the country was even tighter than the year before, but one of my classmates worked out a plan. He found that there was a regular fare train that made the same schedule as expensive, and fast, Super Chief on the Santa Fe line. It was designed to carry only mail and express, but it had half of the last car with passenger seats, left over from the junkyard. We didn't know what kind of facilities there were, but the information said passenger seating was available for a limited number.

He found that by taking the train from Chicago to St. Louis, we could make connections there with this Fast Mail train, and be in Los Angeles as fast as the Super Chief, and it was considerably less expensive. So, he contacted the line for the good reservations from Chicago, and let Santa Fe know that we wanted the Fast Mail from there. Santa Fe replied "No, you don't want the Fast Mail. It's really not designed for anything except moving people from one station to the next one down the line." They offered to make reservations for the group on the Scout, like the Challenger I had come east on, and equally slow. He didn't reply to this offer, and we planned to take the Fast Mail.

We had a very pleasant evening on the first train out of Chicago. There was an entire car for the Coast Guard cadets that evening, I believe it was the Fourth of July, and we each had a group of reclining seats to get some sleeping route to St. Louis.

When we arrived in St. Louis, somehow we never found the Scout, and all headed for the Fast Train/Fast Mail train track. Before it pulled out, a conductor found us, told us that they were holding the Scout for us, and if we didn't board that, we would be reported to our commanding officer. We ignored him, stayed put, and the train pulled out. It had a tough schedule to keep.

There was no air-conditioning in this car; you opened the windows if you were hot, and closed them if you were too cool. There was a potbellied stove in one end of the compartment if it was really cold, but we never had to worry about that. The windows were open all the time, and the dust came blowing in along with the coal remnants from our steam locomotive. If we wanted a meal, we told our conductor, and he would drop off a note as we went through a station, and pick up boxed lunches at the next stop. The seats did not recline, they simply faced one direction or the other, and they were hard.

As the trip neared an end, Bill Wallace from the class behind me, got off in Phoenix, Arizona, and his parents met him. They thought he looked so bad that they immediately bought return tickets for him on a different train, before they even left the station. As we went through Pasadena, California, Frank Carter, a class mate departed, and I really envied him! He had 20 minutes less of this train than we did, going on to Los Angeles.

I had made a date with a girl I'd met a couple of years before, and had kept in touch with, for that first evening in Los Angeles. We were going to the Palladium, where the big bands always played during the war years. That meant that I had to clean up in the train's tiny washroom in change to a white shirt and my blue uniform. The shirt had a detachable collar and French cuffs; we all look pretty good when we arrived in Los Angeles. I had to throw the shirt away after one wearing, however, because it was so filthy around the cuffs and collar band. We wondered if we would ever get clean, but a few showers help that. Needless to say, I did not take the Fast Mail on the return, but joined the hundreds of military personnel on the Scout.

The usual cadet cruises for the summer time more difficult this year, because there were no cutters available to let cadets cruise the coast or to Europe, as had been done often before. However, there were two wonderful sailing vessels, which were available. Mr. Lambert, the owner of Lambert Pharmaceutical Company, donated his huge schooner to the Coast Guard, since he would not be able to use it during the war, and it was getting older.

When the war began, the Danish training ship, Danmark was in St. Petersburg, Florida, and was simply at the dock, doing nothing ever since the German Germans had invaded Denmark some time earlier. It was made available for the Coast Guard, and trained both reserve and regular cadets during the war. We sailed up and down Long Island Sound, calling at various ports, and becoming as familiar with the requirements of seamanship as we could in a short cruise. I spent two weeks in the Atlantic (the schooner) and two weeks on Danmark.

My sail station on Danmark was the fore royal, the second highest position of the masts. It was a thrill to be up there, using one hand for the ship, and one for yourself. We had no safety belts, or lines to prevent falls, but we made it in one piece. We sailed into the harbor at Fishers Island under full sail one time, with Captain Hansen, the Danish commander at the con. There were several Danish seamen around assisting on the lines, and it was a beautiful job of ship handling.

During the first class year, cadet organization was changed several times before hitting on the final one for the last few months. I served as a platoon leader, a squad leader, and a company officer, at least. I ended as a company executive officer, with Bob LaForte as the company commander, and this meant that he was my roommate as well. Lieut. Joe McClelland, who was the tactics officer at this time, told me years later that he didn't really think that I wanted to be any higher in the cadet organization. He was right; I was doing fun doing other things. I was active in a double quartet, and we performed at several cadet functions. I went out for boxing again, more on that later. I managed to go on liberty, usually with a date nearly every time it was available. I was a manager of the football team, and had to keep track of all of the equipment when it was on the field.

Besides, the cadet organization worked hard on battle plans. It wasn't just drilling on the parade field. We went out into the countryside and hiked around, taking cover behind stone fences, deploying against another cadet company, and generally discovering what it was like to use the country's character to find cover, or move in more modern warfare. Also, it was good exercise, I presume.

The ring dance was held much earlier that year, since we would have such a short period when we could wear the rings before we were graduated -- after we had decided what finish, what stone, whether to give an initial engraved on the face of the stone, etc. I had been dating a girl who lived in the Mohican Hotel, downtown, with her parents. She is the only one I ever knew who always lived in a hotel. She had access to her father's car, and by this time, I had a Connecticut driver's license, and first classmen were authorized to drive autos. It was rather a nice arrangement. She pushed very hard to have me give her my miniature ring when I received the large ring, but I wasn't ready for that.

Christmas leave periods were a problem for someone from the West Coast going to school in Connecticut. The first year, I'd gone to the home of two of my mother's sisters. First, I went to Clarksburg, West Virginia where the husband of my aunt was an executive with Standard Oil. My cousin, June, was a senior at Wellesley College, and her fiancé came to Clarksburg for part of the holiday season. It'd been a very nice visit.

Later during that leave, I went to Pittsburgh, and spent some time with my mother's older sister, Alethea. One day I went with my cousin Bob, who is close to my mother's age, on a salt selling trip. Salt to a Californian was something used on food, or to make ice cream, but in this area was used to clean off the sidewalks and streets, and it sold in huge quantities to melt ice on sidewalks and roads in southern Pennsylvania and West Virginia.

On New Year's Eve, my aunt got me together with the young man around my age, and we kept going until midnight without getting into trouble. One of the highlights of this time was a visit to the city morgue--why, I can't remember, but it did impress me.

The second year, the war had begun, and again, there was a problem of distance. This time, I went to Detroit, and spent the time with my mother's youngest sister, Olive. There was at least one other cadet in the area, and I spent one evening with him, his date, and his sister as my date. I don't believe that the leave was as long this year, and we were back in New London for New Year's.

I went out for boxing that last winter with some misgivings. I had not done particularly well in the last year as a light heavyweight, and I didn't like the memory of the knockout at the interclass meet. Stratton decided he was not going to try it for the varsity, as he had some eyesight problems, and his studies were not doing too well, so he was not a concern. There were others, big and strong, but the former varsity heavyweight boxers were gone through graduation. I decided I would give it a try, but I wasn't going to continue if I didn't do fairly well in my first training match. I was matched against Joe Fehrenbacher in my first match of the season, and he outweighed me by about 10 pounds. A good test was my thought. I knocked him out in the first round, with a very short right. I am not sure whether he continued after that match.

That experience merely set me up. For some reason that year, there were a series of broken noses. I had a severe cold for some time, and couldn't consider the first intercollegiate match, and Dan Boone went to the Catholic University matches in Washington DC, although I was listed in the Washington paper is the Coast Guard heavyweight. He lost and I heard he had broken his nose.

I was scheduled the next week to work out with them in a match, I asked the coach, "Isn't he in trouble with a broken nose?" The coach replied, "No, don't worry about that." We boxed, he broke my notice admitted afterwards he already had a broken nose himself. We ended the season with either no heavyweight, or very inexperienced one, who didn't do well. I believe the number of broken noses has something to do with the fact that the Academy dropped boxing as a varsity sport just a few years later.

The spring was bringing graduation, assignment to duties as an officer, and for many, not me, wedding bells. I knew that my parents couldn't make the trip across the country for graduation, and I was resigned to it. I tried my best to convince the girl that I was dating at the time that she should come to graduation and the dance that night. It was questionable for some time, but she and her parents finally agreed that she might attend. We had the Commandant of the Coast Guard present to present our commissions, James Forestal, then the Secretary of the Navy, to be the major speaker, and I had my friend Virginia Bowman, in the audience. It was a good day.

After the ceremonies, as we were standing around outside the gym where the ceremony had been taking place, a Coast Guard photographer saw Ginny and me together, and asked if we would pose for photos. He asked her to give me congratulatory kiss in one, and that the one he chose to send to her hometown newspaper! I doubt that her mother ever forgave me for getting her into that position.

Although we were graduated now and had our commissions as ensigns, we weren't through with school. The entire class stayed on at the Academy, in the barracks room, except those few who were married now, we spent the day experiencing anti-submarine warfare. We had some ancient sonar simulators, and we would go out on 83-foot patrol boats into Long Island Sound to try to hear actual sonar on the subs from the New London Sub-base.

There were a few times when I had trouble giving the course my full attention, because I had run down to Stamford to see Ginny the night before, but I was headed for a larger attack transport in the Pacific anyway. We spent about two to three weeks at this before we left on leave before our real assignments as ensigns.

War in the Pacific

My orders directed me to report to the 12th District Commander of the Coast Guard, in San Francisco. I reported, and was immediately sent to the Navy at the Federal Buildings. They endorsed my orders, told me that transportation to the U. S. S. Hunter Liggett was not readily available, and it could be as much as two weeks before I would go out. They had some rooms that had been made available to such transient officers, and I moved into a dormitory type room in the St. Francis Hotel.

My next weeks were spent going sightseeing, and in the evenings, I would go to the Junior Officers Club. I refused to go to the Officers Club most visitors spoke of, at the Fairmont Hotel, in what had been, and is now, the Cirque Room. I liked the atmosphere of the more junior group.

Eventually I was told to report to the M. S. Weltevreden, a Dutch ship which had been converted into a troop carrier. There were several officers who were to go, and we all went aboard in the afternoon before sailing for Point Hueneme, just down the coast. There we were to pick up a group of Seabees, the construction battalions of the Navy. When we pulled up in Port Hueneme, we were told we were on our own until Sunday night, when we would sail for the Pacific.

There were five of us Coast Guard ensigns, all headed for the Hunter Liggett, and we all headed for Los Angeles. Bob Ruth, a classmate of mine, and Gene McDonald, a reservist who been commissioned just after our class, both were from Los Angeles, and we didn't see them until after we arrived in the city. Phil McFarland, another classmate, and Gordon Lindquist, a reservist and I stuck together for the weekend.

We saw Gordon's fiancé, and went out on the town together, and during Saturday, we shopped for sheath knives. We had seen that the experienced seamen all had knives at their belts. We saw quite a few knives, many of them designed for defense in the city jungle, and I remember the sales pitch of one store, "These knives are weighted for throwing." We reported back to the ship and actually sailed on Monday.

We spent 19 days zigzagging across the Pacific. Most of the time it was sunny and not very rough at all. We never saw land, and life was often boring. We read, sunbathed, and speculated on what the future would hold. Crossing the equator brought the shell-back ceremonies, and most of us were submitted to the requirements of a pollywog (one who has not crossed the equator before). There was often some haircutting in this ceremony but who cared—we would not see anyone who could judge our appearance, other than a new commanding officer, who would understand, for months. The ship had no escort of any kind during this voyage, but we did zigzag, which lengthened the trip. We made port in Noumea, New Caledonia, on August 25, 1943, and our Coast Guard group was taken immediately to the Hunter Liggett, at anchor in the bay.

I never saw the civilized part of Numea, or the military bases there, but I did set foot on foot on New Caledonia, when the chaplain asked if I would like to join a group going ashore to the picnic area for some softball and some beer. The beer didn't interest me, but I was ready to try my shore legs and went with them.

I was assigned to the first division of the ship, which was responsible for loading and unloading the forward part of the ship. We handled the huge tank lighters, but only the best qualified personnel ever gave the signals to hoist them or lower them from their spots on deck. They were very heavy, and came near the capacity of our "jumbo" boom. There were two holds in this area equipped to handle troops, and when we carried troops, there were always men both in the holds, and on deck. I was one of the two assistant division officers, Gale Weaner, being the other, and I also was a junior officer of the deck under way. In port, we junior officers were the officers of the deck, stationed at the gangway.

When we left New Caledonia, we had a group of New Zealand and Australian troops, ANZACs, and their equipment on board. We were with a group of other ships, around nine, with a group of destroyers for escorts. On the second day out of Noumea, I stepped out of the wheelhouse onto the wing of the bridge, at about the time that the navigator and the chief quartermaster were finishing the morning star sights, and the plot of our position. The ship quartermaster was on the wing with me, looked over towards the other ships in our convoy, and said, almost to himself, "What's that?" It's a torpedo!"

It was fired at our convoy, but probably a considerable distance, and went astern of all the ships. It was close enough, however, to get the attention of all of us. The Weltevreden, which I had come to know to Noumea on, was our convoy, and gave the abandon ship signal to their personnel, a series of ship with whistles, which I still recognize.

I spent time as a junior officer of the deck, and spent a great deal of time learning how the ship had to zigzag, in order to make it more difficult for a submarine to estimate the ship's forward speed, and had to maintain formation with a ship ahead as the guide. We would hold a bearing in the line, and turning more to one side or the other could adjust that. The distance astern, we would determine with a stadimeter, because we knew the height of the main mast of the guide ship from the water line. We could adjust that distance by changing the RPM of our propellers by just a few at a time.

It was much more difficult to determine the distance astern at night, when it was too dark to see the main mast clearly, and a stadimeter was ineffective too. Then we would look for the ship and her binoculars, holding them in precisely the same position each time, and see how much of the field of the binoculars ship filled. If it felt too much space, we had moved to close, and we dropped a few RPMs to move farther away. If the ship did not fill in the field, we would change RPM to move ahead. The movements had to be very small, and time had to allowed for the adjustments to take effect.

We went into the harbor at the Efate, in the New Hebrides group, to practice amphibious operations with the ANZACs. Here, although it was assigned to the boat division, all of us ensigns were boat commanders. We would load the troops in the boat, drop a cargo net from the side of the ship, and the wave officer would climb down with them at times. Then we would go to a rendezvous area, and all the boats of the wave would form a circle to await the time to depart for the beach. When the waves were all formed, and the time for the assault came, the group commander would send each wave on its way, with predetermined spacing between the waves. We assaulted the beach several times, to hone the skills of the boat operators and the troops, before we moved on to Guadalcanal with the ANZACs.

I stood officer of the deck watches at the gangway in the port here. It was merely a task of determining who went ashore or came on board, and often it was no one. There was a senior officer on the bridge when we were at anchor here, and it was his responsibility to ensure that our anchor bearing stayed the same, and that we were not attacked by Japanese planes. One of the watches that I liked in particular was that watch on the after deck, when it was just getting light at around 5 AM, which was 0500 to us. It was on the 4 to 8 watch, and the first hour is deadly dull. When it starts to become light, however, you can see the villagers on the shore coming to life, and people coming out of huts. The women would light fires outside the huts, and the men would go off to take care of chores. The sun coming up would be greeted by the birdlife, and we were close enough to shore to see and hear the birds.

After taking this load of troops to Guadalcanal, which was officially secured by the Americans by this time, we went back to Etafe to pick up more troops, and move them to Guadalcanal. At that point, the ship was ordered to New Zealand to go into dry dock and have more wood removed from the interior, go into dry dock to repaint the exterior of the hull and other maintenance work. We were to have radar installed in this availability, and we looked forward to this.

On our trip from Guadalcanal to Auckland, we were alone, except for a destroyer as an escort. Just after noon one day, I was the junior officer on duty, giving the helmsman the zigzag orders with Lieutenant Al Frost as the senior officer on duty. I had just given the order to turn left to a new heading when three bombs landed in the water off the starboard bow, where we would have been if the ship hadn't turned at that moment.

We hit the general alarm immediately, and the guns were always manned with a partial crew. Our 3-inch gun forward, normally my GQ station, was manned by one crew, when at general quarters, both the guns were manned. The crew that was on that watch quickly tried to spot the plane, a Betty which had ducked down out of the clouds, dropped the bombs, and went back above the clouds. They weren't able to get a shot off, but at least they saw the plane, and tried to track it. The escort destroyer called over on the radio to our division command, on watch on the flying bridge, and announced "We are preparing to drop an embarrassing attack depth charge pattern." Our flag watch responded, "Never mind, the depth charges will never get to the plane." We were not bothered again on our voyage to New Zealand.

When we arrived, our first task was to put the Liggett into a floating dry dock. The day was very windy one, and it was a difficult task lining the ship with the dock, where whole blocks had been laid to support the weight of the ship when it was out of the water. The crew labored to haul in on some lines, maneuvering the ship against the wind, and then, since the ship was very low on fuel, and quite light as a result, the hull would flop to one side or the other. It was a long, frustrating job, and the weather did nothing to cooperate.

This was November, late spring here, and cool with a strong wind. Eventually the ship is more or less in place, and the dry dock was pumped out to take us out. This meant the water, and therefore, heads/toilets and showers were secured for all the time we were out of the water. It was a relief when we were back in the water a few days later, and didn't always have to make the trek to the shore side facilities.

I did some sightseeing in this port, but not as much as they would've today. We all ate fresh vegetables in the restaurants and clubs, drank fresh milk, and had New Zealand beef. They prefer lamb to beef, and the beef was usually sold to the Americans, or served to them in the cafés. Fresh lettuce was a treat, and I had never known how much I enjoyed it, I still look for a good salad for lunch treat. One of the first evenings ashore, I went to an officer's club where the New Zealand girls came to dance and meet the visitors. (Our ship's crew, during all the time in the South Pacific, married about 50 of their girls.)

I danced with a New Zealand Wren, their version of the U.S. Waves, who looked at my uniform, saw the Coast Guard shield, and said, "Oh, you must be from the Liggett. You had a single destroyer as an escort down here and were attacked by Japanese plane." I started wondering what she did and didn't know, and kept my mouth closed. She told me that she was in operations at her command, and had tracked the ship down from Guadalcanal. It still made me uncomfortable to have her talking about it.

Shortly after our visit in New Zealand, we were back at Efate, but this time we had a US Marines on board. We trained for some time, and then departed for Bougainville, to make the initial landing on that island. We were reading about huge convoys in the Atlantic at this time, but our force to land on this enemy stronghold was 12 ships. Some of them were AKAs, primarily cargo ships, but with only a few troops to care for the vehicles they might carry. The USS American Legion, sister ship and nearly identical to ours, was the transport flagship on this trip. We must have had some naval support over the horizon; we never saw them, only the destroyers that maintained a close escort.

We went to a cruising general quarter's condition about two days out from Bougainville, about when we passed Guadalcanal. This meant we were either at our gun positions for six hours, with six hours off, or we were just at the gun in a relaxed condition for the entire day. Most of the crew simply slept on the deck near the guns, while most of the officers spent some time in their rooms. There was no ship's work other than being ready to repel an attack.

The initial landing was in Empress Augusta Bay, just north of Cape Toro kina. The ships were set to sail in at right angles to the general shoreline, and the destroyers would fire on the known fortifications at the beach with their less sophisticated guns, without fire control. We had two three-inch guns forward, and I was the gun officer for one of them. We had been warned ahead of time, that when we approached the beach, the range to the area would be reduced by the distance the ship traveled between each round, and that we should spot down each time we fired. My trouble was I needed to spot up after the first round, because it went into the water, short of the beach. I remembered my advice better than my ability to correct the range. All the shots from my gun, and I believe those from

Number 2 three-inch, were short of the shoreline!

The ship went to anchor, and the boats were lowered into the water, and proceeded to their assigned stations. We were loaded troops into the boats, and I was the wave officer of one of the later waves. We hit the beach, but the surf was as rough as most of the boat coxswains had ever seen, and several broached broadside on the beach, and could not return to the ships. There was always a boat assigned to work on retrieving boats in this condition, and it had been a busy day. Shortly after my wave hit the beach, a flight of Japanese planes flew over the beach strafing as they came. I thought that they looked as mean as a plane could possibly look. They did shoot up some of our boats, and injured some of the crews. Our boat group commander, Lt. Will Parker, was hit with shrapnel, and his coxswain died from the wounds he received, and complications from malaria. When the radar of the better equipped ships warned of the approach of these planes, all the ships were told to get underway, and get to sea, where they could maneuver. That meant that when my boats left the beach, we had no place to go. We could see the ships on the horizon, but they were getting farther away, not closer!

As an a side, many years later, when I was at a luncheon in the quarters of the Navy noncommissioned officers, Admiral Jim Holloway, I was told by General Lou Wilson, the Marine Commandant at the time, that he had a great deal of respect for the Coast Guard, because they had put him ashore on Bougainville. I did a double take, and reply, "Lou, there was only one Coast Guard transport there that day. " He responded, "Yes, I know, the Hunter Legate." Thus, it turned out that two future service chiefs were on the ship that same day and hit the beach in boats of the vessel.

Eventually, it seemed hours later, the ships returned, and anchored once more. We unloaded the troops' equipment as fast as we could, but the tropical thunderstorms didn't help. We had not finished when darkness came, and the ships went out to cruise around during the night. That was the night of the battle of Bougainville, between Americans and Japanese destroyers and cruisers. We could see the flare of the guns, and the red-hot shells going back and forth, but we were not involved. I always thought that the conversation on the gun deck that night as we just stood by for whatever might happen was very interesting. Some of our crew was in sick day, being treated for wounds received in those strafing runs. The men standing by the guns were talking just as if their shipmates were in the sick bay because there had been a football game that day, and the wounded had sprained an ankle or broken an arm. The next day we went back for the anchorage, and completed unloading.

We went back to Tulagi, and saw some of the ships that had been in the battle of Bougainville. The USSS Denver had holes through its stack, and had had one eight inch projectile go all the way through the ship near the bow without exploding. If it has exploded, it may have torn off the bow.

We picked up more supplies and some more troops and went back to Bougainville, without incident this time. We spent many hours at general quarters again, and I drank coffee I couldn't have gotten down under normal circumstances.

Following this trip, we went to Espiritu Santo in the New Hebrides group, and then after loading just a few people who needed transportation back to the States for medical care, we headed for San Francisco, via Samoa. Almost no one went ashore in Samoa, but we again picked up person who needed medical care in Oakland. Our voyage into San Francisco was very rough for the last several days. The winds were near hurricane strength, the seas were breaking over the bow, and the poor seasick passengers couldn't find a convenient spot to hang over the rails.

We were low on fuel, as the ship was being lightened to go into dry dock again. When we sailed to San Francisco Bay, the wind flopped the ship from one angle of healing to the opposite when we turned in to go to an anchorage. We went to a dock soon, and then moved to Oakland for work on the ship.

After months in the yard, it was decided that the ship should be assigned to amphibious training in San Diego, along with her sister ship the American Legion. We arrived there in April 1944, started a training routine of 10 days for each group of troops, with four landings in that time. We would land on Coronado Strand the first time, in broad daylight, then retrieve the personnel, and go to sea to San Clemente Island, about 75 miles to the west. Here we would make a full scale landing, but again at a reasonable time, to allow everyone to see errors. We reloaded, but stayed at anchor in the same spot, and the troops would discuss the operation, as performed. The next one, again, was on the San Clemente Island, although all of them in Pyramid Cove, but this one was at dawn. The H hour was adjusted to have the first wave hit the beach at the minute of sunrise.

Often this landing was accompanied by gunfire, and in later

days there were even battleships and the new LSMs with rockets. Our final landing for each group would be at the beach in Santa Margarita, California, now known as Camp Pendleton. By this time, I was the assistant navigator, and it was really a treat to work with Lieut. Glenn Shannon, who was the navigator. He would pick up points of land to determine our position, and our radio operators did very well also, to make certain that our troops at the correct beach.

The radar on the Liggett was an old SH type, and was supposedly not much good, but our operators could pick up floating oil drums at some distance, and little inlets on the shore to position the ship for these landings. We started using it more for station keeping when the ships were underway, but every time we asked for the range to the ship ahead, it interrupted the scan at the vicinity to see if there were other ships that could collide with our group, so we still tried to use the field of the binoculars as the primary method. It was handy however, in confirming our position off the beach if it was foggy when we approach Santa Margarita.

Finally the supplies of troops slowed, we made only three landings, admitting the first at Coronado Strand. Then, the troops didn't arrive at all, and we operated empty beds, with new crews in the boats, and a group of officers observing who would serve as division staffs when they went to new construction. Then, things became really slow, and the ship was tied to two buoys in lower San Diego Bay, and our boats would make landings taking Marines from the Marine training base to Coronado Strand.

This operation was very boring for a young officer, even though

I was promoted to Lieutenant Junior Grade without question. I applied for flight training, but it really wasn't open to my class. Eventually, the executive officer, when he was on leave in San Francisco – Oakland area mentioned to the commanding officer of the training and manning command in Alameda, that he had an officer who was qualified to be a navigator of a ship, and had been assigned as gunnery officer as well.

He came back to the ship when his leave was up, and told me to submit a request for transfer to Alameda for assignment to a newly constructed gunboat. My commanding officer insisted on a different process, and my request went to Coast Guard Headquarters. I received the orders rather promptly, but not to one of the ships under construction. I was to go to the USS Bayfield, another of the attack transports being manned by all Coast Guard crews. I left the Liggett in April 1945 for some leave, and another trip to the Pacific via San Francisco.

The War's End

As I had before, I had a considerable period of time to wait in San Francisco for transportation to my new assignment. I spent one of my first days in the area by going over to Alameda to visit with the commanding officer of the manning section there, because I knew he had expected that he would have an officer reporting from the Liggett. I had known him when I was a cadet, because he had been the Tactics Officer at the Academy when I first arrived. Capt. Hadley Evans told me that he still wanted me for the new ships, and he would send off a message to Headquarters to get my orders changed. He asked how to get in touch with me, and I felt that I might still get on one of those new ships with the guns, fire control, and some interesting duty.

I spent the time waiting by going to schools that were available at Treasure Island, the big Navy base in the area. I took a course in the 5 inch gun, I remember, because I knew we would have them on the Bayfield. Our evenings were free; I would often go to the Junior Officers Club that I had found when I was there earlier.

I was told one day that I should report to a Filipino merchant ship that evening for transportation to the Pacific. I promptly contacted Capt. Evans, and let him know that I would leave that evening if he did not have any new orders for me. He told them me that he would send another message, priority this time, to see if Headquarters had had a change of heart. (Priority messages were not supposed to be used for personnel matters – – deferred, two levels lower, was the usual precedent, and it could take days to arrive in a big command.) He called me late in the afternoon and told me he had authority to change my orders, provided that he sent another officer similarly qualified, to the Bayfield. He said, "I just don't have anyone to substitute for you." So, I boarded the MS Dona Anictea for another long trip to the Pacific.

We spent 18 days across the Pacific to Eniwetok, where we stopped slung enough for someone to come aboard and give information to the captain. Then we went west to Guam, where all the officers who had been on board for transportation left the ship. We had, in addition to the officers, two priests who were to reestablish the Cathedral of Guam. It had been left in ruins when the Japanese took Guam in 1942, and these two were to reestablish the parish, and provide a church for the Chamorros, the natives of Guam. This ship had been chosen, I presume, because of the almost completely Filipino crew, (except for the armed guard detail), and the fact that the Navy chaplain was sent in our passenger group. The chaplain, of course, was a Catholic.

After 18 days crossing the Pacific, it was odd that I spent another 18 days waiting at the Navy Receiving Station at Agama, Guam, doing little but trying to figure out how to pass the days. The officers they were usually assigned to censoring the mail, as was done at that time for all mail leaving the forward areas. Some of the mail was really personal, but it was interesting how many times someone told people back home, "When the war is over, I'm going to put on a pair of oars over my shoulders, walk inland, and when someone asks what those things are, that's where I will stay!"

Together with the officers I'd come out with, I went out to the beach many days. It wasn't a pretty swimming spot, with many sea slugs on the bottom, but it was a pretty beach. Hitchhiking to the beach was never a problem, either. I don't think we ever missed going to a movie at night, and I haven't any idea whether they were good or not. The seats were hard benches, but who cared!

After my 18 days, I was called in to be told that my ship was in Agama Harbor, and I would go for that day. I arrived at noon, about in time for lunch, and was told the ship was about to sail for San Francisco at 4 PM. One of the requirements for Captain Evans to change my orders was another officer, similarly qualified, and I was told I would be the gunnery officer, but not until we returned to San Francisco, because the officer I was to relieve was going back with us. So, I spent the return trip acquainting myself with the department of the ship and again, I had few duties.

The first night in San Francisco, most of the crew celebrated the return to the states after a much longer period in the Pacific than I had had. (They had participated in both the Okinawa and Iwo Jima landings as transport flagship.) I don't remember what I did, because it wasn't long since I left the port. But the next morning, the executive officer called me and because he had a job for me. As a squadron flagship, our transport had a Catholic chaplain on our crew, and he celebrated the first night of our return, to such an extent that he was picked up by the shore patrol, and was incarcerated overnight. They wanted an officer to ask escort him back to his ship. I served in that world, with a very quiet and well behaved lieutenant commander.

We had some minor per repairs performed on the ship and resupply of general stores and ammunition. As we neared our sailing time, the ammunition was brought to the dock, and we had to place it in the magazines. That was the day that the Enola Gay dropped its bomb on Nagasaki, and everyone felt the war was over. The shipyard workers all walked off their jobs and our ammunition was still sitting on the dock. We nearly had to bribe the crane operator to lift it onto the deck of the ship, where we put it under guard overnight, until we could store it properly in the magazines.

When I was going ashore in the (San Francisco) Bay area, I met a classmate of mine from the Academy, Art Perry, who had now been assigned to ashore inside the San Francisco Captain of the Port at Fisherman's Wharf. We got together one night to have dinner, and then we're going to take two girls I had met before out dancing. For dinner, we decided that we would go to the Junior Officers Club, where they always served home-style cooking at a good price.

After dinner, it was too early to depart for our dates, so we played a little ping-pong, and then it was summer, we cooled off as we stood by a window near the ping-pong room. Two attractive girls went by, we commented on the fact that if we came back there on the same evening the following week, they would be there again. We did come back on the following week, and one of those two girls, I saw again, and became acquainted with. She is my wife Bette. We never found the other one that evening but my evening was a genuine success.

We sailed for the Philippines shortly after the war was over, and we had a load of personnel on board were not happy with their lot. Many of them had enough "points" to qualify for immediate release, but most of the others were close. However, we delivered them to Samar as ordered. Someone else would have to wrestle the question of when they went home.

As we were at anchor at SAMA, a boat from a nearby a.k.a. attack cargo ship with a Coast Guard crew came over with another of my Academy classmates, Rufe Drury, who had been the star running back on the football team, and an outstanding boxer in his weight class. He had a copy of an ALCOAST message that said that applications were being accepted from our class for flight training. He told me he was going to submit his application, and asked me if I was interested. I had once sent in an application when I was in San Diego in amphibious training, but I felt certain that the earlier one would not be accepted, because it really didn't apply to our class. This one did, and I arranged to go ashore with Rufe to take a flight physical at a nearby Air Corps base.

When they gave me my chest x-ray, they said there was a film or thickening of the area, and said it was an indication that I had had exposure did to tuberculosis at some time. The corpsmen said that they wouldn't even bother to send it in, if it were an Army man. I told him to send it anyway, but I had to submit my letter of request also. Captain Richards, my commanding officer, endorsed my request with a statement that I could not be spared from the ship until it took was turned over to the Navy, and that date wasn't known at that time. I stayed at sea.

After we had unloaded our personnel, we reloaded the troops

who would go to Japan on occupation duty. We were to go to Amari in Northern Honshu. Our personnel would make the initial landing at that location. We steamed north, and examined operational orders. One new requirement for us was that we were to stream para vanes , to cut loose moored mines that might be in the area. Of course, we would have our degaussing activated to reduce the magnetic field of the ship to avoid activating magnetic mines.

We had one or two destroyers as escorts, but they couldn't really cover all the threats we thought possible, even with the war over. None of the threats applied, however, and we came to anchor in the harbor, and unloaded our troops without incident. I went ashore once, and saw Japanese families, gathered in the ruins of their home, cooking or heating water for tea over little campfires. They were really frightened of the Americans, because they had been gone years of being told how terrible the white men were. I still have a small tea saki bowl that I picked up that day on the shores of Aomori.

At this point in the Pacific operations, we were assigned to the "Magic Carpet" to return troops from the Pacific to the West Coast. Our first test was to pick up troops in Tinian and in Saipan for return. That first night we were assigned to an anchorage off Tinian, and I had gone to bed after the movie. I was awakened early in the morning, but what seem to be a huge giant, striking the ship with an immense hammer. We were dragging anchor, because a sudden typhoon had come up in the early hours.

We had several boats at the boat boom, in the water, to bring the personnel to the ship the next day, and had had no chance to hoist them aboard. Fortunately, we were blown out to sea, when I got to the bridge, we simply hoisted the anchor aboard, and went on out. The typhoon traveled fast, in the afternoon, it had left us behind.

We simply turned back, and returned to our anchorage. On the way back to Tainan, we saw at least two boats on our track line, our boats that had blown away. We just maneuvered alongside, had a boat crew go down a cargo net into the boat where they started the engine without delay and brought the boat under a boat fall. We lost several boats, but it wasn't a big deal to survey a boat at this time.

After we took the people from Tinian and on board, we moved to a dock at Saipan. We spent the day loading, and that night we stayed at the dock. A friend from the Academy class behind me, John Lape, and I went ashore to see if we could find anything that was of interest. We ended up at an officer's club some distance away, and it was on the hill. There wasn't anything interesting for us there, and we weren't interested in just drinking, so we started back to the ship. Usually, it was not too hard to hitchhike, but at night and in a strange area, we weren't too sure. John said, "I know how to do this," and led me to the parking lot. He chose the last Jeep, climbed in and let it coast down the first incline. He explained, "You have to take the next to last, because the last one may have the regular operator too close." Keys were no problem, because none of them had keys. You just switched them on.

As we coasted down that first incline, I looked back, to see an officer going to last Jeep, realize it was not his, looking for his, where we had just departed. He knew we had his Jeep. I shook my boots all the way back to the port director's office, where we bailed out, and walked about a block to the ship. John seemed completely unconcerned and boasted, "I've left a trail of Jeeps behind." When I asked others who had been on the ship longer, it seemed that he had borrowed his Jeep transportation in England, North Africa, Southern France, etc. He knew how it was done!

The Bayfield sailed the next morning for Long Beach California, when we arrived, I asked the executive officer for 10 days during our in port time, in order that I could get back to San Francisco to marry Betty. The Executive Officer Cmdr. Justice P. White, a big man who had been an outstanding lineman in football at the Academy, gave me a big grin, and replied, "Anyone who thinks of marriage should be restricted to the ship for 10 days to think about the advantages of being single." But he gave me the leave, and I flew to San Francisco.

Betty and I went through everything associated with getting married: getting a blood test, getting issued a license, lining laying the church, making the appointment with the minister, getting out invitations, getting her relatives used to the idea, and finally we married in All Saints Episcopal Church, in Palo Alto, California, on October 27, 1945.

We had planned to go to Carmel for a honeymoon, and had rented a Chevrolet coupe to drive down. The first evening, we spent at Betty's sister's house, and we drove there with an escort part of the way with friends who could once more drive without gasoline restrictions. I think thought the car ran a little rough, but the tin cans tied to the rear made so much noise that I couldn't be sure. I went out the next morning, to start the car, and see if it demonstrated any roughness, but it started easily and sounded fine. So we started down the road.

We came to a traffic light, and the engine died at idle. I started it again, but with a little difficulty. We had to stop for a train crossing the road, and the engine died again. This time it didn't start, and I looked around for a service station. In those days, they were service station! There was a mechanic on duty at the station, only a block away. As I walked back to the car, I thought about what could cause such difficult and suddenly, I had it.

There is no such thing as automatic chokes on cars in 1942 through 1946 (I'm not sure what vintage this car was), and there was a choke lever on the dashboard. You could pull it out when the engine was cold, and push it back to the normal position when the engine was warm. My friends, as they arranged the tin cans, had also raised the hood and bent the choke wire, and temperature required, so the engine was always choked. It worked fine while the engine was cold, but when it was warm, the engine was choked excessively, and it died at idle. I quickly raised the hood, confirmed that they had bent the control wire, and straightened again. We had no further trouble with the car, and I drove to the service station to let the mechanic name that his services were not needed.

After three days at the Highlands Inn, we flew to Long Beach to make final arrangements to sail. I was a navigator of the ship, and I went to the Navy office to get our sailing orders. We were to go to Yokosuka, continuing our Magic Carpet trips. We thought that this would be an interesting voyage, since no one had been in Japan for so long. We were to sell direct to 30°

north, 140° west, and then due west until we were near Japan. The reason for this routing was that too many ships had hit extremely rough weather when sailing on a more direct route.

A couple of days out of Long Beach we had some of that extremely rough weather, and if you went down to the crew's mess, you could see that a main fore and beam through that area was working in the seas. We slowed, but continued on our way. About a day later, we had a change in routing. We were to go to Sasebo, Japan. We thought this would be interesting, too, because the Japanese Naval Academy was located there. However, we didn't have the hydro-pacs for this area, and they gave all the latest information on aids to navigation, sightings of mines, and all the things you really wanted to know, other than the charts. He stated all the books and charts we had, and hoped for the best.

A couple of days later, orders were changed again. This time we were to go to Inchon, Korea, or Jinsen as it had been known for all the years of Japanese occupation before the war. We started our study again, looking for both Jinsen or Inchon. We arrived off the entrance to Inchon, which meant about 50 miles from the port area, and were met by an LCI to escort us and another vessel into the port. We followed his track exactly and came to anchor in sight of the city. The docks were long ramps to which our landing craft would moor on one side or the other. You could not leave boat unattended, because the tides were 30 feet or more, and if you left a boat, it could be underwater when you returned, or high and dry on the mud flats.

I went ashore again, to receive our return sailing orders, and pick up the hydro-pace. When we plotted the information, we found that we had sailed through one or two minefields, but we now had exact sailing information to depart. We followed these new directions, and at exactly the spot indicated for us to follow, we sent a floating mine. We sank it by gunfire and I still have an interesting picture of the explosion.

Our return was to Seattle, Washington, the captain, Capt. W. R. Richards, had been at the Academy during part of my time there, and had been stationed in the area before the war. We took the great circle route from just southeast of Tokyo to the entrances of the Straits of Juan de Fuca. Several days it was so clear and calm, that you felt that you should be able to see the Aleutians to the north. We were not that far north, however. Once we were in the Straits, as required by the Navy, we picked up a pilot at Port Angeles, and went into Elliott Bay, off of Seattle.

I went to ashore the first evening and called my bride of a few days and an absence of several weeks, let her know we were in Seattle. We would be in the port for long enough to repair that sprung main beam, so there was an opportunity to be together for some time. I made it a reservation at the Olympic Hotel and returned to the ship.

I had the duty the next day, but I didn't expect Betty for yet another day, since I thought she would take the train. All planes were taken by priority flights. I relieved the department head duty at noon, and sat down for lunch. Suddenly, someone came into the wardroom, and told me that my wife was aboard. She had gotten a flight, a very rough one on the leg into Seattle from Portland, had talked the proprietor of the New Washington Hotel into giving her room, it had to be suite, and then started an inquiry about the location of the Bayfield. She found it was anchored in the Bay, and then worked locating where the boats came in. She eventually talked some sailors were following her into locating the landing our ship used, and she came out to the ship. Doug Armsden volunteered to take my duty that day, and we went ashore just after lunch.

The ship moved soon to Everett, Washington, where we went into a yard. The weather was very poor, and I experienced an ice storm for the first time in my life. We had to move from hotel to hotel, because the wartime rules didn't permit occupation of a room for more than three days. We played musical rooms with other friends from the ship. The best food in town was often on the ship, and Betty and another wife, Betty Dring, often came to the ship for dinner.

I had my first disagreement with Betty has a result of one of these visits. I had a case of hiccups after dinner one evening, and we went through all the usual remedies. I held my breath, I drink water, I tried to drink with my head upside down, she tried to frighten me, and none of the more. Then she suggested that I take a spoonful of sugar. I pooh-pooh that idea, but nothing else had worked, so I tried it. It turned out that someone had filled the sugar bowl with salt, and now I had a mouthful of salt! I spit it out, and ran to the drinking fountain. Since we were in the yard, this was just the time the workers had chosen to cut off the water. I continued to spit, but I also had things to say about old wives' tales about getting rid of hiccups. I continued to say things about the old wives' tales for some time.

We finished the availability in Everett, and sailed again for Inchon. This time the trip was less complicated, we picked up a load of personnel whose time was up, and carried them this time to San Francisco. We were told that we should now turn the ship over to the Navy with a Navy crew, and we would go back to the Coast Guard. We needed up to date inventories of all of our equipment, and since all of the inventorying was done on a rather loose basis during the life of the ship up to this time, it became quite a task.

There was one event that was quite interesting during this period. The department heads on the ship took turns up with the duty, and one evening it was John Lape's turn. He'd ask a girl friend who worked in Alameda to come to the ship for dinner, and he had to figure out how to get her there. He was never at a loss for transportation, as I said before, and he was not this time either. He simply borrowed the captain's gig, since it was in the water alongside the ship, started it up and ran it over the landing at the Naval Air Station Alameda.

Unfortunately for him, someone saw the boat moving away from the ship, and heard the engine running, which proved it was not just drifting down the estuary. The shore patrol in the entire bay was alerted, and everyone on the alert for boat thief. When he returned with his date, he was greeted by either the captain or the exec to be told he would be restricted to the ship for the next two weeks. I think he told the girl involved come onto the ship during the time to visit, so it wasn't too unpleasant.

The Bayfield was never a Coast Guard ship, even though almost everyone on board was in the Coast Guard, so when we turned it back to the Navy, it was simply a matter of relieving the crew, and we left. I went to the Alameda Coast Guard

Station, where Captain Evans was still the commanding officer. I saw the Bayfield again several years later when she was in Pearl Harbor, still training for the time she would be needed for amphibious duty. It was 1953 or 1954, she looked the same but the crew spirit couldn't have been as good.

I Joined the Coast Guard

When the crew descended on the Training and Manning Station in Alameda, I didn't know if there were any plans for the majority of us, but there were many who were simply separated from the service and sent home. I was one of the minority of men who had a regular commission, and didn't ask to be let out. So I became part of the staff at the Station. I was made Personnel Administration Officer, but it made little difference to me -- I didn't know what I was to do in this position.

Fortunately there was a Chief Yeoman Spencer, who really knew what to do in the office, and all he really needed was someone to give the authority of the rank to his actions. In the meantime, I pored over directives, and tried to learn all that should go on in personnel administration.

One of the things that became too readily discernible was that for every personal action, there had to be prepared a forms CG – 2599 which ended in the personnel jacket of the concerned person. This was for every action – if the man was assigned to mess cooking, or if he was entitled to a $50 raise in a draft of people going to the East Coast. This latter resulted in 50 separate forms to be signed. With the number of persons on the station at that time, and reductions in force in effect, there were stacks of 2599's as high as 8 inches tall that had to be signed by an officer. It wasn't long before I learned how to sign my name without lifting my pen, and get it done in a hurry. To take care of the number of signatures that were needed, there were letters of delegation of authority issued to transient officers, for the sole purpose of signing personnel action reports. An officer would spend the entire day or more just signing his name to something he had no other interest in!

Another action that kept my attention was the personnel boards, usually to get someone out of the service. There had been a great surge in enlistments just at the war ended, and some of the young men could not even read. Some could read but had no comprehension. We had personnel unfitness boards, and undesirable boards etc. I don't think with that we were ever turned down if we recommended a discharge. The only thing might be the type of discharge. We tried to recommend the most favorable type, unless the action was a result of a criminal act while not in the jurisdiction of the service – – in the city of Oakland, or on liberty nearby.

The physical for flight training that I had taken when I was in the Philippines caught up with me during this assignment. I was not a selected for the class that was sent to training at this time, because the of the endorsement of Capt. Richards that he could not spare me until the ship was turned back to the Navy, but they had noted the comments on the x-ray. They wanted me to get another chest x-ray.

The station had had a complete medical department, but we were to be decommissioned after the reductions of the services were complete, and the medical area was being reduced in size to make it more compatible with a smaller operating base. The x-ray machine had been moved to a storage area, but it was still in operating condition I was told. I reported to the x-ray technician who told me to put my chin on the top of the movable section, and then he moved it up. It was still about four inches below my chin when he reached maximum height, so he told me to stand with my feet apart to lower my chin.

Unfortunately, the machine was more or less out-of-the-way in this room, and it was located rather close to the wall. I had to stand with one foot under me and the other one well out to the side. Then I twisted my chest back and forth of the photo area. When the results came in from Coast Guard Headquarters this time, they said I had no problem with my chest, but that I did have a curvature of the spine.

One Sunday, Betty and I were driving around, and had parked at the Marina area of San Francisco, when I saw a ship that was entering the Golden Gate. It had an unusual profile, and I couldn't recognize it at first. Then I realized it was the cutter Taney, which I knew was coming to Alameda for its postwar location. We drove over to Alameda to see it arrive at the dock, and I thought what a beautiful ship it was. One reason I had trouble recognizing it as a Coast Guard cutter, was that it was still in wartime gray, as it had come from the yard in postwar conversion in Charleston.

Very shortly afterward, we were told that the Training Station was to be decommissioned (we knew that already), and we would be assigned elsewhere. We could ask for the locations or units we would like. I asked for and was given orders to report to the Taney, right there at Alameda. I reported on June 5, 1946, and was told that I was to be the navigator, and as a collateral duty, the exchange officer.

During the time it was to be at the Training Station, I had just moved into the apartment that Betty had had in San Francisco, and drove over the San Francisco – Oakland bridge morning and evening. It was quite a commute but I didn't mind the drive. The only thing was that traffic at times could be nerve-racking, and as I often fell asleep at night, I would start dreaming of driving traffic. I knew more than once, I dreamt that I had to put the brake on, and raised my knee to put on the brakes on in my dream, only to kick Betty in the family in the bed (no dream!). So when I was assigned to the Taney, we moved to a housing development in East Oakland called Tassafaronga Village, after the area on Guadalcanal. Most of the Taney personnel lived there, except the commanding officer, Capt. Bowman

The Taney made two ocean station patrols to Station November, halfway to Hawaii, and navigating was fun on those patrols, most of the time. The weather was good on station a large part of the time, and since our position didn't change, neither did the general position of the stars. Capt. Bowman suggested that I use one of the advantages of an aviation octant, by averaging three sites on the same body, and since finding the important stress was not difficult, I could usually take a round of three stars on each, compute the intercepts, and plot the fix in a short time.

The senior quartermaster, (the enlisted man who corrected the charts and maintained the navigation bridge) would take my time and record my sights, we had a good routine. There was a stretch of time when I was able to get daytime fixes by sights on the sun in Venus, because it was so bright. I usually had my fix plotted and prepared for delivery to the captain, before the ensigns had completed the observations for the sites that they were to take for training. And the fixes were usually point fixes.

Capt. Bowman didn't like the fact that the ship was still painted wartime gray, and wanted to return to peacetime white with a buff stack as soon as we could. He told the supply officer to get a supply of white paint is money for that purpose became available, and also, course some buff – – a color that had not been seen in years. We bought the best paint available, and simply stored it. Then the message came in on one of our patrols that the paint scheme for cutters was once more the prewar colors. The entire crew turned to, painting everything above the main deck as it should be in the future – – no Coast Guard stripes, however, in those days. We returned from the patrol with only the hull gray, and everything else in the new colors. We were probably the first cutter in Alameda to be painted in Coast Guard white and buff.

When the weather turned bad, especially on the last patrol in December, I had blown up a loran chart, giving it a much larger scale, to try to get more precision. The location of the stations, on the West Coast and Hawaii didn't allow for much error, before you could be several miles off in the intersection of the lines of position. Charlie Shepard, from the class ahead of me, was navigating 250-foot cutter, one of those gunboats that I had hoped for once, that was delivered after the war was over, when the relieved us for the last time on that station, and he said our loran position was an error by about 10 miles. It was easy to do when we hadn't seen stars for several days.

On our one patrol to Station Papa which was due West of the Straits of Juan de Fuca, we were not required to hold position as precisely as on the southern station. On that station, airplanes used the ship as a navigation position on the way to or from Hawaii, but on the northern station, we were just a weather ship. We were required to be within 100 mile circle. There was some drift, regardless of weather, and our weather was almost completely calm for good part of the patrol.

I knew there was drift, because when it so calm, Capt. Bowman decided to hold an abandoned ship drill one day, and put everyone over the sides and lifeboats, except for himself and one other person on the bridge, the radio watch and two other people in the engine room. We had to row hard to keep up with the drift of the ship, even though it was glassy calm. The weather had been so calm that we had both engines secured, as we would have in port, and only one boiler online to get power back.

We were not scheduled to make a patrol in September, but the ship that was scheduled, was one of the new cutters, (ex- gunboats) , that just arrived from the yard. It had many discrepancies that had to be corrected before it could make a patrol, and so – – the dependable Taney had to fill in. This turned out to be the time that Betty was going to have our first child, and I was tempted to ask for leave, but there was really no one to fill in navigator – – so I left her to the last days of her pregnancy alone. Gregory arrived on September 1, and I was in the radio room on the ship when they copied the message that told me that mother and baby were fine – – but I fear lonesome.

On one of the last days of our patrol in that station, the two men who operated the ship's laundry were doing the linens from the officers' country, and one of them was using the mangle, an ironing device, heated by steam to a rather high temperature. One of the sheets or spreads became caught, and he tried to clear it without stopping it. The inevitable happened, he cut his hand in the mangle. Before he and the other man could remove his hand, it was barely burned and partially crushed.

The ocean station vessels usually had a doctor on the ships, frequently for only a single voyage, then the doctors would go back to a public health hospital, (Marine Hospital in those days). We had a doctor, and he was needed this time. Usually he just treated colds or chronic seasickness, but the hand needed attention. The doctor put a cast on the hand, mostly to keep air from the burnt skin, and told the captain that the young man really needed hospital care.

Since no other cutter could get to us to transfer the patient faster than we could go to port, it was up to us. We were due to be relieved very soon, and the captain asked for permission to leave station after sending out our last weather report before we left the hundred mile circle when the relief ship would be inside the circle by the time the next one was due to be sent. That allowed us to crank up full speed about two hours before we were actually relieved on station – –and we passed the other ship going over 20 knots, with following seas and a tail wind. The condition of the hand worsened, and it was a good thing that we had gone on because the doctor had to amputate the tips of two fingers and all the center fingers on the next day. The fellow had only half of his index finger and his little finger left on that hand. We got him to the hospital as fast as we could have in those days of no helicopters.

I received a new set of orders in the fall of 1946. I was to go to shore duty in the district office in Long Beach, where I was to be the assistant communications officer. Once again, I didn't know anything about these new tasks, but I guess the Coast Guard needed communications officers, and I hadn't asked for anything else that was available except aviation, and that had not worked out. Capt. Bowman has encouraged me to ask again for aviation, and my class had been covered by a message that had come in just before Thanksgiving.

I asked for flight training again, but those new orders sent me elsewhere. Now the captain suggested that I ask that my request for aviation be considered in spite of the new orders. I prepared my part of the letter, and sent comments in it to him for his endorsement. When I saw what the ship's office people had typed as the endorsement, I went hurrying to him to ask, "Captain, do you really want to say this?" His endorsement had said," LTJG Siler's request for aviation training should be considered in spite of the fact that he has now been ordered to duty as a communications officer, a specialty for which he is singularly ill adapted." He responded to my inquiry, "Those comments won't hurt you when they look at your fitness report." I guess he was right, because I did go to flight training, and when I saw the fitness report years later, it was a very good report.

We went to Long Beach shortly after 1 January 1947. The first task was to find a place to live. I would drive to an area where there were apartments, park the car, and walk from apartment office to office. Many of them had signs outside, "No children." It was tempting when a manager said, "We take no one with children," to respond "Just a minute, I'll go home and strangle our baby!" and see what the reaction but I didn't, we stayed in a beachfront cottage (dump) for the first three months. It was convenient, but it was cold, and unattractive and expensive for what it provided. It came complete with rats, but not many, fortunately.

In those days in those days, we had been indoctrinated that we were expected to call on our new commanding officer within 48 hours of reporting. You simply asked the boss when you made your first office visit on reporting, "Will you and Mrs. Bennett be at home (either) this evening or tomorrow evening" On one of those evenings Betty and I called on the Commodore and his wife. He, like me, had had a higher rank – Rear Admiral in his case – during the war but, but had reverted to Commodore after 1 July 1946. When we arrived at the lovely home they had on Ocean Boulevard, Mrs. Bennett greeted us and told us the Commodore had had to go to bed, he had such painful bursitis.

So she entertained us alone. She soon said, "Would you like a drink?" To which we agreed, and asked us into the kitchen and she prepared them. She proposed rum and Coke, not a favorite of either Bette or me, but she was the boss's wife. She pulled out iced tea glasses – tall – and filled them with ice cubes. Then she poured in rum to within two inches of the top them, and then touched them with Coke. We talked and sipped for a while, mainly about how hard it was to find a place to live, and she asked if we would like to see her home, (mansion to us). We accepted, mainly to get away from the rum and cokes, and make sure she didn't offer another.

I gradually learn more about communications, but it was

apparent that the communications officer expected to retire before too long, and I would be either tagged as his relief or sent off to advanced communication school, neither of which I was looking forward to. I visited several of the district units, all the way up the coast to Santa Maria, and down to San Diego. It was interesting, but I didn't look forward to a career in this. For some reason, at one time I was selected to attend Treasury intelligence school, to two week course in Los Angeles. I drove up each day with the senior intelligence man from the district, and drove back in the late afternoon.

One of those days when we returned, I went to the offices I always did, even though everyone would be gone except the communications watch and the operations duty officer. As I left the elevator, a man standing in the hall asked me, "Can you tell me where the men's room is?" I told him it was in the opposite direction from where I was going – – and went on to my office.

When I left the building a few minutes later, I realized the man was on the elevator with me but we didn't speak. I started down the street toward where my car was parked, when I heard, "Hey Marine! Hey Marine!" I was wearing the gray uniform that was used during the war, and I paid no attention to the call, but I looked into store windows as I walked past, and saw it was the man who had been on the elevator, who was calling, and he was just behind me. I came to a traffic light, and stopped, which gave him the opportunity to catch up, and he offered to show me a few new things I hadn't experienced before. I offered him returned that I would show him a few things he would remember – – right there! He took the suggestion and headed off but I was steaming so much that Betty knew something was wrong when I drove home.

After three months in that beach cottage, we gave up on the idea of finding a furnished apartment, and decided we would buy some furniture, and look for an unfurnished one. One of the real difficulties was getting stoves and refrigerators – – they hadn't been built in sufficient quantities during the war, and you had to be at the right place at the right time to get your order in. We found an old used stove with the high oven off to one side, and after some welding by a local repair man, it looked as if it would serve.

I went to the Montgomery Wards appliance store every day during my lunch hour, and after some time, I was able to place an in order for a refrigerator that didn't look too bad. We went to a furniture store and bought a sofa and matching chair which didn't look bad but it wasn't stock we would've bought if we had had the luxury of building an inventory of furniture we loved. We bought a mattress from a mattress factory, and were promised a box spring by the chief who was showing us how to handle classified material (and his wife). We found an unfurnished apartment over a garage in a new area where the garages were behind the little homes, and each of them had these apartments. It was nice to move into a new home, and it was only about two blocks from the beach – – very near the Navy's Seal Beach installation.

This didn't last long. I had received orders to go to Corpus Christi for flight training, to report in the middle of June. We had to make arrangements to return the box springs, put most of the furniture in storage, because the orders were for temporary duty and get our car ready to go. On temporary duty orders, you could ship enough things to hold you for short time – 500 pounds – but a household had to be put into storage until you received permanent orders. My orders are for temporary duty in Corpus Christi, and permanent change of station to Pensacola, Florida. We moved everything out of our house exactly two months after we had moved in. I had cleaned all the junk out of the car, and made as much room as they could to take all that we would need in moving to Texas with a nine-month-old baby.

We left with the Ford business coupe – no backseat, but storage space behind the driver seat, and a good-sized trunk – packed to the top. Greg could sleep in a cradle basket on the platform behind the front seat. We didn't go far the first day – Yuma, Arizona. The next day we wanted to go further, but the maps didn't show a good place to stop, so we stopped in Tucson. At least, I wanted to go through Tucson before I quit, so we found a motel with "water cooled" air, on the east side of town. It also had a carport to get the car out of the sun.

The next morning we loaded up, got in the car to head off for a breakfast spot and started to back out of the carport. The car needed more gas than I thought it should, and it went up little incline, quickly dropped down again. I gave it a little more gas, and it started the same routine. I realized that we had a flat tire somewhere. Sure enough, the right rear tire was very flat. I pulled everything out the trunk to get the tire tools, and then pulled out the jack. All these tools were all the way forward in the trunk of this model of the car. I then looked for the handle of the check – and discovered that I must've cleaned it out of the truck before we left Long Beach!

Since it was still rather early in the morning, and we had hoped to make up for the shorter day than we had hoped for the day before, I still wanted to get on the road. I pulled a large screwdriver out, squeezed on my belly under the car to reach the jack, and turned the jack drive with it. It became harder and harder as more weight of the car came on the jack, but I lifted the tire off the ground and loosened the studs on the flat tire, so I could remove it. Then I put the spare in place, and found that an inflated tire was larger, and the car was not high enough for this tire. I hated to crawl under the car when it was supported only by the jack, and I was frustrated enough at this point that I tried to force the tire into place. I suddenly got it to move, not in the correct place, but such that a part of the tire and the wheel came together, with my right middle forefinger between them. It started bleeding, and dripping blood all over the tools. I got a Band-Aid from Bette and went on trying to get the tire into the correct place. Betty came out to watch my effort and saw that I was turning pale, and took me to lie down on the bed, while she went off to find someone – – anyone – – to change that tire.

While I recuperated and watched Greg, she went down the street to where she found three men lounging on the cot in front of a garage. She asked them for assistance, and slowly they got up, adjusting clothing as if they'd slept there in front of the building, and one found a wheeled jack. The man and Betty came back, and with the proper equipment, it was only a few minutes to change the tire.

I don't remember whether we had breakfast, but we felt that I needed to have first aid for the finger, because I had bruised and cut the fleshy part of the finger, and it was still bleeding.

Tetanus shots are probably called for as well. We headed for the Davis – Monthan Air Force Base, and found the clinic. My finger was treated, I received my shot, and much to think about, when the corpsman said, "You may lose the use of that finger, the tendons were damaged." I didn't lose any use, except for the next few days, and we proceeded on our way.

There were many places where homogenized milk for Greg was not available, and some where even pasteurized milk was not available. Diapers were a problem also, and Betty would wash out the ones he had worn during the night or the previous day, before we could leave a place in the morning, and dry them by trailing them out the window list. Disposable diapers were not available but diaper liners were, and we left a polluted trail of diaper liners across the southern part of the United States.

We arrived in Corpus Christi on June 15, 1947, and found a motel on the North Beach side of the city – certainly not the best area of town. We set up in a motel room, to house hunt for the months we would be here, and try to establish ourselves before I reported to the Air Training Command on the 17th. It was hot and humid, with little relief anywhere. Bette wrote to her mother, "I think I have gone to hell a little early." We didn't find much in the way of living quarters, and even went on the radio to be a part of a program set up just for people like us who were military reporting to the commands there. We lived for a couple of nights with the woman who ran that radio program, and then were able to take over the home of a Navy officer who had a child who needed a serious operation, and the family was going to be away for that treatment for at least a month.

Flight Training

Once we were established in the house of the absent naval officer, my greatest concern was on the base, with efforts continually to find somewhere to live when our month was up. I had turned in my orders to say I had reported, and turned in my pay record to the pay office. We had a peculiar pay arrangement, where the Navy would pay us our usual pay, but the travel pay had to be paid by the Coast Guard district office in New Orleans. I found out quickly that I was to take another flight physical – everyone took them whenever we moved from one base to another – and then join the pool of waiting officers for ground school class to start.

House hunting did not go any better after the month we spent in the naval officer's house. We gave up, and moved into the bachelors' officers' quarters (BOQ) where they would allow an officer who is married to have two rooms, interconnected, and an officer with children could have three rooms. We were not to have cooking facilities, except for a two burner hotplate in a central wing at the BOQ. There was also a single refrigerator in this area, and we could use a shelf for milk for the children.

There were several families, most of them with children, who had accepted this option for housing after trying for weeks to find someplace in the city. We were in the wing of the building nearest the club, with a large lawn area outside. In the other direction, from our room, there was the bay, or shallows that were not used now, but once had been a water area for small seaplanes on floats.

The restrictions on hot plates and refrigerator space were not accepted by the residents, and the building supervisors acknowledged that they were not realistic. Each of us had our own hotplate, and we usually cooked with the pressure cooker. Bette discovered more ways to prepare food in that device that we would've imagined earlier. One of our rooms was the kitchen/dining space/living area, we had a bedroom, and a child's room. At times we found that there was a refrigerator that was put in the disposal group, but would still operate. It would be located in one wing of the building, and we could have two or even three shelves for food.

Bathroom facilities were unusual also. They were common spaces originally designed for men only. To accommodate the families, three were now designated women's, and the other three men's. Since the building was a two-story design, one on the first floor would have the opposite designation for the one over it, and the system was carried out throughout the building. With the number of quite small children in the building, the women's head facility was usually used in the morning, the children's toilet this training facility, with the mother sharing gossip and nots on husband's flight training, with the door to a toilet stall propped open while she checked on a small child on the throne.

We've observed Greg's first birthday while we lived here, we bought a cake, which he probably enjoyed without any idea why we thought it a special occasion. When I brought the cake to the building, I took it from the car, and started at the outside steer to our rooms. I don't know what happened, but I was holding it by one hand, under the cake, and as I went up the stairs, it toppled from my hand, upside down on the hood of our car. I'm sure Greg didn't know the difference, it still tasted good, with that a taste of car dirt, as far as I know.

The beginning of the new flight training ground school was to be July 17 – a month waiting around doing nothing but trying to find somewhere where we could live, or go to the officers' club pool. There were three other Coast Guard officers who had been in flight training in Dallas before coming to Corpus Christi. They flew the N2S Stearman biplane, the "yellow peril," before they came to Corpus. We were to start in the SNJ, a more powerful plane with retractable landing gear, and never fly the N2S except for a demonstration flight on how one would recover from an inverted spin – – it was thrilling. But first we had to spend a month on just ground school, learning air navigation, power plants, and flight regulations.

The Coast Guard officers who were ahead of us were finishing their flying of the N2S, and then started into the flying of the SNJ, but our class impatiently waited. We started with about eight of us Coast Guard personnel, and a group of around 30 officers were to make the entire class. That group in Dallas had originally had at least five Coast Guard officers, but one was chronically airsick – he was chronically seasick before, and the other decided he didn't want to stay in the Coast Guard.

On 1 July, I went into the pay office, needing my pay after the travel, and as most new student naval officers did, I had taken out an insurance policy to be paid for by my flight pay, when it started. I needed another letter from Coast Guard Headquarters to start that, however. When I got up to the pay window, the clerk looked through the envelopes, and said "We don't have one for you; let me see what's wrong." She then looked over my pay record and said, "You were overpaid for the last six months, and we believe that you may have been before that."

It been just about a year since I had reported to the Taney and my pay status had changed many times in that year. When I reported to sea duty, I was entitled to sea pay – an increase – on June 9, I had completed three years of service since I graduated, it was entitled to a "fogey" (an increase); on July 1, there had been a pay increase for military personnel, and at the same time I had had reverted to lieutenant, junior class, since the promotion I had to Lieut. was a temporary wartime promotion. The new base pay for lieutenant junior grade was the same as lieutenant had been. However, the rental allowance had not changed for these rans, and there should have been a reduction in that allowance. When I left the Taney, I left sea duty, and my sea pay ceased.

During this same time, there had been two pay officers on the Haney and when I went to Long Beach, there was an entire office of storekeepers who should have seen my pay record at some time. It wasn't until the Navy had my record that the failure to reduce the rental allowance was noted. Now it had gone on for at least the last six months – pay record covered six months.

They sent off to see what the pay record for the six months before said! Today, they would have asked at what rate I plan to repay the overpayment – then, they just took it out! I had no pay, and on the next payday, I was reduced from what I might have expected, to recover the rest of the overpayment during the six months of vacancy. A month later, on August 1, they took out the entire overpayment from the earlier six months, but by this time I was officially in flight orders, and they had to pay me for flight from that time I had arrived at Corpus Christi. It didn't hurt nearly as bad this time.

During the first six months when I had little to do, except wait for the ground school to start, after my flight orders arrive, I went out to the flight lines to see what planes were taking off they could find room for added passengers. There was a rule that if you are airborne for four hours in the months when you were on flight orders, you were entitled to the pay. You could also make up for the fact that you had not flown in the past two months, by flying enough time to equal the required hours for the those past months. I flew in mostly the SNB (Standard Navy Bugsmasher), a small trainer plane that had twin-engines and that could carry about five passengers, or the R4D (better known as a DC-3), most of the time. The other planes that were operated there at the time were mostly single seater, single-engine planes.

After a month of ground school, we reported to Cabaniss Field, nearby to fly for half of the day, and took ground school for the other half. I couldn't of been more tense or nervous about my flying. I remember well, my instructor realizing this condition, said, "This plane is really stable. See you can jiggle the controls around, nothing happens." He nearly shook my hand off the control stick.

We practiced emergency landings onto a practice field, stalls, normal landings – all tail wheel first or you could bounce – and taxiing in this plane. This was an introduction to an aircraft for me, and many of the others. The tail wheel of the SNJ at that time was controllable if you were within 45° of going straight ahead.

If you wanted to make a turn, you could put on the brakes on one wheel, using your front brakes, and the other wheel came forward. At that time, the tail wheel swiveled freely. The only problem with this was that if you lost control in a landing, and had to put on one brake and overpower the forward motion, you can easily put the plane into a free swiveling condition, and it gave you a ground loop, often with damage to one wingtip as you swung around. Thus, taxing, and familiarity with this brake and tail wheel system were imperative. There was so much trouble with ground looping because of the tailwheel configuration that the Navy changed the system about the time I finished all flight training, to a system where you would lock the tail wheel in a "trail" position except when you were on the ground and taxiing. That was long after our class had either finished or been removed from the program.

We had 18 flights with the same instructor, except for two "progress checks" as we went towards the 18th and 19th. The 18th flight was the usual instructor "safe for solo" check of his student and if it went well, the 19th was the official solo check by a check pilot.

If you were not approved, in one of the checks – given a down – you were either given more time, often with a different instructor, or appeared before a board to see if you should continue. I was never given a "down" in my training. I'm not sure how many misgivings my instructor had, but he scheduled me for my check, and I went through the routines. My instructor flew into the station where I was several years later, and told me he felt rather strongly after about 16 flights that I would not be ready on the usual 18th or 19th flights. My regular instructor approved and I was scheduled for the official check.

The check pilot had me land on one of the outlying fields, told me to come to a stop, and climbed out! He told me to make three landings by myself, and on the third, stop and pick him up again. I did as I'd been told – – I was flying by myself! – – and the most amazing thing to me was that the tail wheel would move back and forth when it was on the ground, and it felt just as if someone were riding on the rudder controls, as I knew the instructor had been much of the time before. I nearly looked back to see if the pilot had really gotten out of the back seat. The next flight was a solo flight where I simply went out and practiced what I had learned, and what the instructor had been teaching, only this time by myself. This is my last flight on a Friday afternoon, and then came the weekend. I was the first in my class to solo, and I was "ace" during the weekend to all my classmates.

The next phase of training was to teach us how to do more things with the aircraft, we learn to do loops, barrel rolls, slow rolls, turns, and a reversal of direction while making a climbing half loop. They were all supposed to be done with some speed control, and in the case of the barrel roll, it was a coordinated maneuver, all the way through. I enjoyed that flying, and was always happy flying around the puffy clouds over Texas. We would have one instructed flight, and then two solo, to practice.

The last thing we did in Texas, before moving on to Pensacola, was to get an introduction to instrument flying. We had to control the speed of the plane, and the rate of turns only by instruments. We had learned how to fly – on the beam –, and then it was only with an N or an A signal. When we were on the beam, the two mixed together to give a solid tone. We learned how to orient ourselves using only the sound, and how to make an instrument approach to the field.

In December 1947, Bette and I moved on to Pensacola, and went back to the house hunting routine. There was some flying before Christmas, but it was cold and the heat was always on full when we were up. It was said that we would never have any trouble finding our field, (Saufley) because the odor of paper mills would lead us to it. First, to find a house. I had permanent orders to Pensacola, and I felt it made sense to get all of our things together, in case the next station was on the East Coast. Besides, it appeared that rentals should be lower for a unfurnished home or apartment. This was not necessarily the case in Pensacola. The economy was and may still be based on student aviators, and furnished homes were easier to find.

We stayed in a big home that rented rooms with kitchen privileges to aviation students, for longer than we wanted, and were there over Christmas and New Year's. It was the loneliest that we had ever spent! Eventually we found house that was for rent, unfurnished. It was no prize, but it was available, and the rent was acceptable. Then we needed our furniture. Wouldn't you know, in those days, the train was the method of shipping for long distances, and there was a train strike. We sat and waited and waited for our furniture. Finally, we had to buy some things, anyway, and we did, we borrowed some others, and used packing boxes for tables, until our things arrived.

After formation flying, most naval aviators flew several gunnery flights, firing fixed guns at a towed sleeve. Someone had made the decision that the Coast Guard didn't need gunnery or carrier qualifications, so when Joe Johansen and I finished our formation training, we move to the PBY squadron at the main station in Pensacola. The PBYs that we flew were true seaplanes, and when we would launch them we would go down a ramp with beaching wheels attached, but the line attached to the wheels.

We students, and the enlisted personnel who flew with us in these planes, would detach the wheels when the plane was fully afloat, and the wheels would be pulled back to the beach. At noon, when crews were changed, we would come in parallel to the beach with one of the flight students on the wing tip away from the beach, to hold it down, and let the other wing rise up, so it could come in over the beach. The plane would be taxied very slowly, even turning off the engine and then catching it to start again just before it stopped, to bring the plane over the beach to the spot it was to be beached. When the plane was in position, the ground crew would grab the float and swing the nose into the beach, and the engines would be cut off at the same time. When the afternoon group took the plane, there was still a need for one student on the outboard wing, until the beach crew swung the beached float off the beach, and the plane would proceed to the practice area.

Joe and I were several flights ahead of the rest of our class at this time, and we flew almost the entire syllabus for the plane. We were told we first started, "This plane is a real workhorse. It climbs at 90 knots, glides at 90 knots, cruises at 90 knots, and if you continue to fly it, you will live to be 90." That wasn't all true – – if you raise the wing tip floats to make them part of the wing, it would cruise at 100 knots, but we never did that in flight training except on two navigational training flights.

Joe and I were all through this phase, except for a proficiency check, and our solo flight, which would have been with one of us as pilot, and the others copilot, when the rest of the Coast Guard came to the squadron from formation flying. I guess the number of Coast Guard pilots, and the idea that the PBY was nearly gone from the Navy, brought the decision to cancel all training in that plane. We were sent to Whiting Field where we were to start training in the SNB as an introduction to multi-engine land planes.

Whiting Field is about 30 miles from Pensacola, that it was a better commute than thinking of moving again. The entire group of Coast Guard officers, about 12 of us at this time, went to Whiting, checked in to the squadron, and had a half day of lectures about the SNB and procedures at this field. In the afternoon, they told us they were going to cancel multi-engine land plane flight training, and we should check out again and prepare to go to Jacksonville for PBM training.

The PBM was at that time, the largest seaplane the Navy was operating. It had the PB2Y, a big four engine plane, and it had a few Mars seaplanes for passenger flights to Hawaii from Alameda, but the PBM was now the only operational patrol plane. Flight training in this plane had been at Banana River, in Florida, the year before, but it was now in Jacksonville, at the naval air station. Some fighter planes were being operated there for training as well, but there was a large reconfiguration in the works. We had heard, and knew it to be the case, that the PBM training would move to Corpus Christi in the near future – – probably in a month.

It didn't make much sense for Bette and little Greg to move to Jacksonville, where I was to be on temporary duty once more. So we closed up the house, put our things in storage once more, and Bette and Greg moved in with friends. She lived with Mary Durfee for some time, and then with George and Pat Thometaz. I came back to Pensacola on weekends most of the time, because we were not flying much at all. I had one operational training flight, and one or two flights where I just rode along, during the month we spent at Jacksonville.

With all this time to kill, we did go to ground training on the plane we hoped to fly someday, we had much time to do nothing productive. Someone discovered that the CAA – – the forerunner to the FAA – – would give us single engine commercial pilot's licenses if we passed the written test for the license and showed them the fact, in our logbooks, that we were flying planes as pilots. The entire group of Coast Guard officers decided we would get these licenses, and to make it even easier, someone had got answers to the tests that were given. It was always the same test for every applicant, and the questions are multiple-choice, with four choices. We didn't learn the actual questions, just the answer choices. I remember the order was 4-1-2-3-1-2-3-1-4-3. We knew we shouldn't be too obvious, and determined that each of us would intentionally miss one answer. We all chose the same one, without conferring, because it was the only one that we didn't know without the "crib sheet."

After our month in Jacksonville, we were ordered to Corpus Christi, as anticipated, and we went to Pensacola to pick up families and moved back to Texas. House hunting this time was not much easier than before, but there have been some reductions in the number of military personnel in town, and so we found a place in the city. It had once been a schoolhouse, and the furniture was an antique variety but not desirable antiques. I pulled out the door on the library breakfront one day, and the front of the drawer just came off in my hand.

There was an assortment of large bugs inside the shell of the drawer. We cleaned the house as best we could, and made the best of the situation. One night, however, we had been at the officer's club, and picked up Greg from the babysitter services on the base and came home to the house. The bathroom had only a shower, and the hot water heater for the house was located in the same room. We went into the bathroom and turn on the light, there must have been 50 large cockroaches on the floor, running every direction. Bette climbed on a chair and cried out, "Kill them, do something!" I started swatting and getting a roach spray, but seeing her standing there was too much. I replied, "I'm trying -- what are you doing?"

This was temporary duty again, so none of us had much to make our homes more comfortable. To make things a little less tolerable, there was a polio epidemic in Corpus Christi, and we were told that we should be very careful of contacts with other people, what we put in our mouths, and even that the motion picture theaters would be closed – except for the one on the base.

There was no television at that time, of course. We made life a little easier by getting together at our "schoolhouse" with potluck dinners, and we would borrow 16mm motion picture projectors and films to entertain the group with training films or the series about war in the Pacific. We saw the film of how to row of lifeboat, produced by the Coast Guard with Captain Miles Imlay as the object of the film, time after time. We even ran it backwards for more entertainment. He showed how to operate your oar "by the numbers," and when it was written backwards, it became hilarious.

Meanwhile, we were supposed to learn how to fly the PBM. Unfortunately for us, the Navy was trying to make a quota of new aviators by 1 July, and the Coast Guard aviators would not count towards that quota. So we sat in the ready room for our turn to come. We were told that we must not leave the base without permission, and that would not be given what we were waiting our designations. We played many games of hearts, and spent hours doing little productive work. We went along in a few flights to get enough flight time to be paid for flights duty, and once there were two PBYs that were ready to be ferried from Pensacola to Corpus Christi, and six of us were designated as copilots or navigators of those flights to bring them over.

Finally on July 1 the Coast Guard students rescheduled. We flew every day for the month and ended by flying long navigational flights over the Gulf of Mexico and then into Guantánamo, Cuba. The next day we were to make a night flight back to Corpus Christi, giving us experience in flying and navigating both in the daylight and at night. We had a Navy instructor pilot and four students on each of the two planes that went on these flights, not in formation, but near each other. The plane that I was on had three of us who were married, and then none really looking for a lot of things to bring back from Cuba, except each of us brought one or two bottles of rum.

The other plane had several of our bachelors, each of whom wanted to lay in a supply of booze for the future, but knew the limitations of customs. The instructor pilot, however, had been told by his commanding officer that he wanted a case or two of rum to give a squadron party. The limits for each person were one gallon – five bottles – per person, but this instructor was expected to bring back an extra case, at least.

Knowing this was going to be done, each of the students decided they could manage a case as well, and the instructor told them that he thought two or three cases would be better for the squadron. The enlisted crew had experienced this before, and knew where to hide liquor from customs. The bomb bays in the lower part of the engine area could take several cases, there were spots in the lower part of the plane, around the fuel tanks, that could hide others. It was well hidden when the plane taxied in to the beach at Corpus Christi.

My plane was returning from Panama and Cuba, the squadron duty officer would notify customs, and if there were no conflicting duties at the international airport, the customs officer would meet the plane at the air station. In this case, there was a conflict, and the customs officer asked that the air station duty officer meet the plane, and act as the customs officer. He did so, and the declarations of each of the crew were turned in, with none of them declaring liquor. After the air stations duty officer – acting as the customs inspector – had departed, the instructor pilot ordered the crew to assemble the liquor cases at the entrance to the plane, and prepare to take off and distribute it to the purchasers. At that point, the real customs officer arrived. He had finished his duties at the other airport, and had come out to see the seaplanes, but they were now on the ramp, not in the water.

He picked up the declarations form from the Navy duty officer, and boarded the one plane that was not now secured. He looked around with a flashlight, shining on the cases of liquor next to the entrance, then looked at the declarations form, still by flashlight. He then turned to the pilot said, "I see that none of you has declared any liquor." The pilot responded, "Oh no, we don't carry liquor on a Navy plane."

"I see," the customs officer replied and climbed out of the plane went on his way!

A few days later, on July 28, 1947, eight of us Coast Guard officers received our wings of gold and were sent on our way. We had been allowed to submit our first two choices for our first air stations, and I had asked for San Francisco or San Diego, trying again to be near our homes. I was ordered to Port Angeles Washington, on the Straits of Juan de Fuca, and rather isolated, but a lovely community. It was far enough away, however, that when I told Bette where we were going, she asked me where it was, and many other people do the same. It isn't the best known location.

Port Angeles

We drove across the country from Corpus Christi to California where we would visit my parents and Bette's family before going north to Washington. We bought a new" car (to us) when we were in Pensacola, because our old Ford business coupe was giving us problems, and it was small for an active child right along with us. Air conditioning was a rarity in a car still, but it was a comfortable big Dodge sedan.

To go across the southern part of the country to Southern California, where my family was, we would cross Arizona and New Mexico, and then the Mojave Desert, before reaching the coast. I went to the dispensary, told the doctor he planned to drive across the desert at night, and asked for some Benzedrine to keep awake. He gave them to me with the promise that I would seek a place to catch up on my sleep and we reached California.

In addition, there was a system to cool cars in the dry heat of Texas and the dry Southwest, using evaporative cooling. There would be a supply of water in the tank in a cooler attached to a window of the car, and a method of dampening a pad or curtain, through which the air would come into the car. The evaporation of water would cool the air – somewhat! The problem with this system is that if you parked the car in the sunshine for some time, such as at lunch, the cooling effect could never catch up with the heat gained. Second, you had to continually dampen the pad, in the case of the one we bought by pumping water out of the reservoir onto the pad. It took muscles!

We made it a point not to stop in San Antonio at all. They were having a bad polio time. We stopped in Fort Stockton – – in the middle of the state. There were not many choices of motels, but we chose one, and settled in. During the early evening it was noisy – – we were close to the city's softball stadium, and they must have had an important game. Finally it became quieter – – for short time. Then we heard the train yard, where they must have made up the trains to go either south or west. There would be the sound of the engine, and then the thud of cars hitting, followed by a series of collisions down the entire train. A short silence would be followed by another engine sound, and then bang bang bang bang bang. Over and over!

After couple of days on the road, we stopped at Gallup, New Mexico. We undoubtedly looked, and felt, dirty, tired, and ready for something of a different nature. We chose a good-looking motel, and I went to inquire about the availability of rooms. The desk clerk looked me over, and announced the price, in advance. I was insulted (I was Lieutenant- on flight pay) but I paid and we had a nice room. The place was overrun with movie personnel, because they had just finished filming "Streets of the Laredo" somewhere nearby. I made it a point to put on a clean set of my khaki uniform – with wings – before we went into dinner, but by this time the desk clerk had changed, and I couldn't impress him.

Our drive through the desert was long, hot, and very dark.

We stopped in Needles, California, and filled the car with gas, and water for our cooler. During the night, Betty slept very little, because she was needed to pump that gadget with the cooling water, and if she pumped too much, it would spray back into the car, and she was really awake! It demanded so much, it ran out before we could reach the cooler territory, and we realized how much it actually cooled the car. We eventually came into cooler coastal land, and arrived at my parents' home in Santa Maria around 6 AM. As directed by the doctor in Corpus Christi, we turned our little son over to my mother and Bette and I both went to bed. We were awake by 10, and couldn't sleep anymore then. That night we meet up for the loss of sleep.

We next visited with Bette's family in the Bay area, and then drove up the coast to Port Angeles. The road was not well developed in the road from Olympia to Port Angeles was along the shore of the Puget Sound much of the time. Later we went through some of the lower mountains to arrive in Port Angeles, a town of around 7,000 at that time. There were two wood pulp mills, a plywood company, and the Coast Guard. The ferry ran to Victoria, British Columbia during the summer months, but the tourist trade was much less in the winter months. The salmon and trout fishing brought some fishermen, and the headquarters of the Olympic National Park meant some visitors to the park came through – but it was definitely a small town. We camped with the family of a classmate from the Academy, Tex and Mary John George, while we house hunted. While we were there we did a little exploring of the area, but didn't go far afield.

One afternoon, while Greg was supposed to be napping, Bette

stayed with him until he went to sleep, because he had caught a cold, and when he had colds, they usually became infantile bronchitis. So we had put a pan on a hot plate nearby to moisten the air, Bette stayed with them in this strange location. He finally settled down, and Bette sneaked out. He was quiet but not for long!. He awoke, stirred around, and hit the handle of the pan with hot water in it. It burned the back of his neck, such that he had scars for many years later, especially when he tanned. The scars never tanned.

The house we rented was at 1323 East 4th Street, and directly across the street from another of my Academy classmates, Art Perry, his wife, and two sons. There were vacant lots on each side of our house when we moved in, but later one of them was filled with a new house. Our house had two bedrooms, one on each end of the house, a small dining room in the large kitchen, and a fairly large living room. We had a telephone at the end of the living room, away from everything. If the phone rang in the middle of the night, I would run across the bedroom and the living room to answer the phone. There was no laundry space in the house, but we later bought a Sears washer which had to be bolted to the concrete floor of the garage. It wasn't the most convenient arrangement, but when the weather was freezing, we worried about the innards of the machine, as well as wondering what the temperature of the wash water would be. This was before cold water detergents.

As a new aviator, reporting to my first air station, I was not considered qualified in anything. I had flown the SNJ, but the one here was only waiting to be ferried to some location to be turned back to the Navy. I had flown the PPY, but not the one with wheels, and I was never qualified to be the pilot. I had flown the PBM, but it was too big for a new pilot to be anything but one more copilot. So they assigned me to fly the Grumman amphibians.

That J4F was a nice little plane but a little tricky, especially on the water. I never did fly it off the water. The JRF is a nice utility plane was used as an inter – island transport in the West Indies for many years, and in Southeastern Alaska. It is easy to fly and doesn't require a large crew for operating. I flew this one quite a lot, and shortly after I arrived, I was given my "safe for solo" check by the commanding officer. Commander Snyder and I were the to take a district officer, Commander Schleiter to the Quillaute Air Station, where he would go on to the LaPush Lifeboat Station to check on a civil engineering problem. That series of names, Snyder, Schleiter, and Siler must've been a mind twister for the crew at LaPush, but they made a nice lunch rest.

I flew the JRF quite a little after that, and after I became qualified on the water. It was a nice little utility plane, and we used it for that. There were quite a few times we were requested to evacuate a fisherman from a boat that had been fishing on the Pacific, or up the coast of Vancouver Island, and the man or the master of the fishing vessel believed he should be seen by a doctor. I loved to make those flights to places like Neah Bay, near the northwest corner of the state, up the Vancouver Island coast to Nootka Sound, or in the San Juan Islands to heart Friday Harbor. We had Coast Guard units at Neah Bay and Friday Harbor, but there was nothing up at Nootka Sound.

One time when I meet such a trip, and dropped the man (always in his best suit as if he were more concerned about going hope are down to me to date than his discomfort or pain), I taxied out to return to Port Angeles. We always dropped the patients off at Boeing Field in Seattle, because it was near the Marine Hospital.

There was always a lot going on at Boeing Field, and often several B-52s and 707s would be parked near the taxiway. This time, I made my way back to the takeoff position as usual, and had to make several right angle turns on the taxiway. The breaks of the JRF were the primary means of steering on the ground, although you could use engine power to turn also. I started a turn, and the brakes, being wet from the water landing at the location I had picked up my patient, didn't have any effect. I tromped harder on the brake, and cut back the power on the inside of my turn, because if I didn't make this turn, I was headed for a B-52, which I didn't want to own or repair. I came close, but at last the engines and the brakes made the turn, and I was headed away from the monster plane!

We flew the PPY a great deal at this station, and it was the primary search and rescue plane. We newer aviators wondered how we could be aircraft commanders in the plane, or were always told to get more flight time in it. When we asked how we could get more flight time, the answer was to get better qualifications – a real catch 22!

On one Armed Forces Day, I was assigned to fly as co-pilot for Walsh Tiehen on demonstration flights in several locations, ending up flying over the Port Angeles baseball field, where there was to be an observance in the late afternoon. We made that last part by flying down East 4th Street, where the field was located, but the approach was over our home, and we came over at both at an altitude of around 100 feet. Bette said later that the entire house shook as the plane flew over.

At this time, the agreements with the Air Force weren't as thorough about where the responsibility for each service started and ended. We made many mountain flights to look for lost hikers, or downed planes. I was on one flight near McChord Air Force Base, very close to Tacoma, to look for a lost Air Force C – 47, that had started its approach to McChord but never arrived. We knew it should be somewhere near, but where? It was located by a helicopter, and the plane I was in assisted in guiding ground parties to the plane where it had hit the mountain on its approach. It knocked down only about three trees, as the wings came off, and the fuselage came down.

We did some training for this type of flight, by working with known hikers in the mountains. A couple from Port Angeles, who later signed a contract with Disney Studios, were filming spectacular wildlife movies in the Olympic Mountains, and I made a flight one day in the JRF to drop supplies to them on the ice field of Mount Olympus. It was a beautiful day, and lovely flight.

Another spectacular flight in the JRF was a result of an Air Force disaster. In January, 1950, the Air Force deployed a group of B-36 planes to the Bilson Air Force Base at Fairbanks, Alaska. When they were coming back to McChord, they flew down a large part of the Alaskan and British Columbia coasts and then down Puget Sound to Tacoma. Several of the planes had engine troubles, but they had six reciprocating engines (the older type), and four jet engines, so it was not a real emergency when the engine stopped.

We just monitored their progress until they got into McCord.

One of them, however, lost so many engines, that the pilot ordered the crew to bail out with their parachutes. They later reported their position vert accurately, and jumped. We sent a PBY to the area, and several of them were sighted, but fishing vessels in the area picked them up. The PBY with Walsh Tiehen as the pilot, searched for other survivors, and at one time was in a ravine with a power dam at the end. He had to land on the water to turn around and get out of the ravine – without additional survivors.

I went to the scene in a JRF, which could get into smaller ravines than the PBY, and could land on the water if it seemed advisable. Bill Sale was the pilot, and we had a mechanic and a radioman as crew. We were low enough over the area several times to see tracks in the snow, but we could see that in the location of them made them bear tracks, not man tracks. We spent a night in Bella Bella, British Columbia, where the Royal Canadian Air Force had operated CANSOs – their PBY – during World War II, and there was fuel available. There was no hotel or rooming house, but someone put us up, just out of the goodness of their hearts. On the second night that we were on the search, we stayed in Prince Rupert, at the Naval detachment. The last man who bailed out was not found on that search, and his body was not located until 1952.

I became a patrol commander in the PDY, as time went by and made a good many flights along the coast. I was not fully qualified in the PBM, partially because it was gone to overhaul for some time, and then later there really was no one who is better qualified to say that I was qualified. The other stumbling block was that we could not operate it at night, and an aircraft commander should be qualified to fly it at night. We could not operate on the water in Port Angeles, however, because of the logs that were often a float in the bay. These logs often broke loose from the supply that was to be used to make plywood or pulp at the mills in town. Because of this, I made only one night flight in the PBM in my years of Port Angeles.

On this flight we were to search for a ship that we knew had gone down in the Pacific, the SS Pennsylvania, after reporting that there was a large crack across the main deck. We moved the plane to Seattle, to the Naval Air Station and spent a short night there. At 4 AM, we launched the plane, and flew out to the location where the ship must have gone down. We were not the first plane to be there, but no one had sighted anything to indicate the ship or survivors were there. We did sight a lifeboat, capsized, but it was so far from the ships that were searching, that it could not be investigated. We returned from the flight again at Naval Air Station Seattle, at 11 PM, for flight for 19 hours exactly.

The pilot on this flight, was a man I had done for some time before he came to Port Angeles. He liked to fly the PBM but some of his habits frightened me. We would take off, climb to 300 feet, and then bring up the flaps from the takeoff position. Not him! He would get the plane into the air, and about 50 feet, throw the flaps switch into the up position! He kept the nose of the plane such that the altitude remained the same, and the speed increased slightly, but it wasn't as safe as a climb to 300 feet. He later had such continuing arguments with a commanding officer, that he was reassigned out of aviation. He had had an interesting career in aviation, remaining one letter of commendation ahead of his letters of reprimand! He moved on to other activities in the Coast Guard, commanded a high endurance cutter, and then retired and was the operator of the air cushion craft being developed by Bill Aircraft for the Navy and Marine Corps.

The PBM had a hatch on the lower side of the base of the tail, where it was necessary to attach or detach the tail beaching gear, when the plane was put into the water. After the beaching gear was removed for takeoff, the vertical hatch, just forward of this particular hatch was closed, and part of the crew normally found positions in the "after station," just forward of that. There were side hatches here where, during the war machine guns could be mounted, and the main access in and the plane was here

I went to Elizabeth city, North Carolina pick up the PBM after it's overhaul in around 1950, we flew the first leg to St. Petersburg, Florida where they also operated the PBM for the Coast Guard. When we took off from St. Petersburg, I was flying, the plane seemed to take a long time to go over on the step, so I pushed on the yoke to lower the nose. We let the water, and one of the crew asked permission to go all the way back in the tail, and take pictures the Naval Air Station, and the city as we left. He didn't get to the tail, however, because when he opened the hatch to go to the tail, water poured into the after station from tail hatch area. We scooped up water as we started the takeoff and if I hadn't push the nose down, it could have been dangerously tail heavy. The tail hatch had come open somehow during the takeoff run.

I mentioned before that the body of the last man from the B–36 had not been discovered until 1952, and the Port Angeles PBM was sent to return the man's body to the United States, with an Air Force man going up to British Columbia and back as the escort for the man's remains. I had been transferred by the time that this happened, but I knew all the crew who were assigned, and heard about the flight when I arrived in Hawaii. The tail hatch came open, as it had in St. Petersburg, but this time the pilot didn't push it over, and the plane went nose up and then stalled into the water with a terrible crash. The plane was a total loss, there were three of the crew who lost their lives. I never flew in a PBM again after I left Los Angeles, not because of anything but the assignment of aircraft to the stations where I went.

I knew I should be getting orders when I had spent three years in Port Angeles, the Korean War had started and there were negotiations going on about how the Coast Guard would be involved. It appeared that there would be additional responsibility for search and rescue, but just how this would be handled was up in the air for some time.

In the meantime, Marsha was arrived on the scene. She was born on April 25, 1951, in the old Port Angeles General Hospital, which is long gone. I had the duty the night before she was born, so I spent the night of her birth at the hospital. Mother-to-be played cards with me for some time but labor pains went on, and as the nurses gave her medication to assist with the pains, resemblance to regular card games became less and less. Finally, at 11:20, she arrived, and Betty heard the nurse say, "Won't Mrs. Siler be happy that it's a girl!" To which Betty responded, "Oh, Dr. Hamilton, I love you," but I don't think he had much to do with the sex of the baby.

Shortly before Marsha was due to be born, we received orders on the station to deliver one PBY to overhaul, and pick up another to replace it in Port Angeles. Often these flights in those days, with lesser instrument flying capabilities of both planes and pilots, would take several weeks to complete, complete, because of weather delays. I felt that this was not the time to be gone, especially since I had been at sea when Greg was born, so I asked to be dropped off from the ferry crew, even though was my turn to go on such a flight. I was dropped from the crew, but I paid for it by receiving the lowest marks on my fitness report that I ever received.

We had a B-17 or PB–1G assigned to Port Angeles some of the time, although the runway was about as short as could be used by this plane. At one time, the plane had an engine failure when the pilots (I was one of them), were practicing landings at Whidbey Island, about a 30 minute fly away. We made the next landing while the engine was inspected. It needed changing, and the spare engine was at Port Angeles. Somehow, the engine had to be transported to Whidbey, or the plane had to be moved to Port Angeles. With only three engines operative, the second alternative seemed not available, but Bob Cromwell, the engineering officer, knew this plane well, and assured the commanding officer that he could move the plane, with a minimum of fuel and some of the normal equipment removed, back to Port Angeles. He did it, and the engine change was made in Port Angeles, without complications.

I flew in the PB–1G on a very long flight one time in 1951, with Walt Kerwin as the pilot, since I was not qualified in this plane, except as an additional pilot or navigator. The third pilot on this mission was Charlie Muelle, a very well-qualified pilot, especially in helicopters, but not in this plane. We were sent out to locate a fishing vessel that had lost its spirit generator, and it's built upon was operating on questionable electronic power, .while it was taking on water, it had also lost one of its main interest, and was not sure that it could continue to port, although it was trying we located about, and circled over it until near dark, when we need to refuel her plane.

We then went to a Canadian field at the north tip of Vancouver Island, and refute refueled, and grab some food. We knew we would be airborne a long time. We went out, and circled of the bed all night, until a Coast Guard vessel which was sent out told us that they had the fishing vessel insight. That was a very long night, and what was it only qualified pilot. Charlie and I traded often navigator fly the plane, was little easier to stay awake, but my eyes crept toward the close position at times, Walt waited in stayed awake all night. It was a long mission, and we had over 20 hours of flight time on the entire trip.

Around Labor Day in 1951, there were quite a few transfers being made, and I ended up as administrative officer, personnel officer, and operations officer for some time. I still stood my regular watches, usually one day on and two days off – – after the regular work day was over – – and we had standby duty in case the duty crew was dispatched to a flight even when we were at home on one of those days. We had a new commanding officer report for duty, and I had an argument with him on the day he reported. He said he had to report before noon, and I told him that the regulations required only that he report by midnight. He lost his temper very easily, and was noted for it. He growled, "Show me the regulation!" I knew exactly where it was, and showed him, which put me one up on him. I needed it before the weekend was over. This occurred on Friday, and I had the duty on Sunday

Around noon on Sunday, we were called to tell our operations watch a forest fire lookout in a tower on a peak, north of Seattle, had fallen, and needed evacuation. We were asked for a helicopter, a HQ3S, could lift him out and get him to the hospital. Charlie Mueller had the duty with me, and was the duty helicopter pilot. I knew that if it could be done, he should be the one to do it. He asked the altitude at the location where they proposed that he pick the injured man, and was told that it was a designated peak at 4800 feet. Charlie said he felt he could do it, and prepared for the flight. While this went on, the station doctor came aboard, and he loved to fly when he could assist in any way. He had just come from church, and had no flight gear, but he borrowed a flight suit, and went along with no other crew in the helicopter. We sent a JRF along to be communications guard for the helicopter, and it had a radioman to relay to us at the station.

The helicopter found the clearing in the mountains, and went over at altitude to survey it. Then he told the JRF that he was going to fly over slower, and if all seemed well, he would land. When he slowed, the altitude is too great, and the air too thin for the hover. The helicopter stalled, and crashed down, cart-wheeling as the main rotor caught bushes. It ended up, upside down on the brink of a steep incline down the side of the mountain. The two crew got out immediately, to make sure there was no fire, since this helicopter used gasoline for fuel. When it seemed safe, Charlie went back in, turned the radios on, and reported to the JRF, "We're okay. No injuries."

Then there was a delay, the doctor came on the radio and

said, Don't believe him. He was hit on the head and he says that he is a fruitcake." The doctor didn't mention the fact that he had injured his hand, and as it turned out he had broken some bones in it. We learned that the mountain was actually 5,500 feet high, and was above the safe operating ceiling for the helicopter.

It also seemed that the man was not severely injured after all, and he was assisted out playground party the next day. The most painful injury for the helicopter crew was the blisters that formed on the doctor's feet as he walked down the mountain in boots several sizes too large, slipping into the toes on each step. He had departed from the station in the same shoes that he had worn to the church that morning, and these boots were loaned by some on the forestry crew. That was a way we received our new commanding officer!!

In February 1952 I was ordered to All Weather Flight Training, a real choice opportunity to learn about instrument flying under all kinds of conditions. This was for two months in Corpus Christi. With the weather Port Angeles, rain mixed with some snow, Bette thought it was a good time for her to spend some time at my parents in California, while I went off to Texas. She spent the next two months in Santa Maria, while I went to All Weather Flight.

Shortly after I arrived in Corpus Christi, I received orders to Sangley Point, in the Philippines. The timing was very bad in that they ignored the fact that I was in Texas. The orders authorized 30 days leave en route, but didn't indicate that I couldn't leave Port Angeles until I finished schooling, then about a week later, I received a change in orders that was better in one way and worse in another. I was to go to Barber's Point, Hawaii, now but the reporting date specified was such that I could only have four of the authorized 30 days leave.

I asked for and was authorized an extension in the reporting date to allow for 10 days leave and the usual four days proceed time. But the San Francisco Coast Guard office said that I needed to allow for 10 days between reporting there and the required date in Hawaii. I actually arrived in Hawaii on the original date, even after taking the whole 10 days leave. I arrived in Hawaii on May 23, 1952, but without family, and thereby lies another chapter.

Hawaiian Duty

My orders, now to Hawaii rather than the Philippines, told me to report to the Barber's Point Coast Guard Air Detachment on 23 May, 1952. The way to get there was to report to the Coast Guard in San Francisco, and let them provide transportation. For me to be in Hawaii on the 23rd, I had to know when to be in San Francisco. They responded to a message to say that I had to be in San Francisco a week earlier. There was no time for leave, after I had finished my training in Corpus Christi. So I asked for and was given an extension of 10 days in the reporting date.

I went back to Los Angeles, without taking Bette back from California. I checked out of the station, had our household goods packed up, and drove back to Santa Maria to join the family. We seldom did anything on our leaves any time over the years, but visit the families, and we did the same this time, spending more time in Santa Maria, and thence some time with Bette's sister and mother in the area of Palo Alto and the bay area.

It wasn't Greg's birthday, and it may have occurred a year or two earlier when we took some leave to go from Port Angeles to the California area, but Greg had a second birthday cake incident that's worth recording. We bought a cake for him, and were going to go to Bette's father's cottage in the hills nearby. We loaded the cake in the car, and everyone got in, and Bette's mother being the last to get in. She was large, to put it mildly, and she maneuvered into the car with difficulty. When she thought she was in the proper location, she relaxed – and sat on the cake! It was a second time that Greg had scrambled cake for his birthday. He didn't mind, he probably squeezed it even more before he ate it.

When we looked into transportation to Hawaii, it appeared that I would be flown out to meet the reporting date, and Bette, Greg, and Marsha would be sent out one of the ocean transports that the Military Sealift Command still operated. It was going to be some time before my departure and Bette's. Bette's sister made no offers or suggestions about where to live in the interim, and a friend from Bette's high school days was living nearby, and had sufficient room to crowd our group in. Irma, the friend, had two children, and her husband was doing well in the insurance line –(he later was convicted of submitting fraudulent insurance claims, for which he kept the payments, and he spent some time in San Quentin. Irma divorced him. So Bette moved in with Irma, and the next day, Irma's children came down with chickenpox!

I still had to depart, and on the new (later) reporting date, I reported to the Coast Guard. They sent me to the Navy, who sent me to Moffett Field, near Sunnyvale, and I was to depart the next day on an admiral's R5D (C – 54 or DC-4) that was just coming back from overhaul. I reported to the plane in the morning, and we flew to Barber's Point that day, without incident. The plane had just come from of refurbishing, was like new. The only bad item was the crew have brought fresh fruit including many flats of strawberries while in California, and the strawberries better were getting old didn't smell very good.

The plane was not pressurized, so we had plenty of outside air to dilute the odor. However, I arrived at Barber's Point on the original reporting date of May 23, even though I took my 10 days leave beyond what the offices wanted to me to have.

I moved in to the Bachelors Officers Quarters (BOQ) and reported to the Air Detachment. It became obvious that I needed some type of transportation around the station and to Honolulu or wherever I would go, and I bought an old junker Pontiac. One of the men at the station help me to weld some additional metal on the fender, and I spray painted parts of the car to make it a little more presentable. It kept me, later us, going until our Buick arrived on the Navy ship.

I spent my spare time looking into where our family could live when they eventually arrived, and found a little house next to the Episcopal Church in Wahiawa, in the center of Oahu. The town is the site of Schowfield Barracks now and to drive to Barber's Point. I went by Wheeler Field that had been active at the time of the Pearl Harbor attack. I also drove past fields of pineapple and sugarcane, and finally by the little town of Ewa, the home of the US sugar plantation which gave the name to the World War II Ewa Marine Corps Air Station, which was now Barber's Point Naval Air Station.

It may not have been the best idea to rent that house, because if you didn't housing when you arrived, you were entitled to per diem which covered most of the cost to staying in a Waikiki hotel for a few weeks. An alternative to the house I rented would've been waiting for a vacancy in government housing on the base, while we lived in a hotel. It was hard to tell when government housing would be available, however, and when it became available, all the Coast Guard people who were waiting were assigned together in this little enclave where everyone knew the others' business.

I had to learn to fly the airplanes at the Air Detachment, and they were different from what I had been flying. We had that PB–1G or B–17, and the R5D for transporting personnel and cargo to the loran stations all over the Pacific. The PB–1G was our search and rescue plane, and we used it mostly to intercept and escort the commercial DC–4s that were transporting military personnel out of Korea and back. We often would have three intercept flights in a single day.

On one of my intercept flights in the PB–1G, at night, we were flying out of Hawaii toward San Francisco at a good speed, and the flight mechanic would make routine checks of the engines, using a strong flashlight or electric torch. He came up to the cockpit, and said there appeared to be oil coming from out of the engine, and running back over the wing. The pilot, Russ Lentner, decided that we would feather the engine, to try not to damage as the oil level dropped to too low. We punched the propeller feathering button, but nothing happened.

We then watched the engine as we punched the button again. The oil line going to the propeller feathering was the broken line, and we simply set sent oil out in the air ahead of the engine as we tried to feather the propeller. We quit trying then, and simply brought the power back to the engine as we headed home. The oil pressure in the engine itself started dropping as we approached the coastline of Oahu, and we decided to land at Kaneohe Marine field, on the eastern shore of Oahu. When we touched down at Kaneohe, the oil pressure on that engine dropped to zero, and the engine stopped. We taxied in, called for oil, and a new prop feathering line, and the engine was all okay. It was a longer day than we had planned, but it was still a good plane.

I called for, and was assigned to a flight in the R5D, out of Japan, the Philippines, and Guam, during that time before Bette arrived, so that I would not be eligible for that assignment since so soon after she arrived. I went on a flight with Jerry McGovern, an older and well experienced pilot who had flown the photo plane that the Coast Guard operated for the Coast and Geodetic Survey, in past years. He was really smooth in the R5D, and I tried to learn how he did it. We went out on this flight from Barber's Point, to Johnson Island, to Kwajalein the first day. The next day we were in Guam, there was a Coast Guard Air Detachment there that flew PBYs to Saipan, UIithi, and Palau, although if we had enough cargo, sometimes we in the R5D would go to Palau. We stayed two days in Guam, and then went to Japan, with a short stay at Iwo Jima with supplies for the loran station.

By this time, it was time to make a routine examination of the engines of the plane, so we stayed in Tokyo for about four days. Sometimes there would be cargo that we needed to deliver to loran stations in Japan, and we would go to the stations in Korea, Hokkaido, and to stations on the main Japanese island. Then we are off for Okinawa, the Philippines, and back to Guam, and Kwajalein again. It was usually about a 15 day trip. Later we would often go through Midway and Wake Islands instead of Kwajalein again, because we had then we had Coast Guard air units in those islands.

The shopping for goods from Japan and other locations was truly outstanding at that time, because the currency of Japan was stabilized at 360 yen to the dollar, and the Philippine peso was firm and at two to the dollar. There was some black market activity in the peso, but the currency in Japan was in military procurement certificates, the MPC, and you could use nothing else. I bought some Japanese crystal glasses which were fabulous bargains on the first trip, and added to them later. We still have some of them today. Cameras were another good deal, as was some furniture. Hong Kong goods were always chancy, because much of the desirable material came from Communist China, and you usually had to have a certificate of origin or lose it at customs on your return.

Meanwhile, back in California – – both of the children got chickenpox. It didn't bother Greg very much, and he was a good patient. Marsha was so young, she couldn't figure out what made her feel so bad, and she fussed constantly. This in someone else's home!

When Greg was feeling better, he went out for a walk in the neighborhood, and since he was a stranger there, he became lost. He had enough good sense to get a house, ring the bell, and announce that he was lost. The woman at the door called the police, and he was driven up and down the streets until he recognized the house he was staying in. The police congratulated him, and told Bette that she was not to scold him, since he had done so well.

Bette was called one day by the Navy to say that there was a flight to Hawaii that enough space for the three of them. She told them that the children were nearly over their chickenpox, and took them to a local doctor, who said they were not contagious. When she got to the Navy doctor for clearance, however, he said not until the scabs had all gone. So she sat still longer.

Finally, on the first of July, Bette was given space on a ship, the General Norton. It was to sail from Fort Mason in San Francisco. There was another complicating factor. The daughter of her host had come down with mumps! Probably one or both of our little ones would have it soon. Can you imagine exposing a ship load of military personnel to mumps?! Bette didn't mention it, and neither of the children had any symptoms yet, so they boarded a bus to go to Fort Mason. The kids were both dressed nicely, and behaved well on the bus, the ship was not ready for them when they pulled up to the gangway. So they sat on the hot bus, until to top off the boarding procedure, Marsha threw up on the woman who sat next to her!

The first exercise on any ship is an abandon ship drill to make sure that all passengers knew where to go, and how to get into lifejackets. Marsha was so small that she slipped through the life jacket, and she was still not walking, so she had to be carried everywhere. She usually accused anyone in uniform of being "Daddy" which made friends with some, and scared others. The days were long what with carrying Marsha everywhere, and Betty never went to the bingo games held in the evenings for the passengers. The weather was rough enough the first night that many of the troops on board were looking for seasick relief the following morning, but Bette and Greg had good breakfasts, and had no trouble. It was six long days from the West Coast to Pearl Harbor, though.

On the morning of July 6, I went to the unloading docks of Pearl Harbor to meet the ship. It wasn't hard to pick out Bette at the rail. She was the only one on the entire ship who was wearing a hat. She and the children were dressed to arrive in New York in 1929 – fit to go the Ritz. The only thing was, I was driving my clunker, and we went to the tiny house in Wahiawa. We spent the rest of the day looking around Oahu, and learning how to pronounce Hawaiian words.

Greg came down with the months of mumps about two days after arriving in Hawaii, and we were told that the best thing for Marsha would be for her to have them at an early age, so we didn't try to separate them. Greg was a good patient again, Marsha crawled all over spend all the time. She never had the mumps, and hasn't to this day. When he recuperated, we saw more the beach at Barber's Point, but the first days were not too great.

One interesting item having to do with transportation from San Francisco to Hawaii, and not really affecting us at all, bothered me for some time. Ham McNatt received orders just like mine, to report to Barber's Point on June 23. He arrived in San Francisco, I'm not sure on what date, but he was held in San Francisco until a plane from Barbers Point was there with our district commander, Rear Admiral Perkins. He, McNatt, was held in San Francisco to fly, with his family, on the admiral's plane to Hawaii, arriving after the date he was ordered to be in Hawaii. Their entire family arrived at the same time as Bette arrived on her ship. I couldn't avoid resenting the difference in treatment of our two transfers, even though Ham had nothing to do with it.

I had been promoted back to lieutenant in June, 1949, in Port Angeles. They gave us back our date of rank that we had had during the war, so I dated from November 1, 1945. That made me a historic lieutenant, and made Bette the second "most senior dependent" on the trip out to Hawaii. I was promoted to Lieutenant Commander in August 1952, which complicated our waiting for government quarters. I had waited up to near the top of the lieutenant list for quarters, and if I now announced that I was promoted, I would go to the bottom of lieutenant commander list. So, I kept quiet and moved into a Quonset hut as a lieutenant. The service did take all of my rental allowance as a lieutenant commander, however.

We had bought a new washing machine when we were in Port Angeles – one of the ones that spun the clothes to remove the water. It had to be bolted to the floor, which was no problem in Port Angeles, we just bolted it down in the garage. In a Quonset hut, however, there was no solid floor – it set on blocks at the edges and corners. To mount the washing machine properly, we had to have a hole cut in the floor, and a concrete block poured in the kitchen area. This was at our expense, so we owned a concrete block in the housing area, and it's probably still there.

The Coast Guard was assigned search and rescue responsibility for most of the Pacific during the Korean War, and so we also got a different airplane, which was faster than the PB – 1G. We were to fly the P-24, which was a single tail B – 24 or the Navy had called them PB4Y–2s. It was a replacement for the PB–1G because it was faster, and these planes were newer because they had been delivered to the Navy much later, and were being reconfigured for us. We in the Coast Guard were to operate these planes out of Barbers Point, Midway, Wake, and Guam.

The plane was to operate from Sangley Point in the Philippines was the seaplane, the PBM, until the P5Ms were available. The P5M never did get to Sangley, but they were operated by the Coast Guard in Bermuda because of this build up.

The date for us to take responsibility for Wake was set for October 1, 1952, and the Air Force SA–16 would leave on that date. We didn't get our P4Ys in time to make the reliefs, so we arranged for the loan of Navy planes of that type, but it was much heavier and slower than our planes would be. At the time we were seriously planning for this deployment from Barbers Point, we had the additional crews come in, with PBYS as an interim plane, and a hurricane hit Wake Island.

There was construction going on to build a barracks for the Coast Guard crew, but after the hurricane, there was almost no sign of the beginning of the building. There were a large number of good-sized tents flown in, and for several months, the Coast Guard lived in tents. Food was served by Pan American (Airlines), as they had a mess hall to serve hot meals to passengers and crews who were overnighting on their flights to Japan and the Philippines. The mess hall lost a part of its roof in the hurricane, but it was still operational. The office for the Coast Guard was in the island operations building, and was not affected by the hurricane.

The first crew with its borrowed plane did get to Wake on October 1 and spent its time escorting many of the DC-4s going or coming from Hawaii or Japan. I had the pleasure of going for November and by this time we had a plane which was our own. When it was about 30 knots faster than the Navy version, and flew well, although is not as forgiving as the PB–

1G. It was designed for speed and we were able to keep up with the DC–6s six with no trouble.

The DC–7, which was around Hawaii, would leave us, even if they had trouble with one engine. The barracks and the BOQ at Wake were redesigned and completed about six months after we started serving as the rescue crews. We had enough crews that we would have one day off in four and we could go swimming or hiking around the gun replacements left after the Japanese occupation. There were some guns which had been moved from the defense of Singapore, and many underground developments. I mentioned that I went for November – this is the time I was assigned that Quonset hat, which meant that Bette had to move in there alone.

While the PBYs were in Hawaii, waiting for all the P4Ys to arrive, we had an interesting search one night. There had been a small mail plane sent from Honolulu to the dirt field Kalaupapa on Molokai, where the leper colony was. The plane hadn't arrived, and we had searched for signs of it during the late afternoon, and we were to send out a PBY to search at night for any flares or fires, since such things can be seen at a long distance at night. I was the pilot of the plane, and we went to the North Shore of Molokai, along the route that the plane would've flown, and flew back and forth to see if we could find anything.

There were many flashes of phosphorescence, but most of the time they were obviously not caused by a plane's wreckage. One flash we could not identify, so I wanted to go to a little lower altitude. The PBY and the flight engineer in the "tower," the connector between the boat hull and the high wing, and the pilot had to ask him on the intercom to change engine mixtures if you were to go to higher power settings. I called and asked for a "auto rich mixtures." He responded, with an affirmative answer, and shifted both controls the wrong direction – to idle cutoff! That shut off both engines when we were at 500 feet on a moonless night off of Molokai! It didn't take long for him to realize what he'd done, and move the controls back where we wanted them but it seemed like an hour, and it was the quietest I have ever spent a PBY in flight!

There were not too many ways that we could practice instrument flying on the airways around the islands, so we would from time to time fly from Oahu to Hilo or Maui. Hilo was the preferred location, because we could have lunch there, buy some meat from the Parker Ranch, the second biggest beef raising ranch in the US, and buy some orchids at the nurseries and Hilo. We always went to the same nursery, the proprietor got to know us, and gave us some beautiful flowers. I brought home so many orchids that Bette told me one time near the end of the trip duty, not to bring any purple or white ones, they were too common!

I became an aircraft commander in both the P4Y and the R5D as time went on, and made some interesting flights in them. When in the P4Y, was to Wake Island, where we were to spend two weeks. Originally the tours were for a month, but the planes suffered such corrosion from the salt spray blowing across the low island, that the tours were shortened to only two weeks. One evening I was standing on the porch of our barracks/BOQ as a thunderstorm passed over. I was standing about 10 feet from the flagpole where the Coast Guard ensign flew along with the U.S. ensign during sunlight. It was shortly after dark, but the lightning from the storm gave interesting light to the field often. Suddenly flash of lightning hit the flagpole, making the loudest hisses that I ever heard. It was followed immediately by a crash of thunder that nearly deafened me. I went inside, needlessly to say, immediately.

The commanding officer at Wake, was not qualified in the P4Y, was several years senior to me. He had been qualified in several other types of aircraft, and wanted to become qualified in this one. As an aircraft commander, and there to do his bidding, I took him out to let them go through the maneuvers he needed to qualify. We did several normal landings without incident, and then he was going to try a landing simulating what might be necessary if you were to land when there was a low thin fog over a field. You flew over the field at 1000 feet with the field in sight nearly straight down, but the visibility supposedly was poor as you got to lower altitude. So, you dove for the field, as it passed under the nose, then rounded out to land more or less normally.

Mike did fine, until we dove for the field. It always seemed that you were going to crash, so he pulled the nose up – too soon, and the plane stalled above the runway, instead of flying onto the wheels. The only thing to do in this case is to add power at the last moment or let the plane come down harder, and we do the latter. We also wiped off the tail skid from the rear of the plane. Since I was the responsible pilot, it was noted my logbook is my first aircraft "incident."

On one of my R5D flights into San Francisco, I was the third pilot with Jerry McGovern as the pilot, the commanding officer listed as copilot, and I was a navigator, and third pilot. We were scheduled to take off at 8 PM and fly through the night to land at San Francisco in the morning. Unfortunately, engine trouble held us up for two or three hours, and Jerry never went back to meteorology to check the weather. They extended his clearance by phone calls. Actually headwinds were getting stronger, and our fuel was became marginal, but we were not aware of it.

As we navigated across the Pacific, I gave the pilots several course corrections, as we were being sent farther south, and we were required to approach San Francisco in "channels" for air identification. These wind alteration sure that the winds were stronger than forecast, but our speed didn't seem to be too bad. As we got over San Francisco, we were told to hold that at a designated fix, with a "non-standard" holding pattern.

The non-standard pattern was shown in the charts, but the captain, who was flying didn't know what a non-standard pattern was, and flew the standard one. There was ice in the clouds, and we were using our anti-ice boots, and eventually, got down. The captain made such a bad landing that Jerry, sitting in the copilot's seat, had to put it down after a hard bounce. We finally landed about 7 PM instead of arriving in the morning.

The next morning the flight mechanic went up to run up the engines, and make sure everything was in good shape for our return. There is so little gas in one of the tanks that he couldn't get one engine started off its own fuel supply. We had landed just in time. Icing was so bad over Oakland that night that a plane crashed on that side of the bay, but we had had no trouble of that kind.

I liked flying the P4Y and since I lived close to the Air

Detachment than any of the regular duty standers, the duty pilots usually called me first if they needed someone from the stand by group of watch standers. This was not bad most of the time, it was usually simply a matter of being at the unit while the crew was gone with one of the planes. One night it didn't work out that way. They called me at about five in the morning with the information that they had an intercept of a DC –four just a little closer to Hawaii than half way, and it had lost an engine, and needed an escort. Since it was going to be a long flight, the present duty crew would like to get home at 9 on that Saturday morning, would I mind taking the flight. I must been groggy with sleep, because I said, "I'll be right there," and I took the flight.

It was over five hours before I returned from that flight. That evening there was another intercept flight, but it was a short one – only a little less than two hours. Betty and I had had an invitation to go sailing with some relatives of friends we had known in Port Angeles, and it was to be on Sunday around noon. Early Sunday morning, I had the regular duty still, and we were called on yet another intercept. I didn't realize how long this flight would be, but it was so far out, and the fuel situation was so critical on the plane we intercepted that he had to divert to Hilo, which is just a little shorter than Honolulu if you change course soon enough. That meant that we had to escort him to Hilo, then return to Barber's point, adding a couple more hours for our flight time. I didn't get back to be relieved of the duty until about noon time, again over five hours of flight time and by then our invitation to go sailing was canceled – and it was never reissued.

The R5P flights were often interesting. Once when I was

the aircraft commander into San Francisco, had just had our instrument landing systems receiver changed before we went on the flight. The flight was strictly routine, except we had the usual morning fog in San Francisco on our arrival. We were cleared for an ILS on the usual runway, headed in from the over the Bay towards the west. I had more trouble correcting my heading than I had ever had before, and the signals seemed to make me zigzag into the landing area.

I could see the runway at a fairly good height and distance, and we landed and off loaded our passengers at the San Francisco Air Station. My crew checked the ILS to see if it was working all right, and discovered that the antenna was not connected. It received signals only when they were so strong that the antenna really was not needed, and the signal said to go to the other side of the beam! I'm glad we didn't have to go in with lower weather conditions.

On one flight to Palau, which was just south of the island where the savage fighting took place on the island of Peleliu, and we now had a loran station, it had seemed like a routine flight, but the landings there were always a little interesting. When the plane went below the jungle tree line, there was always a little less wind, and the plane landed a little harder than the pilot had expected. I prided myself on smooth landings, but this was never the case here.

We off loaded the cargo, always taking a look around at the junk left from the war, and we were ready to return to Guam. We started the first two engines as usual, but one engine didn't react to the energizing of the starter. Apparently the starter motor was burned out and we needed a new starter. I turned to the flight engineer and said "What do we do now?" Knowing that he had no spare starter with his spare parts kit, he replied after short time of considering it, "How about a taxi start?" And he explained that by taxiing fast enough, the defective engine would have the propeller windmill, and it could possibly be started. This was usually done in a very long runway, if it had to be done. This was wasn't that long, and the wind was no help.

However with little alternative, we taxied to the end of the runway, knowing that we would needed considerable speed, and then would have to stop to check out the engine completely before we made the next real takeoff. We added full power to three engines, and the engine did windmill. The flight engineer switched the engine on, primed it, and the engine was running! I hit the brakes hard, came to a stop, and turned around to return to a takeoff position where we took off and returned to Guam to replace that starter.

In March 1954, I was the aircraft commander for a flight to take Rear Admiral Perkins on a farewell inspection trip of the far reaches of his district. On a trip of this nature, we would also go into Hong Kong, when the VIPs on the trip would visit the British command and also the senior US Navy officials. We never went into Hong Kong on the regular Coast Guard supply runs, and I had never made a trip as the pilot.

On March 18, getting an early start, we left Sangley Point, and following an instrument flight plans, since we would be flying near communist China and entering a British Crown colony, we climbed to altitude. We were assigned to an altitude several thousand feet lower than we had requested, but we could tell from the radio traffic that an airplane from Manila

International Airport was just ahead of us at a higher altitude, and as he cleared an altitude, we would be cleared higher. We would level off, reduce the power, and start normal flight when air traffic control would clear us to 2,000 feet higher, to report when we reached it. We did this for several steps, leveling, changing power, and going to cruise configuration, when we were nearly up to our requested altitude.

This time when we reduced power an engine started backfiring – – loudly. We reduced power further on that engine, changed the engine fuel mixture, but nothing helped. We had no choice but to feather the propeller, call air traffic control, and return to Sangley. When we landed and examined the engine, it was apparent that an engine valve pushrod had stuck, and was bent as the pushrod was pushed by the drive. Fortunately, supply had a spare, and the crew work most of the night to be ready to depart the next morning. The crew was anxious to get to the shopping of Hong Kong, and worked without relief until all was well for departure, just a day later.

Since I had never flown into Hong Kong, and the approach was a little unusual, one of the pilots at Sangley (who wanted to go again), and had been to the Kai Tak airport several times on Navy planes, volunteered to sit in the cockpit and help us with procedures. As we approached, it was actual instrument conditions, and if you simply followed the printed plans, he couldn't help. If it had been clear, he might have been able to point out landmarks that would've been useful.

We were on instruments, and I was flying "on the gauges." Curt Kelly, my copilot, was on the radio talking to approach control in the tower, and was busy! I wanted to call to the flight engineer for approach flaps, but the flight engineer was not there, and John, our visiting pilot didn't know the cockpit procedures. I reached over and put the flap control in the down position, and went back on the instruments. I realized that the controls felt odd, and looked at the flaps. They were in full down position– – not approach. So, I reached over and put the control in the up position, but was busy again, and when I noticed, they were all the way up again. I put them down once one more time, and this time, Curt was available to stop them when they reached the correct position. I hope that I had no airsick passengers because of this odd flight path!

When we went over the ocean, we would rotate the flight positions of the three pilots we usually had. One time on this flight, I was navigating, and one of the senior passengers came up to the cockpit to see how things are going. It was Captain W. P. Hawley, who had been my navigation instructor at the Academy, when I was a cadet, and he had been lieutenant Commander. He was now the chief of operations for the district. He couldn't resist saying, " I hope I taught you all you needed to know when you are my student. Where are we?"

It was tempting to put my hand down flat on the chart, and say "Somewhere about here!" but I resisted the temptation and showed him where we really were.

On my last flight out to Japan and the Far East, in May 1954, we were in route from Guam to Tokyo on the 23rd. We made our usual stop at Iwo Jima, to take supplies to the loran station there, and while we were on the ground the flight engineer came to me with disturbing information. He said, "We have an oil leak on Number four engine." I

I replied, "How bad is it?" knowing that we would have time on the ground in Tokyo to make our usual inspection of all the engines and the equipment of the plane. If we could go on to Tokyo, we could probably replace a gasket if that was all that was necessary.

His response I have always remembered, "It's only about a two rag leak," meaning he could wipe up all the oil with only two of the standard size issue rags that were provided by a supply company. In that case, I decided, we should go on and fix it in Tokyo during the next days.

We went on and I put Joe Stephany, who was not fully qualified in the plane in the pilot seat, I was navigating and the third pilot had left the cockpit. Joe called me back into the cockpit to show me that the oil pressure was dropping on – not number four, but now number three engine. I told him to watch it carefully, and I kept my eyes the cockpit as much as on the navigating table just aft of the cockpit. The pressure kept dropping, and when it reached the limit of good operating pressure, we punched the feather button.

The prop feathered as advertised, it may increase power on the other engines, watching the oil pressures on number four, in particular. Everything worked fine, except the airspeed seemed to be a little lower than it should have been, and I suspected that it may have been how our plane's cargo was loaded. (We calibrated the airspeed gauges when we returned to Barbers Point, and they indicated low all the time. That didn't help much at this time!) We called in air traffic control, because we would not be moving through the control space at the speed we should have, and they asked if we needed an intercept. When we had been on the other end so many times, it seemed like a good thing to do, we asked for and had an Air Force intercept. They arrived in a Grumman Albatross, could stay near us all the way to Tokyo's Haneda Airport.

Next, air traffic control asked if we wanted to GCA, (radar steers all the way to the ground, with altitude control on the final approach). I asked what the weather was like at Haneda, and they must have been dreaming or wishing for the weather they reported. I said, "No, we do not need a GCA," and planned for regular instrument approach. When I arrived over the Tokyo radio station, the weather was nothing like they had reported, and I was near the mid-minimum altitude when we could see the field. But we did get in, the engine was changed on the ground at Tokyo, and we made the return flight without incident.

The Navy in Hawaii had some family oriented recreation trips that could be made to the neighboring islands. If you took the LST that was available to Kawai, you had to make your own arrangements on the island when you got there. If you get to Hawaii, there was a military camp we could have a cabin for a family, and then you could use that as your base of operations while you were there. The trip to Kauaii would be for about three days, and you could take your car on the LST. We took the trip, and stayed at the Kauaii Inn, which was a lovely break in the Honolulu routine. The trip to Hawaii was for a week and we were on the list to go, and thought we would enjoy it but –

In late 1953, things started facing down in Korea. The need for all the search and rescue was decreased, and we started moving people and planes out of the Pacific. We were asked to Barbers

Point whether we wanted to stay for only two years or whether we are happy to stay longer. I replied I would be happy to stay longer, if I could go to San Francisco or San Diego. Someone must have thought it was time for me to go to the east, because I received orders to Elizabeth City, North Carolina to leave in the summer of 1954.

Before I left, I thought I would get some medical care that I had been putting off, but was available at Tripler Hospital there on Oahu. I arranged for a nasal resection, hoping that I would be able to breathe easier. I went into the hospital and had the minor operation without complications.

While I was in the hospital, it was announced that the Assistant Commandant of the Coast Guard and the Chief of Personnel, both from Washington, would be coming through on a trip from the Far East, and would spend several days in Honolulu, where there would be a reception for them. Since I would not be able to go, Bette said she would not go, but our commanding officer live just across the street, and his wife insisted that Bette should go with them.

While Bette was at the reception, she of course met all the VIPs in the receiving line, but when they were not lined up, she could not remember who was who. Everyone who is in civilian clothes, probably Hawaiian shirts, and she saw a man standing alone, with no one talking to him. She approached him, and asked "Where are you stationed?"

He replied, "At Headquarters," and Betty said, "Oh, downtown here." At that point, Mary, the commanding officer's wife came up, heard Bette's response and said, "You met Admiral Richmond, the Assistant Commandant, didn't you?" And Bette looked for a hole to climb into. Two days later, after the VIP party had flown onto the West Coast of the US, it was announced that Rear Admiral Richmond would be the next Commandant, and Rear Admiral Hirschfield, the Chief of Personnel, would be the next Assistant Commandant.

As the time for us to Hawaii became shorter, we packed up a bunch of things that we felt we would need when we first arrived in Elizabeth City, and had them shipped by express, as was allowed with a small amount. We didn't know when our household furniture and everything else would get there.

One day when I had the duty at the air station, I knew Bette had taken the children and gone to the beach which was on the reservation of Barbers Point. A message came in on the teletype from the district office in Honolulu to the air station, relayed from Coast Guard Headquarters changing my orders from Elizabeth City to Washington DC, where I was to be the personal aide and pilot for the commandant. This was Admiral Richmond who had just been in Hawaii, and I had not even met him!

I called Bette at the beach, frightening her badly when she was paged. I said, "You must really impress people when you meet them at cocktail parties!" She had no idea what I meant and I told her what my new orders were. She thought she would have to change her identity somehow, and she didn't mention the earlier meeting with Admiral Richmond for years afterwards.

We left Barbers Point in late July, and were to fly on MATS from Hickam Field to Travis Field north of San Francisco. I sent the car ahead, with arrangements for a friend to pick up the car in San Francisco, and he would hopefully be able to meet his Travis.

We went to Hickam early, and learned that the flight was delayed. We were going on a C–97, the military version of a stratocruiser that Pan American flew. There are about 100 passengers, and many of them were children. We had many of the friends from Barbers Point down to see us off, with leis until our necks ached. Most of them had left before the plane was ready, near midnight, only about four of our friends were left at the terminal. We also removed the leis and put them in a box which we carried aboard with us. We left most of them at the terminal at Travis Field the next day.

We sat in the C–97 in seats with Marsha next to Bette and Greg next to me. The children were sleepy, but we were given a box lunch to start the flight. It had been ordered for 8 or 7 o'clock and had to be eaten or thrown away by 2 AM. So the flight attendants gave them to us to do with them as we pleased. A chicken leg and a bologna sandwich didn't do much for anyone at midnight, but there they were. The children found the cookies, and that was enough to satisfy them. We had a screamer across the aisle, probably with ear trouble, and that took the first couple of hours to get quiet to get some sleep on the flight.

The C–97 took about eight hours to arrive over California. It was daylight of course and Greg looked out the window of the plane and said, "There sure are a lot of volcanoes here!" In Hawaii, all the hills were green and only the former volcanoes are covered by brown grasses and patches of bare earth. Dry California looked to Greg like a country of volcanoes.

When we arrived in Travis Field, there was no car for us, and no message to say where it was. I called to the San Francisco Air Station, and I found that my friend had had the duty the night before, and had a late flight, so he was given the day off, and had not received the message that we were coming on this flight. The car was there, as were the keys, but our friend was not. They were holding the message to deliver when he next came to the air station. So, we took a taxi from Travis Field of the San Francisco Airport, where our car was waiting for us. We were off on leave, and then to cross the country to Washington.

HEADQUARTERS DUTY AS AIDE

When I first reported to Headquarters and reported to Vice Admiral Richmond as his aide, (he was promoted to full admiral in 1959, after I had left) he made it very clear that he wanted first of all, a safe and reliable pilot, and second, an aide. He stated at the first meeting, "When we're on a trip, or planning one, I want you to tell me if it's safe to go, and you have the decisions on that." It was a very good arrangement, and I had to tell him only once in the five years of that duty, that we should not go.

He also told me that he wasn't much for using an aide, and he was not demanding in that regard. He lived in a house in Arlington, Virginia that his mother owned, and there was no government quarters or stewards assigned to the Commandant. When we made a trip, I was the pilot first and the aide second. In fact, on some long trips, he had Captain I. J. Stephens as the aide, and I really concentrated on the plane and flight plans.

Bette and I found a furnished apartment in Alexandria, Presidential Gardens, and we existed in that for the months that it took to look for a house, get our furniture from Hawaii, and move in. We decided on a small house in Falls Church, and cashed in my Service Life Insurance to make the down payment. Officers who had never been discharged from the service were not considered as veterans at that time, and I was ineligible for an in-service loan to buy the house. That was changed later, but my insurance was gone then. The house was 45 feet long, had three bedrooms, one bath and a full basement. We kicked ourselves many times later for not having a second bathroom blanked in the basement. There was no air conditioning, but a couple years later, we bought a window unit that we installed in the dining room, and by putting an exhaust fan in the master bedroom, we had some cool air through part of the house – not in the children's rooms.

I had to learn to fly in the Martin 404 aircraft first of all. It was the primary plane for transport of the VIPs of the Coast Guard and treasury at that time. There were only two of them in the military of any kind at that time, and the rest were all owned by TWA or Eastern Airlines, or the prototype by Martin. It was a nice plane to fly and had some characteristics that were better by far than the Corvair that was flying as a competitor.

It had a water injection on take-off to give it more power to get in the air and it had a hot-wing for anti-icing. Our planes had the only engines of the type we used, because we had spare engines for the PBM seaplanes, and to save money, the Coast Guard had used them. We couldn't fly as high or as fast as Eastern or TWA, they were still good engines. The last years I flew the plane, we ran out of those engines, and had by newer and better engines.

As the last item of my "check–out" for the new position, I made a flight to the West Coast with my predecessor, Bill Jenkins, as the pilot, and I was the copilot. We visited the three districts on the West Coast, and also went to the Disney Studios where we were shown a bit around by Walt Disney himself. He was just planning Disneyland at that time, but he showed us some plans, and the motels in the models of the sea monster that would be used on the submarine ride – – that same one that had been used in "Twenty Thousand Leagues Under the Sea." He was planning a movie as a short subject, to feature the two icebreakers of the Coast Guard that had reached a new northern point in polar exploration by ship in the previous year. It showed later with the feature film "The Great Locomotive Chase."

Of course, the trip left for the West Coast at the same time that we were told we could move into our house, and while I was there for the moving in, I couldn't stay for the unpacking of all the dishes, clothes, pans, and other things. There had been no telephone installed when I left, and the road was not paved to our location. Bette had to park a block or two away and trudge over the dirt for the last many yards. By the time I returned, the pavement was in, the phone was in, and Betty had unpacked.

One of the first flights I had as a pilot of the plane when we returned from the West Coast trip was to take a planeload of people to the christening of the Great Lakes Carrier, the George M. Humphrey. He, Mr. Humphrey, had just taken over as secretary of the treasury, and the ship was being put into service by his former company, the Hanna Corporation. I guess that he was already in the Cleveland area, but Mrs. Humphrey was to go on our plane along with the Commandant, Mrs. Richmond, and many other flag officers. My copilot on this trip was Lieutenant Loren V. Perry, who had been in as an enlisted pilot, and had been around a long time. He had served as copilot for Bill Jenkins, and had given me some of my instructions as I checked out in the 404. He was a good pilot!

The morning of the flight come all the passengers arrived, we taxied out just behind the plane of Postmaster General Summerfield, who was also going to the christening. His plane had some discrepancy, and they called over to ask if he could go on our plane. We taxied back in, and took him aboard.

The weather was bad all the way up, and when we arrived in Cleveland, the weather required an instrument landing system approach. This gave me no problem, but when I broke out of the overcast, and made the landing, I forgot to crank in back trim tab for the elevator, and you couldn't just pull back on the controls. I landed nose wheel first, and bounced several times before I really had the plane on the ground. It was the worst landing I ever made with that with Admiral Richmond, and he never let me forget it. He was still laughing about the landing when we went to the quarters for dinner when I was Commandant.

A flight had been planned for the Admiral and the House Appropriations Subcommittee for November, as they liked to do every year. This gave them a good feeling for the needs of the Coast Guard, and it was a good vacation, after elections were over. This year they had discussed a trip to South America, and the group usually included Post Office Subcommittee members, since this was the organization of the committee, and it made it possible for them to visit other locations.

They had made arrangements with Elizabeth City for one of the pilots there to be the pilot on this flight, since they didn't know what planning time that I would be fully qualified. Admiral Richmond asked if I would like to go along as another pilot, or if I would like to stay behind. I told him that I felt it would give me a chance to be better established in the Washington area, and I opted to stay behind. The flight did not go as planned, and we made a full schedule in the Martin instead.

By the end of October, I had a new regular co-pilot, Jim Maher, who had been a year behind me at the Academy. He was a well-qualified pilot, and had a great sense of humor. He was fun to fly with. We made flights to Chicago, the Academy, New York, Boston, Cincinnati, and to San Juan and Miami. The passengers often included an assistant secretary of the treasury, but the Secretary of the Treasury, when he flew usually had the other pilots at the Air Station at the National Airport fly him. It was just a matter of having pilot you knew when they knew what to expect the passenger.

In January 1955, we meet a flight to New York to take Rear Admiral Cowart to the Society of Naval Architects and Marine Engineers annual banquet where he was to be the speaker or at least to be at the head table. We put his bag which had his dinner dress uniform in a rack at the tail of the airplane, and when we deplaned all the passengers, we couldn't find his bag. We felt certainly had taken off all the bags, but there was none for him. When we arrived in Washington, after flying back empty, his bag was in the rack——we just hadn't seen it because it was small, and was partially hidden behind a partition. We felt very small we went back to pick him up the next evening! He was very forgiving about it, and accepted our apologies.

In November 1955, we made one of the Congressional trips to the Caribbean this time. We had J. Vaughn Gary, the chairman, from Virginia, a Republican from New Jersey who didn't get reelected the next time, and one or two of the staff with Admiral Richmond and a couple of other Coast Guard officers. We went to San Juan first, then to Ponce and visited the offshore island there. It is Isla Caja de los Muertas or Coffin Island. The parrots and other birds are beautiful, as is the jungle. We had a barbecue on the island, and then flew back to San Juan. The field at Ponce was just about as short a runway as the Martin could possibly take off on, especially with the heat and humidity which affect the power output of an aircraft engine! From San Juan we went to Barbados, Trinidad, Curacao, Kingston, Havana, and back to Washington

On very long flights, such as from San Francisco to Honolulu or sometimes just to cross the country, I would borrow a plane from another station, such as Elizabeth City or San Francisco. I had a copilot was also qualified in the R5D, and on the long flights, we usually brought along two other pilots who would serve as copilots or navigators. The plane which was the preferred plane was the one that Secretary Snyder had had during the Truman days. It had been General Eisenhower's plane in Europe during the last of World War II and was a nicely outfitted plane. Secretary Humphrey didn't want such plane, and it was moved out of Washington. In September 1956, I borrow that R5D from Elizabeth City, and we made a trip to the West Coast and Alaska, and tried to visit every loran station in commission at that time in those locations. I stopped in Santa Maria, and the newspaper had a picture of me, Admiral Richmond, and Mother on the front page. The caption was "Hello Mother." In the small print it said that the commandant of the Coast Guard was visiting the loran station at Point Arguello.

We had a really tough time getting into Attu on that flight.

The weather was bad enough that the crews of the Coast Guard loran station were betting with the small Navy airfield crew on whether or not we would make it. I made an approach on a radio station that was officially not in operation, but it did work. When I approached the field, over water, Ham McNatt, my copilot on this trip, kept saying "Take a little lower's, Si." I would ease down and then would tense up and returned to the official minimum. The radar operator was very good, and he thought he could see the runway, give me "steers" to get me lined up.

Finally Ham said, "I have the runway in sight!" and I eased down a little lower where we could see we were lined up on a taxiway − − not the runway. I turned the plane around with the wingtip almost in the windows of the operation center, and went out and did it again. This time, we knew where the runway was, and landed without trouble. That night we went back to Adak where we could make a Control Approach− on radar − to near minimums. Adak's weather is seldom good, but we were glad to be on the ground that evening.

In 1956, we meet another Congressional trip, this one a little different. The Congressmen and their party went first to New Orleans on our plane. The passengers boarded a Coast Guard cutter to cruise over the Campeche banks where the American fishermen went to catch shrimp, with quite a few altercations with Mexicans—either other fishermen or the gunboats of Mexico. My new copilot, Chris Weitzel, and I had returned to Washington, while they went to sea. A few days later, we flew to Havana, where we stayed overnight at the National Hotel, that had once been so lovely. Castro had just arrived in Havana and had not yet clamp down on everything, but the hotel was not great. We flew on the next day to Managua, Nicaragua, and the next day, went to the Puerto Cabezavisa, on the Caribbean coast of that country.

The Coast Guard was considering putting a loran station there, but it never came to pass. This had been a banana port, but now it was an export port for mahogany for the states. We landed the belly with large wet mahogany boards – that stunk as only mahogany can. Admiral Richmond did cabinet work as a hobby, and welcomed this opportunity to get some good Nicaraguan mahogany – and it didn't stink as much as it dried out. We went from there to Guatemala City, Montego Bay, and to Cuidad Trujillo (now Santa Domingo) – before going back to Washington.

In January 1957, I guess the name of Coast Guard aviation was on the lips of a good many commercial pilots in New York. We made many flights to New York, where Admiral Richmond went regularly to be to the meetings of the American Bureau of Shipping and the National Cargo Bureau. My copilots and I knew the courses and the radio frequencies by heart. We normally went to Floyd Bennett Field, which was a naval air station and the Coast Guard had an air station there. Admiral Richmond would be met by the rear admiral from New York and they would drive on into the city.

On this flight, there was a very low overcast over the entire area, we asked for a Ground Control Approach to get us in. We worked our way down in the air traffic, and were cleared for our approach, but even at only 100 feet over the runway, we couldn't see enough to land. We took our wave–off, climbed back up to some altitude. We were cleared for a second approach, and once more, we saw parts of the runway as we leveled off at 100 feet, but we were not seeing enough to land.

This time air-traffic approach control asked if we would like to try to go into Idlewild (the name of Kennedy Airport at that time). We asked for their weather, and it was just at instrument landing system minimums. We said," Yes, give us clearance over there." Between the time we started our approach and the time we should have been near the end of the runway, the weather visibility went below minimums. Then almost immediately afterward, they reported that had gone back to minimums. The strobe lights marking the runway came in very clearly, we went into land. In the meantime, I don't know how many planes were holding all over the east while we made our three approaches!

The car came over from Floyd Bennett to Idlewild to pick up Admiral Richmond, Chris and I thought we would see if we could move the plane to Floyd Bennett, just a short distance closer to the city. In a while, the fog lifted and we could see over to Floyd Bennett. We asked if we could take off, fly at 100 feet over there, and land on the other field, but they would not allow that. It was not in accordance with visual flight rules. We filed an instrument flight plan then, which required us to climb out, go to altitude, probably join a stack of planes waiting their turns to make an approach, and then try again to go into Floyd Bennett. We got to the end of the runway, while we awaited take-off clearance, the fog came back down, and the tail of a Convair, with its rotating beacon on the top of the tail, was out of sight in the fog before it left the runway. We decided the smart thing to do was to stay at Idlewild overnight. The next morning would not be difficult to get out to return to Washington.

I have spoken almost entirely about the flying, but the office work was interesting, as well. Headquarters at that time was in the building that had once been built for the Southern railway system, at 13ᵗʰ and Pennsylvania, Northwest, and Washington. The building was old, and the offices were not air-conditioned. The commandant had his office, with a back office where he could go for privacy or to study a subject was in a corner of the building. Mrs. Selma Strawser and I were in the outer office. A chief yeoman, Pokorney, who had come from England to this assignment, was in the next office which was very small. Then there was a large office/waiting room with the administrative aide and the secretary for the assistant commandant had their desks.

Beyond that was the assistant commandant's office. The administrative aide was Commander Russell R. Waesche, Junior, the son of the wartime commandant of the Coast Guard. He had been associated with the Coast Guard all his life, and he had one brother who had been in the Academy at the same time as he, but who decided he wanted to be an Air Force officer, yet another who served in the Coast Guard reserve. Rest was 200% Coast Guard! His wife was the daughter of retired captain also.

Ms. Farr, the secretary to rear Adm. Hirschfield, had been the secretary for Vice Admiral O'Neil when he was commandant, then, and her feelings were hurt when she had to go back to being the secretary for the assistant commandant. It was a year or more before she would join us for coffee in the morning. The commandant would usually go out to the deputy chief of staff's office for coffee every morning, I should say most morning. Sometimes he had his coffee in the office and it would be my job to get the coffee for the admirals who were invited in to discuss something. The coffee-klatch in the deputy chief of staff office had almost all the senior captains and flag officers in. That was where I would get the coffee for my stay-ins, so they knew me well. Mrs. Strawser, Russ Waesche, and sometimes Commander Quennie Walsh, the aide to the secretary of the treasury, would have coffee while the bosses were out of their offices.

A funny thing occurred regarding my getting the coffee for the visitors when they stayed in the office. When I first arrived, Admiral Richmond would take his coffee with cream and sugar, and Admiral Hirschfield would take his black. It didn't take me long to get those orders straight. A few months later, Admiral Richmond would not have coffee, while the others would have their cups, and the discussions went on. I asked Admiral Richmond what happened with his coffee drinking, and he told me, "My wife suggested that I try my coffee black and see if I didn't like it that way. I tried it, and I discovered that I just don't like coffee." About a year later, he started drinking it again – black this time.

When papers came into the top offices, they were routed to the administrative aide, then to the assistant commandant, and then, if they were in all respects ready, to my desk. I would move them to Admiral Richmond's desk for signature as appropriate. Once in a long while, I would have a chance to make some input, other than making sure that the important things were on the top of the stack. People knew that I could rearrange the order, and at times, tried to get earlier attention by asking for that rearrangement.

The most notable of these input cases had to do with the promotion exam program for officers. Someone decided that all Coast Guard officers should be general duty officers, except those who had backgrounds that limited them, and even of them, 23 would be allowed to be promoted above commander, the maximum rank for those who accepted the "limited" status. In addition, there was a question about how to phase in the Merchant Marine officers who had been brought in to administer the Merchant Marine safety program. The decision here was to make them general duty, and to exempt them from any of the promotion exams. Academy officers, on the other hand, had to take all the exams, regardless of the fact that some of them are now serving as lieutenant commanders – my rank. Admiral Hirschfield put a notice on this directive saying "Some academy officers will resent this treatment!" and sent it on for signature.

I saw the note, examined the proposal, and added my note, "We sure will!" Adm. Richmond saw my note and called me in to make some explanations, and tell me why there were to be the 23 odd exceptions, and asked me to take the directive to Captain Roland, who was Deputy Chief of Staff, to see if he could make some adjustments. I did as I was told, trying to get out of the inner office as quickly as I could, because I knew there were five admirals and captains waiting in the outer office while this half-hour explanation was given to me. When Captain Roland came back with to me with some modification, a week or so later, he was Rear Admiral Roland. He asked if anything was all right and I couldn't have said, "No, give it more work!" Incidentally, Admiral Roland was the officer who eventually relieved Admiral Richmond as commandant.

Socially, the Richmond's didn't entertain officially at their home. He belonged to the Metropolitan club in Washington, and the Army and Navy Country Club, and the military clubs were available. Bette and I went to the Metropolitan Club several times for delightful dinners, and I was always in the receiving line when there were big receptions. We knew the flag officers and their lives wives very well, and were invited to many parties that few other officers of my rank attended.

When President Eisenhower was inaugurated in 1957, Betty and I were invited to observe the inaugural parade from the office of the commandant and the vice commandant, and so we had to go into Admiral Hirschfield's office to see the parade up Pennsylvania Avenue, but the view from the seventh floor was just great. There was some food brought in, we spent the entire day there. When we were about to leave, Admiral Richmond asked if we would like to have his tickets for the inaugural Ball, but we were not prepared to go to that – – it had to wait.

In August 1957, Admiral Richmond made the second of his loran station visiting trips. I made a note in my flight log that on the passenger list, we had Admiral Richmond, three other rear admirals, and four captains. One of the captains was Donald B. MacDairmid, who was the operations officer of the 14th District, encompassing all of the Pacific beyond the limits of the U.S. Pacific Coast. He drank a lot of Scotch whiskey each night, and I would frequently hear him trying to tell all the admirals how they should do their work. It would shock me at the time. He had been a very good aviator in earlier years but was about due to retire at this time.

We flew on this trip from Washington to San Francisco, to

Hickam Field in Honolulu, to Wake Island, Iwo Jima and on to Tokyo. While we were based in Tokyo, we made local flights to Niigata, Misawa, to Miho, and Pusan. Then we flew onto Okinawa, Hong Kong and into Sangley Point in the Philippines. We couldn't take the R5D to the Philippine stations, so there were a few days of rest for us while the party went to the stations by Grumman Albatross.

Then after four days, we went on to Angura, Saipan, Guam and then to Kwajalein. After staying overnight at Kwajalein, we went to Eniwetok, and spent a night at Truk. From there, our plane went on to Momote, in the Marcus Islands, while the inspection group took Albatrosses to Ponape and joined us in Momote. We flew overnight from a Momote to Fiji, then went on to Samoa, where they had a native kava ceremony for the official visitors, and we picked up the Governor Peter Tali Coleman, who was a native Samoan to take him back to Washington with us. We returned via Canton, Johnston Island, Hickam, San Francisco, Long Beach and back to Washington. It was a very long, but interesting trip.

In 1957, I made it to trips to St. Kitts, in the islands just south of Puerto Rico. On the first one, was taking a group of dignitaries to commemorate the birth date of Alexander Hamilton, and one of the passengers was Laurens Hamilton, a distant descendent. The flight was made in January, and besides Hamilton, we had Congressman Gary, our appropriations chairman, and the commandant. We used the R5D, and flew from Washington to Puerto Rico, largely at night. Then we went in to St. Kitts, where the only air service was by DeHavilland Dove, a small two engine plane. I have never known whether the BWI people passed the word that our plane couldn't make it, and the crowd came out to see the crash, or whether they were there to see the big plane and the VIPs arrive, but the runway was lined with spectators. I landed short, because it was a short runway, but I was stopped just over halfway down the runway. I came back and parked at the terminal, and our passengers got off to be greeted by the governor of the island.

In June that year, we went back to St. Kitts, and several other islands in the area, because the Coast Guard was thinking about establishing a loran chain in this area, there were negotiations going on about where to put the stations, and how much the US would pay for the rights. This time when I landed St. Kitts, the BWIA people came out to ask me if I could land the R5D there regularly, and how much weight I can load on the plane when I did it. I didn't have time to work it out with them, but I know the island is serviced by jets today.

Occasionally I was allowed to take Bette with us on a flight. She made one of the trips to the West Coast to visit family and meet a few of the Academy trips. One time, when it was to be Secretary's Day at a football game at the Academy, I had left the house early and she was to come to the Coast Guard hangar and join us before departure time.

We had gone to the animal shelter in Alexandria shortly before that time, and had gotten a beautiful boxer that was been too much for the previous owners in an apartment. I took him out to give him his morning airing before I left, but he ran off and I couldn't get him back before I had to leave to prepare the plane. I told Bette what had happened, and asked her to get the dog back in the basement before she left. We were ready to leave as scheduled and Bette still had not arrived at the hangar, and

I asked Admiral Richmond if he wanted to go ahead without her, the only missing passenger. He said we would wait a little longer, and she arrived soon and let me know she hadn't gotten the dog in. We never saw it again

In May 1957, the annual visit of the Congressional Board of Visitors was scheduled to go to the Academy to spend the day, visiting, interviewing cadets and instructors, and to make their recommendations. We would fly them from Washington to New London for the day, and then returned them either that afternoon or later that evening, if they stayed for dinner. Unfortunately, one of the Martin 404's was in overhaul at that time, and at the last minute, the secretary said he wanted to use one of the planes that morning. We sent for the R5D from Elizabeth City and I flew the party at the Groton in that big plane. I'd flown in and out of Groton so many times, that it was routine.

I had taxied up to the terminal, in doing so, we passed an old fire truck garage. I'd forgotten the wingspan on the R5P was considerably greater than the Martin, and didn't get over to the side of the taxiway as I would have to. The plane came to a sudden stop, as the wingtip of the plane hit the garage. On this flight, I had asked for and received permission to take Greg with us, and Russell Waesche III, the son of the administrative aide, also went with us. None of the passengers were shaken up at all as we stopped, but they deplaned some distance from the terminal, and Captain Hammond, who was a very aviator assigned to the Academy at that time took the kids in tow until I could make all the reports I needed to.

After all the passengers were gone, my copilot on the trip, Joe

Covington from Elizabeth City said, "Let's take it up and see how it flies now." I said "Let's take a good look at it first," and we taxied to the parking area. As we turned the plane around to park it, gasoline spewed out of the damaged wing. If we had flown in that condition, it could well have exploded from the air being forced into the hole. Needless to say, we were flown back to Washington that afternoon and another plane – – the Martin now through the Secretary's flight. I had an entry my flight log about the ground incident, and was kidded about it years later by one of the congressmen who was on the plane that day.

The plane had a patch on the wing in then was flown the next week to Corpus Christi, where it received a new wing. When he arrived home that evening, Bette asked Greg, "How was the trip to the Academy?" And he replied, "Daddy goofed!" She hadn't heard about it until then.

The following Monday, I was flying the commandant and Rear Admiral Kenner, the Chief of Operations, to New York for some meeting, and as I taxied out from the terminal, Admiral Kenner ran up from the passengers seats to say, "Look out for the fast taxiing boarding ladder over there!" It was a boarding ladder that was being towed by a tractor from one airline boarding spot to another, and he didn't want me to hit another fast taxing garage or boarding ladder!" He signed the entry in my log!

In the summer of 1958, Admiral Richmond decided to visit the units in Europe. We picked up the R5D, and started from Washington with a flight to Argentina. There we had a lobster dinner and started a flight across the Atlantic while the passengers slept. I didn't know it, but we had blown a tire on the take-off from Argentina. The plane had just had a brake replaced before our departure and apparently grabbed, just as the plane left the ground.

When we arrived in the London area, we were given a radar approach to the airport, which was good, since I had no idea what the field was, and we went in to land. I made one of my typically smooth landings, fortunately, and we went to the parking area. I noted the parking man looking at the left wheel as we parked, but thought nothing of it. Then, when the passengers were gone, the crew called me to look at the wheel. There were dual mount wheels and tires on that plane, one of the tires had a hole in it, big enough to put your head through it!

The plane had had a new brake put on just before we left, and it was apparently tight. There was a strong cross wind in Argentina, which makes the take-off a little difficult, and apparently, just as we left the ground, it had stopped rolling, while we made our take-off. The crew found a new tire, in the next morning we continued our expedition.

One of the passengers on this trip was my office mate, Russ Waesche. He had been selected for captain, and had his new assignment as Commander, Activities, and Europe. This would be a familiarization trip for him, to see most of the units he would command. He wanted to make the trip as a captain, the rank he would have when he was on duty, but he would not actually make the rank until 1 July, and we were leaving on June 17th. He asked Admiral Richmond for permission to wear the stripes of a captain, and was told the admiral would think about it. Admiral Richmond, with his wry sense of humor, didn't tell him that he would go as a captain, until the admiral figured out he had about reached the limit of his uniforms striped. Russ went as a captain, but there was still a goodly amount of celebration on the night of June 30 – July 1, judging from the bloodshot eyes the next morning.

We flew to Bremen and to Hamburg, where the Germans recognized the efforts of a Coast Guard cutter to rescue the survivors of the cadet training vessel that had capsized during a storm the previous year. We went on to Copenhagen, Antwerp, where it was possible to visit the Brussels World's Fair. All of these stops were to visit the Merchant Marine details that the Coast Guard had in connection with the US Consulates at that time. The next stop was to visit the Coast Guard ship that was the mobile transmitter in or near Rhodes for the Voice of America, until a station was built in Turkey.

The approach to Rhodes was handled entirely by a Greek radio operator – not a tower operator or air traffic controller. It was the only time on the trip when we had trouble understanding the English of radio operators. The next worse was the very thick and clipped English of operators in London.

We went on to Naples where a loran chain that had recently been completed the Mediterranean was being administered and supplied. The air unit that did most of the supply delivery was of interest to me as a possible assignment in the future. We went on to Rome, and Paris, the latter as the officers of the international Association of Lighthouse Authorities. Then it was back to London, where many of her passengers dropped out for a while. Admiral Richmond however, wanted to make a part of the cadet cruise with his classmate, Rear Admiral Lemby, who was now Superintendent of the Academy, and we went to Dublin, where he joined the cruise.

Six days later, we picked up the passengers, who had business in London, and went to Lisbon, via Dublin. We diverted via Dublin, because a cadet had had a case for appendicitis there, and had had an operation. He was now ready to rejoin the cruise, so we took him along.

When we left Dublin, we were going to Bermuda, where the Coast Guard had run a search and rescue establishment since the Korean War. We flew from Lisbon during the night, and landed in Bermuda for a daytime visit. The airplane crew was going to use Air Force facilities to sleep during the day, but the commanding officer of the cutter on standpoint pointed out that the BOQ was not air-conditioned, and we might want to use space on his ship.

We took him up on the use of spaces on the ship, but he didn't tell us that they were chipping paint off the decks, and the chipping hammers would be going over our heads all day, except when the crew stopped for lunch or inspection by our VIPs. I can't say much for rest and that ship! We did arrive back in Washington that night after being gone for a month.

It's time that I said something about the passengers that we had on the many flights. Usually the senior ones were the easiest to get along with. We did try to keep them happy. When we were late, or couldn't get into a field, they never complained. I think the funniest incident was when we are headed for Miami, once for Propeller Club conference, and the plane was full. We stood around in the waiting area, waiting for the last arrival –

usually the admiral, and everyone had a cup of coffee. When we reached our cruising altitude, my co-pilot would check with me and turn off the seatbelt light. The rush would start for the restrooms, two of them, one on each side. We had rough weather for some time, and had to keep the light on, to avoid injuring someone, but the light finally could be turned off.

We had the Chief Medical Officer of the Coast Guard, Rear Admiral Van Ackeren and his wife on the plane, and she was a big woman who had once been Miss Norway, I guess in the Miss Universe contest. When the seatbelt light went off, she headed for the lavatory. That evening in Miami, there had been a reception at the air station, and she was in a conversation with my co-pilot Jim Maher in the group. She said she had trouble getting out of the laboratory and she replied," Oh, that's the one on the port side. It does stick, but if you push hard it will open." She replied indignantly and in her Norwegian accent, "Listen, I push and when I push, I really really push, all 200 pounds of me!"

Later in the summer, Rear Admiral Roland, now the commander of the district in Boston and continuing to the north, talked Admiral Richmond into seeing the loran stations up there. We went to Frobisher where the terminal was at one time expected to be on the polar route from Europe to the states, over the pole. The jet age, and the range of the newer planes made Frobisher unneeded.

We were to be met by a small plane that would fly at low altitude over a range of mountains, then landed a loran station where we could not land, and we would fly onto Thule. The field and the route over the mountains closed in, the small plane couldn't go either, so we took them onto Thule. The sun never went down when I was up, but it was August 27 so it must've gone down sometime.

The spring of 1958, when the orders for the summer were being prepared, Harry Solberg, who controlled the personnel side of aviation had come to me, to ask whether I wanted to be transferred that summer. There were a couple of reasons that he wanted to know. He wanted to go to San Juan, he knew that I had looked at it as a possibility for my next assignment. Someone would have to be ordered in as a replacement for me, and it could leave a big hole somewhere else. So, I took a quiet time and when in to ask Admiral Richmond if I should tell aviation I was going, and if so, if I might steer the choices.

He replied, "I've been meaning to talk to you about that. Mr. Gary (the appropriations chairman) wants to make an around the world trip and he would like you to be the pilot. He can't justify trip all the way around the world, unless he takes a member who was also who is also on the Land–Lease Committee, and the one he has in mind won't do it unless he goes in a pressurized plane. His solution is for the Coast Guard to borrow a DC6 (R6D in the military). "Have you checked out in that plane, and then make the trip in the R6D. Does that appeal to you and would you be willing to be the pilot?"

It was appealing as a challenge to my piloting abilities, and I thought the trip could be fascinating. So that is why we were still in Washington in the summer of 1958. The trip didn't go as planned, because the Air Force and the Navy said they had no plans available for loan, and the trip finally went after I was gone, in a C – 130, that was Coast Guard owned.

In November 1958, both Assistant Secretary Flues and the commandant were invited to the dedication of the American Chapel in St. Paul's Cathedral in London. Mr. Flues needed to attend a meeting of *Interpol* in Istanbul just before the dedication, would fly over earlier. But he had never seen any of the Coast Guard units in Europe, so we were off again.

We flew overnight from Argentina to the Azores, and then overnight again to Naples. Then onto Istanbul, where we picked up Assistant Secretary Flues. Then to Rhodes to visit that transmitter ship, to Athens to visit a Merchant Marine detail and on to London. I did see the Queen and Vice President Nixon parade down the aisle just a few feet away, as they headed for the chapel. No one could see the actual dedication, because the chapel was immediately behind the main altar. We all watched on closed-circuit TV.

The plans called for us to be airborne around 7 PM London time that night, the night before Thanksgiving, and for us to be home for a late dinner that evening. There was a late invitation extended to the VIPs and then we were going to take off around 10. The head winds across the Atlantic made it impossible to fly direct to Argentina, so we filed for the Azores. When the passengers arrived, the winds had increased if anything, and at Lajes, Azores, we had to file our flight plan for Boston. We couldn't make it to Washington. We flew to the Azores and then filed our flight plan to Boston.

We taxied out to the end of runway, and the tower called, "We have your clearance."

"Go ahead."

"Santa Maria air traffic control – the clearance point for the Azores control area clears you to the Bermuda airport." I didn't know what the rest was, I was so angry and confused. We waited for him to finish, then said "We aren't going to Bermuda, we are going to Boston."

He said he would call Santa Maria – on another island – and let us know. We asked for and were given permission to shut down the engines where we were at the end of the runway. It was now about 3 AM.

We got our clearance to Boston, and were on our way. We had hoped that the winds would die down little, and we might change our flight plan to overfly Boston and go into Washington – about two more hours. They did not change, and we landed in Boston.

Boston had figured a way to make money on the military when they landed. Commercial fields were prohibited to charge government planes landing fees when they used the field, but Boston charged fees for using the foreign clearance area. We taxied into the foreign clearance area, headed in with all the clearance papers. None of us have had anything to eat except the two box lunches we had ordered, even though it was now about 6 PM on Thanksgiving evening.

The customs officer looked at the clearance documents, and said, "You have passengers on the plane." "Yes." "They will have to come in and clear individually."

I asked him, "Would you like to go out and tell the assistant secretary of the treasury that he is to come in, or do you want me to go?"

"I guess I'll just go out." By the time I finished filing, his visit and our clearance were all through.

We went on, got to Washington about 10:30, and Chris Weitzel and the rest of the plane crew went on to Elizabeth City. I know they had no Thanksgiving turkey. Only the dry chicken that was standard in those lunches.

I made a bunch more routine flights in the Martin, and one more R5D flight to Alaska, but I don't remember any details about. I do remember one Martin the flight that Chris Weitzel and I made, when it was to be just a routine training flight, but in instrument conditions with snow in the area. We went to Wilmington, Delaware, Baltimore, making instrument Landing Systems approaches, and asked for clearance back to Washington. Washington had had a wind shift, the ILS was inoperative, and the snow was putting it at minimum.

An airliner had to divert to his alternate, and the clearance was to the wrong direction. We were held, circling, for some time, just north of Washington, and when we reached the point where we asked for clearance to Floyd Bennett, they said, "Winds are now very light and the ILS is now operating. Would you like to try an approach?" We took it, and where the first plane to make it after a long period of no planes.

Bette was very active in the Wives Club, and was often used as a photo model in publicity. I was in the receiving line for one of the Wives Club receptions, and for some reason, I couldn't remember the name of my old friends. I usually knew the names of almost all persons assigned to Headquarters, but I didn't know how to reply to Harriet Smith, the Wives Club presidents, when she said," I'm not getting the names from you, Si."

In early August, 1959, a fascinating assignment came to an end. We sold our house in Camp Algier Avenue in Falls Church to a buyer who paid us several thousand dollars more than we had when we had bought it. We pondered about keeping it, because we knew we would be in quarters in Corpus Christi but sold it, because of the fact that it had only one bath. That came back to haunt us later!

Corpus Christi

Our trip to Corpus Christi we tried to make as pleasant as possible. After all, there hadn't been much vacation time in the past five years. We had gone to West Virginia state park one time, but it wasn't a rip-roaring time for all. This time, we stopped at places like Natural Bridge, and spent time at souvenir stands. We purchased a new (for us) Buick Riviera not long before departure, and had air-conditioning installed in. It was one of the early ones, the frosted up at times, and we had to watch it to see that it was actually working, but it made life much more comfortable as we drove through the heat and humidity of the southeastern US.

When we arrived in New Orleans, we were going to spend a few days, and my classmate friend, George Sohm, was stationed here. He had made arrangements for us to have guest quarters at the Naval Station across the river from downtown New Orleans, and we checked in there, and Bette and I went somewhere with George, while the kids went to the movie on the station. It was a ghost type, and Marsha had nightmares the rest of the night with encouragement from Greg.

We returned to the guest quarters and went to bed, in non-air-conditioned spaces, where the pillows on the bed smelled so strongly of mildew, that we slept better without pillows. We decided the next morning that we would move to the Monteleone Hotel where we could have two adjoining rooms.

Each room had a TV, so the kids could choose which program each wanted and there were no arguments about that subject.

We enjoyed a few more days in New Orleans, and one evening, the Admiral of the district, Carl Olson and his wife asked Bette and me to dinner, which we enjoyed very much. Our last evening before we went on to Corpus Christi, we told the kids, "This is your night." We took them to Kolb's, an established restaurant in downtown New Orleans, and let them choose their own entrées. Greg chose Oysters Rockefeller and enjoyed them so much that when the waiter was clearing the dishes Greg said, "I think I'd like some more of those." I quickly said, "No, you don't!" So Marsha said, "I'd like to keep those shells," and the waiter brought them back in a plastic bag

We went into the amusement park on the shore of Lake Pontchartrain, and the first thing that struck the eye of both children was a booth where the prizes included large blue teddy bears. Greg immediately said "I'm going to get one for Marsha." I tried to dissuade him, saying "You'll just waste your money." He won on his first turn and gave Marsha her teddy bear. So much for the lesson!

They enjoyed a few rides and on the way out, we once again passed the teddy bear booth. Greg said, "I think I'll get Marsha another one." This time I let him go ahead and he lost a few coins without any return. Then I was able to give my lecture about how much chance he had to lose his money on those things.

The next day we started on our way over to Texas, and the first time we stopped, as I walked around the car, I detected a strong odor of old seafood in the trunk. It was Marsha's oyster shells! Without a word, and as quickly as I could, I removed the shells and dumped them in a trash can. The entire car could have been detected by odor if we kept them much longer.

We checked into a very nice motel on the shores of Corpus Christi Bay when we arrived, and I called Art Perry, whom I was relieving. He told me that our quarters were ready on the base, if that was what we wanted. We were pleased not to house hunt, and the next night we were back in our own beds. The move was very easy, the van line found one one piece of furniture that was nicked, and would not deliver it until it was properly repaired. There was no air conditioning in the quarters, but we could buy as many air-conditioners as we wanted to come and put them in the windows, and there was no change in electric bills – in fact no electric bills. We paid for our phone, and turned the rental allowance over to the government. We eventually had a big air-conditioner in the dining/living room, one in the bedroom and in Greg's room, and one on the screen porch where we had a television.

Art and I made a courtesy call the Navy admiral who was there at the time, Joe Clifton, and then Art and I went flying in the planes we had. We called them UFs then, the designation was changed to HU–16 later. Part of what I needed to do was get oriented in the area again, and I had to learn to fly the plane. Also, since I hadn't flown during the month, I needed flight time for pay. I went out again a couple of times shortly after that, and never had any trouble getting enough flight time. One of the flights in the first week was over six hours.

The executive officer that I inherited from Art was a good pilot, and very bright, but he had a unique ability to rub people the wrong way. He had alienated the operations department of the Naval Air Station, because they didn't call us for every search and rescue call but used their own helicopter. (We had no helicopter at that time.) The Navy wanted to change hangar assignments, to do more maintenance on their planes in an orderly fashion, and they wanted to move us at their expense to newly renovated space in another hangar, where we would have more space, and it would be arranged as we desired. Tom fought this move every inch of the way. We did make the move, now the Coast Guard has the entire hangar at the air station.

One of the main functions of the air station here was to provide some protection for the shrimp boats that operated all along the coast of Texas, and down into the Mexican waters. Just how much authority the Mexicans had to seize them was not clear at that time, but we would circle just over 12 miles offshore, and monitor radio traffic as we observed what went on. There was a large number of the shrimpers who had flooding problems, partly due to overloading with shrimp cargo and ice and we would fly out and drop pumps to them. We had a lot of developing our own pump systems then, because there was no standardized system of packing when into a container with parachutes. If the boat made it back to shore, then we had to retrieve it somehow.

In April 1960, we were tasked with a flight around the entire Gulf of Mexico, to be made every week except once each month, the air unit in Biloxi, Mississippi would make the flight instead of our plane. We were to stay outside of Mexican waters, but to locate concentrations of shrimp boats, and especially to see if there were any problems with the Mexican patrol boats. These flights were about 12 hours in length, and we took three pilots on them at first. Later, we found we could shorten the flights a little to just over 10 hours, and we made them with only two pilots. On either two or three of these patrols, the plane developed engine trouble and had to land in Mexico. I know one landed in Merida and one at Campeche. When the crews came back, they were gaunt and looked terrible, because Montezuma's revenge had gotten to them.

Since we had airplanes and could fly officers to where they were needed, we were often asked by the district office to serve on physical disability boards relating to the Coast Guard personnel at the Fort Worth Public Health Hospital. These were very depressing, for the members in the counsels. It seemed like the doctors had made their minds up about how fast these young men should be thrown out, and it made you wonder what would become of them in the future.

On a couple of occasions, I was sent down to Brownsville to give promotion exams to the officers on the two boats there in Brownsville or Port Isabel. It was a long and uninteresting drive through much of the King Ranch, but a visit to Mexico could be fun.

In May 1960, we started conversion to the UF–2G. It had a longer wing, better anti-icing system, and a little faster acting landing gear. I decided I would get that first plane from the factory, and fly one of our UF-1s in for modification. We waited until a front had gone through, thinking that it should clear the weather out as it went east. The front stopped just past New Orleans. The next morning, I was sure we would have no trouble getting through, but the front stopped just beyond Roanoke, Virginia. In those days, Roanoke rolled up all the sidewalks at

6 PM. The next morning we tried again, and this time we went as far as for Fort Belvoir, Virginia near Washington. We went into Headquarters and visited and checked with the weather again. Later that afternoon, we delivered the plane to the Coast Guard Air Station at Floyd Bennett.

The next morning we accepted a UF–2G at the plant, and tested it in the air and flew over to Floyd Bennett. The crew wanted to stay there and renew old friendships, but I knew the district would think that we had been gone long enough. That same afternoon, we flew to Baltimore. We were on our way! This plane could fly through weather, and was not nearly so restricted in a ferry flight. The next morning, we flew back to Corpus Christi.

When I submitted my orders with a voucher to be paid for the expenses of my absence, the pay officer returned them with a note that the airline schedules showed that the flight time from Corpus Christi to New York should be only one day, when we had taken several. He wanted to know what hijinks we had been involved in. I sent the orders back to the Chief of Staff, and reminded him that the primary purpose of the flight was safe and expeditious delivery of the plane. He responded to that by saying that the pay officer probably didn't know the difference between a ferry and a fairy. That time I was paid and promptly.

The Navy admiral who had been there when we arrived was replaced by one who was a very likable individual, Rear Admiral Kirn. By this time Bette and I had become established as part of the station society, and we would be included in the group of commanding officers of the squadron parties, be included in the group of commanding officers of the squadron parties, and the admiral and some of his staff. We would go together to the Little Theater shows, and would party before and after. I met an individual at one of the yacht club affairs, who introduced himself as John Pitcairn, and I learned at dinner that he was the son of the inventor of the Pitcairn Autogiro, and that manufacturers were still using the patents of that aircraft in helicopters.

Then we learned the family had used the earlier profits from that venture to buy or establish Pittsburgh Plate Glass, and then PPG Industries. They had some lovely parties. We came to know a family in town who were involved in the oil industry in the area, and we were invited to the "coming out" of their daughter – some affair! We were really enjoying Corpus Christi at this time, and if someone had said, "I have just the position for you here," I would have been sorely tempted.

Greg had become very interested in age–group swimming, and was doing very well at it. He could usually place highly in both breast stroke and the butterfly stroke and we thought he looked great at it as he'd grown, and become tanned in the Texas sun. He hadn't had any interest in swimming when we first arrived in Texas, but a girl about his age had suggested it to him, and after he started, the coach, a young Navy enlisted man, had him hooked.

We planned to trip to Mexico in the summer of 1961, and Greg would have none of it. He had a swim meet that he wanted to attend, and besides, he thought he didn't like the Mexicans. We went without him, and saw many of the sights around Mexico City, including the National Museum, as it was then. One of the features then was a simulated tomb of an Aztec nobleman, where you had to go down into the tomb by stairs. Marsha slipped on the stairs, injured her coccyx, and I think it still bothers her.

On one of the evenings we had dinner at our hotel, where they had Aztec dancers as a floor show. The waiter was so pleased with how well Marsha had behaved at dinner, he brought her a dish of ice cream, without our ordering it. The next day she's suffered Montezuma's revenge, all day. She still made it through the day of seeing Mexico, however, and went to the bullfights with us. These were fascinating to her – – she couldn't quite figure out why they were doing these things to a confused bull.

In late August 1961, we were threatened by Hurricane Carla. We watched it for several days, then the training command either hangered or flew out all its plane. It was time for us to do something too. We flew one of our planes to a field to the north, and pulled another all the way into the hangar. The third one, we left the tail out of the hangar, in order that we could use the antennas of the plane to communicate if the phones went out. The phones did go out, before the worst of the hurricane reached us, and we had the only communications on the field, through New Orleans.

I slept on the floor at the station, as Bette and the children had done at their shelter, the Navy Supplies building. We had new mattresses that were destined for our new location in the hangar that the Navy wanted us in, so it wasn't too uncomfortable, if you could forget why you were there. Fortunately, no damage was done to our quarters, and none of the planes or the hangers. Our fliers went out to survey what damage was done up and down the coast, and the worst was just the east, Port O'Connor, where the station at Matagorda Island was almost completely demolished.

I was asked by the chief operations in the district office to go to Port O'Connor, and see what they needed, and to make a recommendation about where their operations should be continued. I flew up in an Army helicopter, and found that there were snakes everywhere. A mound, about 8 feet above sea level, had about 20 rattlesnakes on it, and someone – a good shot – had killed them. There were snakes in the water supply of the Coast Guard station, and the crew was using canned water designed for use in a life raft. The cook was cooking over a small fire on the beach. Some of the men had moved ashore probably to their homes on the mainland, and some had gone to homes where they rented space. This didn't solve their problems instantly, because water had been around three feet deep in each of the houses that remained standing.

A new station was built there, elevated so high water would go under it, and it was on the mainland – not Matagorda Island. Sometime later, in the spring of 1962, I received a phone call one day at the station from a friend I had gotten to know when we were in Washington. He was now the Chief of Staff of the Seventh Coast Guard District in Juneau, Alaska.

He, Captain Bill Harned, had gotten a copy of my orders to the Seventeenth District, and wanted to make sure that we didn't think that we were going to the end of the earth, or that it wouldn't be all bad, because he was enjoying his hunting and fishing there. Of course, I hadn't gotten my orders, or even heard about them from the district where I was, and it made me a little aggravated to say the least. The next correspondence was from the Thirteenth District, who would normally arrange transportation to Alaska, and it was addressed not to me, but to Bette as "Dear Madam." It practically said, "Now is not a good time to go through Seattle, because there is a World's Fair here, but if you want rooms on a cruise ship anchored in the bay, we can put you up at $200 per room per night. It became the subject of conversation at every spring cocktail party at the air station.

Eventually my orders did come, and we seriously looked at where we would stay when we were in Seattle enroute. Yet another new Navy admiral arrived, and said he would arrange for quarters at the Naval Air Station, Sand Point, on Lake Washington. It was difficult to turn him down when he was obviously trying so hard to work something out for us. A friend on one of the staffs had relatives in the Seattle area, and they said they would make an apartment available – one that they had developed in their basement. We accepted the letter, and after we were away from the base in Corpus Christi, sent a telegram to the Navy command in Seattle to let them know we would not need their quarters. They were actually in the enlisted area, we would have to check out bedding, and pots and pans from the temporary supplies.

So we were on our way to Alaska. We had another new car – a Pontiac sedan (we needed the space for Greg's legs now) which had air-conditioning installed, and seemed a good car to head for Alaska, even if we never used the air-conditioning in Juneau.

ALASKA

In route to Seattle, our jumping off spot, we visited with my mother and with Bette's mother in Palo Alto. Mother said she had something bothering her that she couldn't identify, but wasn't terribly concerned by it, didn't seem to be losing or gaining weight, and she would see her doctor as soon as my brother Win and his family came for a visit shortly after we left. Everyone in the family went to the big house and the space of Santa Maria for vacations. We went to Palo Alto, and wondered why Bette's mother let her other daughter run her life so completely.

We went up the coast to Seattle, and visited the World's Fair. It was a lot to see, and not that much time to see it. The Space Needle frightened Bette (she is afraid of heights) but the housing was not nearly what the district office there had made us believe we should expect. We turned our car in for transportation to Alaska by ship, and took a motel in the downtown area, within walking distance of the monorail train terminal to the fair, at a very reasonable price. We flew to Juneau on Pan American Airlines, and we were in the city which would be our home for the next two years.

Housing was desperately short in supply in 1962. Some enterprising individual had built a tract of homes in Mendenhall Valley, the area just downstream from Mendenhall Glacier, but they are all sold and occupied, and when you knew you would only stay two years, it was hard to see the value of buying that housing. My predecessor, Dave Oliver, had lined up a house that was owned by an official of the Fish and Wildlife Service, that we could rent while he and his family went to Minnesota. It had several faults, but it was one of the most attractive homes in or near Juneau.

It was three miles out of the city proper, but the roads were plowed in the winter. It had its own water supply, since it was out in the "country," and this was a well, with a pump in the space under the house. The water was put into a pressure tank, and pressurized, for use. The only problem with this, as the landlady pointed out, was that the well was around 200 feet deep, and the pump could become air bound if too much water was drawn out at one time. The supply of water had never been very great, and that made the possibility of being air bound a definite possibility. If this occurred, she suggested that we watch the gauge on the pump to see if it were pumping, or if it was dropping to zero, which would overheat it and start a fire – under the house! The landlady also pointed out that she had a water line installed in the kitchen to provide water from a catchment area in the yard of the neighbor just up the hill, and this brought in the pure stream waters from the snows and springs of the mountains above.

The other disadvantage of the house was that it had a flat roof, and in Juneau, you can have snow. Our landlord was the Alaska expert, however, and he had designed the house this way. It had advantages too, there was a possibility of converting space into an apartment in the basement next to the garage – this was often done in Juneau – but we made the area into Greg's bedroom. It had a hot water heater, one of the most expensive systems to install, but one of the systems that gives very even heat. It was draped and carpeted, and we accepted it, with relief.

There was some little time before we could move into the house on the highway, so we moved into the Baranoff Hotel when we first arrived in Juneau. The Baranoff was by far the nicest hotel in town, there were no motels, and the couple of other hotels didn't impress anyone! There was a new district commander who had just arrived, and he and the area commander from San Francisco were planning an inspection and familiarization trip around the Alaska district, and I was listed as an additional passenger.

The first Sunday we were in the Baronoff, I received a call from Win, my brother, to let me know that Mother had died in the hospital after an exploratory operation. I was really undecided about what to do under the circumstances. We had only had a few days to move into the house before the scheduled trip, the family was in a new location, and I was expected to make the trip. Finally, after much soul-searching, this I stayed to help move in and went on the trip, missing Mother's funeral.

The new district commander, Rear Admiral W. D. Shields, had been an aviator as had the Chief of Staff, Bill Harned. The chief operations was not an aviator, but was a surface operations man. He depended on my advice for anything that related to aircraft. I was the Chief of Search and Rescue for the district.

We had very few vessels that could do anything regarding search and rescue, so we had to make sure that the buoy tenders in the area were available to be diverted. The only pure search and rescue vehicles were two 95-footers, and the STORIS which was used more as a cruising cutter on Alaska patrol. Besides that, the tenders had to be scheduled to provide supply trips to some of the lighthouses along the waterways of Alaska where we still had manned lighthouses. That part of the task was taking care of by the Aids to Navigation section. I also wrote the operations order for vessels that was sent to Seattle for maintenance, repair or conversion. I had my hand in many of the offices of the district a good part of the time.

The Chief of Operations at this time was confronted with a situation which needed correction, and to his credit, he did. The quarterly operating budgets were prepared by the engineering division, since they had the money, rather than operations. By the time operations saw the budget, it was too late to change. The revised procedure put operations in charge with engineering having full input, but not the final word. It was working that way when I left Alaska.

Very shortly after the trip around the district, I was introduced to one of the problems of Alaska search and rescue. A couple of men had gone fishing in a small boat at the Knik Arm, that led to a glacier. Apparently the glacier "calved" a "bergie" bit, and either it hit the men's boat or the swells upset and swamped the boat. We set our 95- footer and several Coast Guard Auxiliary boats to look, but all that was ever found a man' jacket. The cold water didn't allow for many mistakes.

Another new aspect of being in the district came home very quickly. I was now an administrative aviator, and the aircraft was not readily available the fly. Fortunately, there was a supply trip that went from Ketchikan, via the air unit in Annette Island, to the Yakutat Loran Station every two weeks, and it usually stopped in Juneau to pick up materials or personnel when it was enroute. This allowed the aviator assigned to the district to replace one of the pilots, who would then go to the district office to conduct business not easily taken care of by phone. He would send spent his time there visiting while the plane was gone, and the exchange would be made again after flying to Yakutat and back.

Yakutat was always an interesting spot to visit, but especially in some seasons, because there were so many moose on the plains below the mountains. There was a former commanding officer of the loran station who asked to return for a second tour, and then retired in Yakatat. He built a lodge at the airport, had his own small plane which was beefed up to land on the plains near the settlement, and he would guarantee a hunter a moose if he, the hunter, came to his lodge and used his plane to bag this. On one occasion, the hunter arrived on the airline, checked into the lodge, and 30 minutes later, he was dressing the moose to return to Seattle or Anchorage with meat for most of the winter.

On one of the trips to Yakatat and return, the weather came down somewhat on the return flight. The Alaska pilots were used to flying Victor Fox Radar – a corruption of the VFR or for visual flight rules – and would keep an eye out from the pilot's seat, and a radar operator at the control of the radar. I was flying with my old friend from Port Angeles, Walt Curwen, and I had not been in Alaska long, while he had been there over two years, and knew the land well. We flew down the coast of Alaska with no problem, and saw Cape Spencer on our left. Here we turned inland to follow the inlets and waterways to Juneau. Walt told me, "Just keep the land in sight on your side there, and we will follow it in." I did as he told me, until we suddenly saw through a small break that we had gone into a small inlet, and there was a mountain ahead. At that point we asked for an instrument clearance, and came in at a high altitude. We did that and made our let down at Sister's Island, near Juneau. Even from there it is an interesting trip to the airport.

The DC-7 was used for flights to Alaska and on to the Orient at this time, at least by Northwest Airlines. This plane must have been pushing some of the technology available at the time, but it still had propellers. One of the planes, in the fall of 1962, had a propeller runway on a flight from Seattle to Anchorage, with a plane full of military personnel and dependents, headed for Japan eventually. It was approximately over Sitka when this happened, and at that time, Sitka had no airport. It had had seaplanes during World War II, but there was only a facility for the little inter-city Alaska operations now.

The pilot of the Northwest plane put the plane down in Sitka harbor, and a great deal of scrambling took place to remove all of the passengers before the plane went down. The loran station at Sitka had a boat and that was used, as was the Coast Guard auxiliary and many fishermen. There was no loss of life in this incident.

Greg, in the first summer, just after we arrived, had heard that there was a city swimming pool, and he headed there when the weather was good. If the water heater failed, the water was icy, and there would be no swimming but if the sun shone and the heater worked, it was fun. At the end of the season, there was a swimming meet, and Greg entered every event he could qualify for. He took first in every event. There was no swimming pool in the fall or winter, since this was outdoor. During the time we were in Alaska, there was an election to decide whether the city should build a pool, and it failed. Greg was without his strong sport in Alaska.

I joined the Elks while we were in Juneau as almost the only outlet available. One day in the summer of 1963, there was a picnic for Elks and their families in Auke Bay, near the Mendenhall Glacier, but along the shore of the ocean inlets there. There were quite a few teenagers who attended the picnic, and they went wading in the cold water of the outlet. Greg looked very impressive in his swimmer's bathing suit, and although he had no tan by this time, he knew he could swim better than any of the others. He told us later, that he struck out from the shore (we saw that) and then suddenly turned around. The cold weather was causing his muscles to cramp seriously. He made it back to wading depth, but it gave him a real scare, although he did look good while he was swimming.

In December, it was time for me to have an instrument check. An active aviator was required to make a designated number of instrument approaches, a number of Ground Control Approaches (GCA) on radar, and to have logged in a number of hours of instrument time. The instrument time was not hard to get in Alaska, but GCAs are almost nonexistent except in Kodiak, or Anchorage. The flight time was almost equal, so the pilots from Annette Island always went to Seattle, where they could do some shopping, get some fresh food, and get those GCAs. I went to Annette the night before I was scheduled for my check, with Gene Farley as my check pilot.

We flew south along the airway for some time, but then we noticed that the airspeed didn't seem to change much, but we were getting some ice at the top of the clouds. We asked and were given a clearance to climb to a higher altitude, where we should be at the top of the clouds. As I pulled the nose of the plane up, when the airspeed should have reduced, it went up, and then reached the zero point and stayed there. Apparently the pilot heater had failed. We asked for clearance to let down to the airport in Sanspit, British Columbia I made the approach with no airspeed indicator, just altitude of the claim

We landed at Sanspit, there was a dish of ice about 2 inches thick on the nose of the plane, and we had seen ice in our pitot tube before we landed, about four inches in front of the tube. We stayed there for a while, letting ice melt, then flew to Seattle under the weather, down the channel inside Vancouver Island. We landed first to Port Angeles, and let them replace the defective heater.

We took care of the GCAs at Naval Air Station Seattle, and then went out to get some fresh foods and look for Christmas presents. I don't recall anything I bought that the family had ordered, but as I walked along a street in downtown Seattle, I passed a pet store. Everyone Alaska has a dog, but we hadn't. I went in and asked about the parentage of the pups, and was told that they were a mixed breed, water spaniel and cocker. I chose a black and white little fellow, and took him in a box to head for the North country. He didn't suffer for attention on the return trip, and when I dropped off in Juneau, I went by the house, and put him in the kitchen. Bette saw him the moment she walked in, it was just as hooked as I. I took him to a vet for a check and shots, and asked that the vet bob his tail, but the vet said since the tail was all blacks except for a white tip, that it would become part of the pup's personality. He became "Taku," named for the wind that comes off the Taku glacier, just about 75% of all the dogs in Alaska.

That first winter in Juneau, we did have snow several times, but there were two that were worse than the others. The first time, it snowed in heavy showers for about a week, until there is about 45 inches of it on the ground. Then, as is so likely in southern Alaska it turned to rain. The 45 inches of snow with all the rain, was just too much water for the flat roof of our house. Greg and I went up and shoveled some of it off nearly every evening, but some of the melt would go to the overhang of the roof, and freeze up again, making it dam to hold the water on the roof. The designated drains, were out in the air and frozen solid as well. Water poured down inside Marsha's room, making one wall a waterfall. We contacted the landlord, and he had the roof re-tarred, very shortly afterward.

The second heavy snow, once again was about 45 inches but this time it came in one continuous snowfall. I would shovel the drive in the morning, so I could drive to work with chains on the tires of the car. Bette would shovel the drive just before she expected me home, and I would shovel it again before I went to bed. The snow was so deep, we had difficulty finding a place to throw it when we shoveled out. This time, after the heavy snow, the sun came out and it melted slowly.

Marsha went to school on Douglas Island while we lived here. She had to take the bus, and all winter long, both children went down to the highway with flashlights. It wouldn't be light for nearly two hours after they were picked up by the bus. Marsha

also took piano lessons during this time, and she was getting along rather well, when she began to object to practicing –
– the usual reason why we don't all play piano well. We had a lovely piano that Mother had given us when she came to Corpus Christi for a visit one year. I tried to play it some, but I was never even as good as when I played as a child.

In early June 1963, my old co-pilot from Washington and I decided to go to Anchorage to the Air Force Base to get them GCA practice. (Jim Maher was now the executive officer at Annette. We started from Annette, and were flying the airways to Anchorage, when we were contacted both through the Coast Guard radio channels and the FAA air traffic channels, to see if we could contact Northwest flight 293, that was in route from Seattle to Anchorage with military dependents. This flight was just like the one that had landed in Sitka Harbor earlier. We started a series of radio calls on the frequencies that we could expect Northwest planes to be using, and then the Coast Guard in Juneau asked that we reverse our course and fly back to Annette Island, so we flew back there, at low altitude, calling on the radio, and for the possibility that the plane gone down on the water. We saw nothing and heard nothing.

When we landed at Annette, the district operations officer contacted me and told me he wanted me to assume the duties of on scene coordinator of the search for the plane, which was assumed to be in trouble by this time. An Air Force C–124 landed at Annette, and told us he was available for search if we could use him. It was nearly dark when we were able to set up search areas, and assign aircraft and ships to them, but we were ready to go at first light, which comes early in Alaska.

During the night a Japanese fighter Japanese freighter radioed to the Coast Guard that they were passing through an area of much debris, including many suitcases. It was apparently the area of wreckage from the plane. We sent ships to the area to recover what they could and look for survivors but found no survivors. The largest piece of what had been a human being was a piece of thigh bone penetrating a seat cushion. The bone was about 10 to 12 inches long. It had to be assumed that the plane had another runaway propeller, lost control and the plane came straight in from over 20,000 feet.

In July 1963, broke my arm under circumstances better not related. Only two days after it was broken, and I had not taken any time off work, I was in my office when the chief of operations came into my office and said, "Si, go home!" I couldn't tell whether he was joking or not but he went on to tell me that the Chief of Safety from Washington headquarters was visiting the district, and I was to stay out of sight, since we didn't want to make a formal report of the broken arm.

I didn't fly at all that month or most of August, but made one flight late in August. Then in September, I made an inspection trip with a plane from Kodiak, and visited Kodiak, Attu, Shemya, Adak, St. Paul, and Sitkanak, visiting the loran stations in the Aleutian chain. I flew this series of flights as copilot, because the strength in my right arm (the one I had broken) was questionable, but I could do all the duties of the copilot with the left arm being the important one.

In October Bette and I went to the Academy's homecoming for the 20th reunion of my class. We flew across country – – Bette a few days ahead of me, then I was there for the weekend.

Bette borrowed a fur parka to wear at the football game, and showed what we were doing Alaska. The only problem was the temperature went up to 80 during the game, and Bette had a heat rash. She didn't put the parka on!

Winter this year was not as snowy as last year, but it was cold. The temperature frequently went down to zero, and went to a few group degrees above all too often for us. The house was warm, but the water supply was a real problem. The pipe that brought water to the kitchen, (by now I had convinced the landlords that they would be wise to have that available in the garage as well) and I could run a hose to the pump, but this was frozen solid. I got permission from the neighbor just up the hill to run another pipe from his catchment, but it froze, too. Many nights I would come home from the office and use a torch to thaw the pipe, so we could at least know there was one full pressurized tank. There were a few times that winter when it went below zero, but several when it went down to around six above.

I bought a second car, a Buick that one of my fellow workers had until he left Alaska. Was a good car, but getting old and by this time Greg was driving, and often worked until little later than when I finished. He was a stock boy from Montgomery Wards. One of the reasons I wanted a second car was that he had not learned the width and length of our car, and he had a series of very minor accidents. With the Buick he seemed to get around all right – until near Christmas.

There was a youth carol sing in town, and Bette and I were giving a cocktail party, just after the morning period for President Kennedy. Greg went into town to participate in the caroling and we had our party and then cleaned up. Greg called later in the evening to let us know that he was had gone off the road where it was elevated considerably and ended up just missing a log that was apparently washed up to shore there. The log was around five feet in diameter, and would have given him a very sudden stop. As it was, he had only wrenched his back since he ended up on the wrong side of the front seat, he realized he could have benefited from seatbelts. We installed them the next weekend, after the car was pulled out of the woods by a wrecker. He insisted on three seatbelts, so if he had a girl with him, she could sit in the middle, and still have a seatbelt on.

Greg could have been a member of the Junior National Honor Scholarship Society when he had been in Corpus Christi, but to qualify for the one in Juneau, one had to participate in sports. There were two – basketball and cross-country. Greg was not wwell enough coordinated to be a good basketball player – neither was I – and he tried out for the cross country, but an injury to an ankle back when we lived in Falls Church bothered him, and he couldn't do well.

He needed to apply for a college, become accepted, and be prepared for it without ever seeing the college, because of our location. He had very good grades, among the top in his class, and some of the Alaskans were being given autos for graduation but were officially considered needy. Greg, on the other hand, was considered as not in need, because I did get service pay. He blanketed the country which college applications, was accepted at every one he completed. He never sent in his final transcript to UCLA, and refused to complete an application to Georgetown. He was strongly tempted to go to University of

Southern California, when they accepted him with honors on entrance, but once again, he would have been at a disadvantage in his swimming. Southern California has one of the powerhouse teams, and Greg hadn't been swimming for these two years. He would have had a long way to go to catch up.

I finally suggested strongly that he apply to Texas, where he might have been with classmates he had been with before, with Connecticut as a fallback, in case we were on the East Coast. He was accepted at both schools, but Texas had only non-air-conditioned dorms for freshman, and going to Texas from Alaska in August with no air conditioning didn't sound good for a beginning freshman. He didn't like the idea of Connecticut, especially when we went all the way to Florida, but I told him that if he did well, I would try to help him transfer to the Harvard **B**usiness School with advanced grades, if he went and was eligible.

We went to an Elks picnic on the Fourth of July, and when we came back, we let our pup out for some air. He went down to the neighbors just below us, and while he was there, he saw a bird and chased it — out into the road in front of a car. That was the end of Taku. We had resigned ourselves to no more dogs, when the butcher at the store Bette used regularly told her that there were some fine pups in the "Indian village" in town. That evening she and I had little to do, and we went in to see the dog saying "We won't consider what this unless it is a really good dog." When Bette saw the pup for the first time, there was only one now, she immediately said, "Let's take it!" Thus we became the owners of Taku II or Takutoo, we never figured out how to spell it.

The Cuban missile crisis affected operations even here in Alaska. Someone had the idea that with all the Russian fishing vessels off the coast of Alaska, that country would take steps to remove them and bring them closer to the Russian coast if there really wasn't a danger of all-out war. So we were sent a message one evening, it must've been in the middle of the night in Washington, telling us to keep all the Russian fishing vessels under surveillance in the Gulf of Alaska and the Bering Sea. We were also told not to count on assistance from the Navy in this operation. I looked at the message when the duty officer called it to my attention, and said, "Let's get the chief of operations in here!" He arrived shortly after, and told us to get the chief of staff and the admiral.

It was apparent that we couldn't do the job with only our planes. We had four HU–16s in Kodiak, and helicopters on only one ship. We drafted a message (I drafted and had it approved by all my supervisors) saying we would need a fleet of C–130s to do this job. We all went home after sending the message, feeling that we could put the load back on Headquarters, and we could relax. When I came into the office the following morning, there was a message from San Francisco Air Station saying that a C-130 was in route.

My boss told me that he wanted me to go to Kodiak to coordinate the efforts of the C-130s, so I called Bette to have her pack a bag, which I would pick up on my way to the airport. We sent a message to the C–130, telling him to stop at Cordova to pick me up, and got my orders to Kodiak, via commercial air to Cordova, and Coast Guard air to Kodiak. I met the plane, shortly after the commercial plane delivered me to Cordova.

We watched the radar in route to Kodiak, and counted and plotted where the ships were. We had a good picture, and I felt we would be able to provide some meaningful information. When we arrived at Kodiak, the commanding officer there, whom I knew well, met me at the plane and told me, "The Navy admiral here wants to see us as soon as possible after you arrived. Let's go." It turned out that the Navy had not been alerted to the fact that the Coast Guard would be intensifying its patrols, and the admiral was a little unhappy about this.

A little later, we received a flight plan for a C–130 coming from Hawaii for this duty. It was followed, not much later by message saying that the plane had had engine trouble, and it was believed it would need an engine replacement. So, a third C–130 started for Kodiak from Hawaii.

I set up a plan for the next day for the C–130 that we had that could fly, and then all we could do was wait for a report or developments. The next development was the end of the missile crisis, when the Russian ship was seen removing its missiles, and a message from Coast Guard Headquarters, canceling the requirements for patrol. We did have the report from the one plane, and it showed how well that plane could patrol areas of concern.

We got a new district commander in Juneau in the summer of 1964, and housing had really become tough. Knowing at the chief of operations wanted to leave that summer anyway, the admiral arranged to have him leave in order that the admiral and his wife could move out of a motel room. They then took his house. There was a rental tenant in the basement, next to the garage, and no door on the apartment, such that when the admiral came in, he could look into their bedroom as he went up to living space upstairs.

This admiral was sharp! The icebreaker North Wind damaged her steering and sent messages regarding what was wrong, and as the drawings are being explained to the admiral who was in command earlier, he broke in, "You have the drawing upside down!" And he was right! He didn't hesitate to tell people how he believed it should be done.

Many people remember Good Friday 1964 in Alaska, but the little Coast Guard community in Juneau had a special reason to remember. My yeoman until a short time before, Dan Cherry, had now been moved next door to work for the chief of operations. He drove a Volkswagen to work, carpooling with another Coast Guard man. This morning there had been a little snow on the Glacier Highway, but not enough to bother most Alaskans who drive in snow often, and the front wheel drive Volkswagen is good in it. However, as Dan went around a turn, he skidded into the path of an oncoming car, and had a head-on collision.

They took both young men to the hospital in town, and worked on Dan for some time – hours – but it was to no avail. The other man did sleight-of-hand to entertain children while being dressed as a clown. Obviously this required manual dexterity, now his hand and arm were crushed. I never knew how he came out of it in the long run.

That evening Bette and I decided to go to dinner rather than sitting in concerning ourselves with Dan and his young wife. We went to the Baronof, it was almost the only place to go except for the seafood place across the channel in Douglas.

While we were eating, I was paged to call the district office. We had lost communication with Kodiak and its radio station, and it appeared that we might have lost communication with a number of stations to the north. It was not something to be concerned about – yet. Shortly after, I was paged again. This time, it was to be informed that the stations to the north were coming in by radio to let us know there had been an earthquake and a tidal wave was forecast.

As I went to answer the second page, the state senator from Juneau, Millie Banfield, whom we knew, said as I went by, "Some people will do anything to get attention!" But this time when I came back, I told Bette I thought I had better get to the office, and she could come home alone.

We had a buoy tender in maintenance status in Cordova that had one engine torn down, and many of the crew's families on board to see a movie that evening. Before the tidal wave hit, they were cleared the ship of the dependents– most of them-gotten one engine on line and moved out where they thought they would have plenty of water to operate in. They went aground where they should have had 15 feet or more under the keel.

The parking area outside the hangar in Kodiak dropped about 9 feet and water from the tidal wave went into the hangar, and went over the deck of a C-123 parked there. It also went into electronic shop in the hangar, soaking the electronics in salt water. The Light Station at Eldred Rock had just had the dock extended by several feet, in order to make it possible to load and unload stores at low tide. Now it was high and dry once more. The station was bothered by bears almost every day after the quake, because the bears were awakened from hibernation early, and their usual food was not available. They inspected the garbage daily.

The only military man killed in the earthquake was a man at the light station at Cape St. Elias. The man, with a companion, had gone out to climb the pinnacle that marks the cap. The earthquake knocked him off it, and the companion went back to get a stretcher and one other of the crew to bring the injured man in. They believed that he had broken his leg. The tidal wave picked him up, and he was drowned before they could recover him.

For the next several days the cutter that had been in repair status, and the aircraft from Kodiak, patrolled the area that we knew had been hit by the earthquake to see if anyone needed help and we hadn't heard about. The Alaskans are fiercely independent and there were few if any who asked for any help. In Juneau, we hardly knew there was an earthquake; was hardly felt. The effect of the tidal wave was about a 12 inch variation in the tide.

In July there was an airplane from Annette Island that came to Juneau in the morning with logistics, and then had a short search in midday. Late in the afternoon, a call came in from a fishing boat that was unsure of its position, but it was taking on water and wanted a pump. The same crew went out with a pump and tried to find the boat. They didn't find it, and fog was setting in about sunset. The plane came back to Annette, and trying to cut corners, decided to make a semi-instrument approach. You don't do that to Annette because you need to clear the mountains just off the field.

The crew in Annette Island started searching right away, but found nothing for a while. They felt sure they were looking in the right place, because there had been radio communications right up to the last minute. We had volunteers from as far south as San Francisco to come to look, but we felt the plane was on Annette, if we could just part of the trees and look down. I was relieved as chief of search and rescue tasks during the afternoon of the second day. The admiral came in and just said, "Si, go out and get some air." I went out with my family to see the Fourth of July Parade.

The fourth parade fourth parade had been postponed for a day because it rained so hard on the fourth. Now all the decorations were bedraggled, but the parade went on. It went twice, in fact, around the center part of the city. No one can say that the citizens didn't get a chance to see the floats.

I went back to the search and rescue center, and the plane was sighted that evening. Then next morning a ground crew went in, and that there was no one who made through the crash. The flight time limitations have been adopted by the Coast Guard came about because of the long man-hours that were put in by this crew on a Saturday.

As the time came close for us to leave Juneau, we had some concerns. The chief of operations decided to retire, rather than coming to Juneau. The chief of didn't pass his physical, and had to go to the hospital before he could come. We had made reservations to leave on a Canadian cruise vessel, going down to Vancouver, and wanted after all this time in Juneau to make that trip. The Admiral came to me and said, "Si, count on it. You can go on the date you have your reservations on the ship."

Bette cried as we left Juneau on August 12. She wore a camel's hair suit that was not a bit too warm, and the children explored the ship. Bette's crying was because she thought she would never make it out of Alaska alive. She was happy! It was very interesting and demanding tour of duty, but I was glad to be going back to an operating command, rather than an oversight one. We had a pleasant trip to Vancouver, took the train to Seattle, and picked up our car for the trip across country. We sent the dog out by air a few days later and picked her up in San Francisco

MIAMI

When we shipped the car back to the states, it was to be picked up by Russ Waesche's brother's firm in Seattle, and checked over preparatory to making our trip across the country. We had no concerns about the car, it hadn't been driven much while we were in Alaska and was now checked over.

Before the Alaska tour, I had built a sailboat in the hobby shop of the Naval Air Station in Corpus Christi. I had some troubles, getting a mast of the correct length, getting sails, and finding a trailer, but all those things were cleared up, and I had sailed in Corpus Christi Bay for some time before we left.

When we were in Alaska, I asked Mother for permission to put the boat in her garage, while I was located where I didn't believe I would use it. She agreed, and it almost fit into her garage. The door had to be partly open for it.

When Mother died, my sister Kathy and my brother Win felt that the best thing to do with the house, after checking real estate prices, was to rent it. A boat did not go with the rental agreement, however, and neither did keeping one stall of the garage vacant or with the door partly open. I wrote to my old friend Jim Maher, now the executive officer in San Francisco Air Station, and asked if the boat might be parked somewhere on the air station during the remainder of my tour. Jim gave me permission. Win moved it there, and now we needed to pick up the boat to take it to Miami.

When I arrived at the Miami Air Station, the crew was busy with the search of some kind, but I found an officer had known years earlier, and he directed me to where the boat was parked. Someone else had found it earlier, and it had the tires, mounted on wheels, removed – stolen. I had planned on greasing the axles, but I had not planned on buying new wheels and tires as I now had to do. I blurted out to the officer who had taken me to the location of the boat, "I hope no one steals the tires off your airplane some night when you're not looking."

While I was running around to procure the needed tires, the car started acting in a peculiar manner, and we had to put it back in a repair facility. It had apparently developed slack in the timing chain for the distributor, and it wasn't providing spark to the cylinders at the time needed. It was repaired, and we had no more trouble there.

As I said earlier, our dog was shipped to San Francisco by air. She must have been given some tranquilizer before she left Alaska, because we saw firsthand what the expression "sick as a dog" meant. She tried to eat, but nothing stayed down, and when we're driving down the highway, she tried her best to let us know that she needed to find a patch of grass, but we couldn't always find a place to stop in time. She eventually cleared up when we arrived in Florida, she was chasing balls with all of the enthusiasm she had before.

Our transfers were the nearest things to vacations for us often, and so we tried to find nice motels. We made a reservation in Reno, and then in Wendover, Nevada, all the way across the state. There were no interstate highways at that time, and all the way across the state was good progress. The latter motel did not hold our reservation, even though we were not late, and sent us down the road to another motel which was not as nice. The following night we made it a point that we were going to stay at a Holiday Inn and added the mileage up to see how far we would go. Bette did the final adding and I have never let her forget, because she made an error of 100 miles.

We should've stopped at Laramie, but went on in the dark to Cheyenne. That was quite a task, with the boat being pulled behind, the road under repair, a sick dog on the seat between Bette and me, and two teenagers in the back. The Holiday Inn where we made a reservation this night had held our reservation, but the dining room closed as soon as we were seated. It became so cool outside that evening that the air-conditioning stopped functioning, and there were no windows to open in Holiday Inns. That was not one of our best nights, either.

We arrived in Miami and began our house hunting. Fortunately, the district commander here was now the man who had many trips with me when I was flying the commandant several years earlier. We moved in with the Stephens for a few nights until we could find a more permanent camping ground. We found a motel, the Tiger Tail in Coconut Grove, not far from the Coast Guard Air station and made that our headquarters.

Greg had to leave for Storrs, Connecticut before long, and we just let him go with a farewell and hoped for the best, while we continued to look for somewhere to live. There were many homes, but not much charm to the majority. Finally we found a group of homes being built, nicely, but none was ready to move in. This latter was just as well, because we were able to have a swimming pool put in, and move some walls a few feet, as well as pick out paneling, wallpaper, and kitchen cabinets. Marsha had had to start school in the meantime, and went to junior high first from the Stephens house, then from ours at Palmetto Junior High School.

The air station was busy as could be, trying to keep track of Cubans wanting to sneak into the states, and former Cubans, wanting to make raids on Cuba, and all the boaters who use Florida's as a base of operations. I had to learn the new area quickly, and take on the tasks of an executive officer of a large station. We had patrols designated as several colors, the Red patrol, the Yellow patrol, the Green patrol, etc. The frequency of each varied, but none were made with less frequency than once a week. We had a fleet of six Grumman amphibians, and four helicopters. The latter were used almost completely for search and rescue of recreational boaters, while the Grummans were off on patrols every day.

A few month earlier, the press of patrols to determine what was going on with the Cubans, nearer to the time of the missile crisis, had made it necessary to assign even more planes to the air station, on a temporary basis. At that time the planes had to be operated out of the Air National Guard facility at the Miami international Airport. Now, with only the six, we operated off the water, and when the planes were at the station, they were parked about three feet between wingtips.

I was made commanding officer of the station before long, when my friend, Ice Sansbury, was transferred to the Coast Guard Repair and Supply Base. I was still commander, but was promoted to captain in July 1965. One day, another officer who was promoted to captain at the same time was visiting the base, when the chief of staff from the district office was on board. He looked at the two of us and crowed, "I've caught two at one time with their eagles backward!" The collar devices are supposed to look forward but we hadn't paid any attention to that and just pinned them on – backward.

From the time I had reported, people were talking about moving the air station to Opa Locka, where we would operate off land instead of water, and would not be limited in space. There was work going on at Opa Locka Airport, which had been Navy in World War II, and Marine in the Korean War, and now was occupied by an assortment of unconnected facilities. The blimp hangers were still there from World War II, but probably could not be used. We were taking over the hangar, building a barracks, and a BOQ, and modernizing several other buildings. The date when we could move kept being moved back and back, and it didn't appear that we were ever going to make the move.

One week, when I attended the admiral's weekly staff conference, it was remarked that the Air Force would be engaged in an exercise, and would like the cooperation of the Coast Guard, if we were at Opa Locka at that time. The admiral, now Rear Admiral Thayer said in response, "They certainly should be by that time!" I went back to the air station, and told my exec at this time, Al Yates, "We're going to be at Opa Locka by the first of November." We looked over the planning dates, and set moving dates of October 25, 26, and 27 with all operations to be at Opa Locka on the 28th. We told the contractor, and all the planning was for those dates. I flew the last HU–16 out of Coconut Grove on the 27th.

Even that last flight didn't go quite as planned. Earlier in the day, a boat needed assistance from one of the helicopters. The helicopter flew over it, lowered a pump, and then had a chip warning light that indicates that there are chips of metal in the oil. This can lead to failure of the engine, and since the helicopter had both floats, inflatable bags, it set down on the water. When I took off from the water, I called in to say that I would take a look at the helicopter, which needed to be towed to a boat ramp, and across town to be repaired but before I arrived there, I had a chip warning light on the HU–16, and went directly to Opa Locka. It was a long day before the helicopter arrived there.

About a week after we were in Opa Locka, and before the telephones were installed all of the base, or the intercom system, or the public address system, one of the biggest search and rescue operations came upon us. The SS Yarmouth Castle burn between Miami and Nassau. It was one of the cruises that went out one afternoon, gave the passengers the next day in Nassau, and then came back the following night. One of those nights, the ship caught fire! (Admiral Thayer analyzed the incident thoroughly and became famous for his speech on what happened. It led to his becoming one of the first members of the National Transportation Safety Board.) The duty officer that night, received a call from the duty officer in the district office, and he ran in his underwear out to the gate watch, told him to close the gate, ran over to the barracks and get everyone up to go to the hangar. In the meantime, the duty officer went back to the BOQ, got the duty pilots up and headed for the operations office.

The evacuation of the Yarmouth Castle by helicopter and

ship led to the decoration of several of the pilots involved. They hovered so close to the rigging of the ship, that a little movement one way or another would have meant the death of all the evacuees. They did it for some hours.

I wasn't qualified to fly the holiday helicopters, but I felt I needed to know something about them, to be the commanding officer in that station. I asked for the manual on the engines, the T–58 turbine, in the pilot's manual for the helicopter itself, and started studying. I couldn't do the entire job by myself, but the engine part was not that difficult, since I had studied turbines for ship direct before.

Next, I was asked the operations officer to take me up and let me see how each step of the flight syllabus was done. He put me in the pilot seat and not only let me see how it was done, but had me do it. Before too long, I was comfortable about flying the H–52 helicopter, and made auto rotations in the water simulating loss of power – (this plane had only one turbine), an experienced ground resonance with a helicopter. This last was not intentional, I got into it, and my instructor that day told me to pull up and get out of it! Once I got through the syllabus, I didn't insist on flying missions since I had no designation, but I could speak with knowledge about the maneuvers.

At Christmas 1965, an invitation was extended by the Cuban community in Miami to the Coast Guard in the area to attend their Christmas program. Bette and I went, as did a few of the officers from the district office. Few could understand Spanish, and Cuban Spanish is harder to understand that in some other countries, since they usually speak so rapidly. The scenes they portrayed in their pageant were stirring and the costumes were beautiful. They expressed their appreciation to the Coast Guard at one place in the program, and asked those present to stand, but I'm afraid not all of us understood what was being said.

We went through two near hurricanes while we lived in Miami. In both cases, we partially drained the swimming pool, get all the movable things off the patio, and inside the garage and taped windows, and then waited for developments. In one case, we were still at Dinner Key but the one that came closer was when we were in Opa Locka. Bette and Marsha were at home, hoping that all would be all right, and I was at the air station, hoping that we didn't lose a plane. The funny thing about that one when we were in Opa Locka was that Marsha had a friend whose family had an avocado tree in the yard, and the best advice for those people was to remove as many of the fruit as possible. They could be bullets moving at 100 mph if they were blown off the tree. We ate free avocados for many a day after it was over.

Neither storm came close enough to cause us trouble. Heavy rains in October created more problems, because the area was supposed to be drained by dry wells at the intersections of the streets, and those were not nearly enough. The streets were so full of water, that when Taku wanted to cross the street to follow Marsha, she had to swim.

One of my patrol flights is particularly memorable, as we came on a small sailboat, headed north, but not for any of the Bahama Islands, just generally north. I knew that there were Coast Guard and British vessels on patrol in the area, but not in sight. I prepared a message block, a balsa wood block with a hole drilled in one end, and a yellow streamer attached to call attention to it. I wrote a note, saying (I hoped) "Fly in the direction the plane flies." We dropped the note, and saw them pick it up. Then we rocked the wings, and flew off in the direction of the nearest of the Bahamas. We sent a message to the patrol vessel to let them know the boat was there.

Another interesting patrol was one made with the District Commander Rear Admiral Thayer, the Assistant Secretary of State for Latin American Affairs, and a man from AID. We mapped out a flight that would show all the points that were referred too often. We didn't get to the first point! This was just after Castro had announced that any Cubans who were not satisfied with his regime could leave, and they were leaving in droves! We came on a boat, not looking very seaworthy, not too far from the Coast Guard cutter that was on patrol with a helicopter. We escorted the helicopter to the boat, and tried to go on with the patrol. We diverted again when we heard of another boat needing a pump, and dropped it. The only thing we did as scheduled was to end the flight in to Key West. Admiral Thayer was delighted with the way it turned out!

In December 1965, a decision was made to supply the loran stations at Grand Turk, San Salvador, and South Cacos from Miami instead of shipping all their supplies to San Juan and bringing back them back halfway. We needed a different kind of plane to do that job, and the C–123 that had been in San Juan was transferred to us. In December, a group of us went to ground school at Eglin Air Force Base and then in January we started flying the new plane. Of course, it wasn't a new plane, it had been in the Coast Guard for quite a few years, and had flown thousands of miles in Vietnam as a combat delivery plane. I had made several delivery trips to San Salvador, Grand

Turk, and South Cacos. The latter station had a good supply of warm water lobsters, readily available, from what I heard, but I never brought any home. We had to chase the cattle off the runway there every time we landed, or it could have been dangerous.

As the commanding officer of the air station, I was an honorary member of Biscayne Bay Yacht Club, since we had been neighbors on the bay when the air station was at Dinner Key in Coconut Grove. We were invited to a party there one evening in the spring of 1966 it was a lovely evening. Bette and I have been talking about what I would like to do next in the Coast Guard a few days earlier, and I told her that I would like to go to the National War College. She had been to a wives' club party since then, but I had not put in an application for the War College yet, as we agreed I should.

Shortly after all of us arrived, including the USCG Chief of Staff and his wife, and the chief of operations from the district, who was a graduate of the National War College, the wife of the chief of staff said to me," I hear you are going to the National War College." My first thought was that Bette had been talking to the wives, a had I would like to, and that was misinterpreted. I thought, wives do talk, and told her I knew nothing of it. A few minutes later, her husband confirmed that I would be going, and he just hadn't gotten around to sending me the orders.

We've been are in our house for only a little less than two years and enjoyed it very much. We considered keeping it, but housing in Washington is almost always very hard to find, we knew we would need a down payment on something, and so put the house in the market. It sat for two or three months, and we never had a prospective buyer look at it. Finally at almost the last minute, a couple came and feel in love, made an offer of almost exactly what we had paid for it, and we took it. He was the head of the CIA watching the Cubans, and the day I took the key to him as we left it for the last time, he said he had orders to Laos, and would be leaving very soon. The house then was bought by the agent who had sold it to the CIA people, and they lived there until he died.

NATIONAL WAR COLLEGE

The name is not really correct, because we never studied tactics at all in the year I spent at Fort McNair at the National War College. It was more of a foreign relations school. We wondered many times as we did our studying and debating, why we went to a school with that name. We would have chosen the National Peace College, I believe, but when it was started in 1946, I think the idea came from General Eisenhower. and it was designed to bring all the services together to look at what threatened the nation and how. Since that time, there have been additions, such as a Coast Guard in the second year, the Departments of the Treasury, Interior, Commerce, and several from the CIA, almost all of whom are listed as State Department.

Bette and I had taken some leave ahead of time, and gone to Washington to look at the housing situation. We couldn't get the Coast Guard to say that I would stay in Washington after the year at the War College, but they said it was likely. We looked around, knowing that I would be busy studying until late at night often, and decided to rent a townhouse in the vicinity of where we had lived before, in Virginia. We signed a one-year lease, with an option for two more years, so we were set for three years if we wanted to stay there. There were two other students at the War College who were living nearby, and it made a convenient carpool for that year, and then I would take a bus to Coast Guard Headquarters, if I stayed.

Marsha was in high school by this time and went to Falls Church High School. Greg decided he wanted to be married when he was in his sophomore year of college, and we saw less of him, but we enjoyed his in-laws. Marsha told us there was a societal division in the school of homeowners, town home owners, and apartment dwellers. When she spoke of the swimming pool we had had in Miami, it opened the eyes of some, but not many of her classmates.

My class at the War College consisted of some outstanding individuals. There were two would become Chief of Staff of the Army, one who would be Chief of Naval Operations, and one who would be a lieutenant general in the Air Force as the superintendent of the Academy. There were many who became generals and admirals, as time went by and one Air Force officer was a brigadier general even before we finished the course. It was very nice to be able to contact classmates as time went by to do business with a friend.

Once again, I had to rethink my aviation career and operations. There was no time for just going out to go flying. If I flew, it had to be on weekends or at night. Fortunately, I didn't have to fly a lot, just enough to get paid for flight. I flew to Elizabeth City one time, with Hap Easter as copilot (he was at the Pentagon as a helicopter expert) and made arrangements for my boat to be brought to Washington. Another time I flew to Hartford, where Greg picked us up and we went to University of Connecticut football team. Often, it was just a night flight, with nowhere in particular to go. In December, I received a letter from the Coast Guard, telling me I would receive flight pay without the four hours flight time that had previously been necessary. I also was told that I was no longer required, nor permitted to fly for proficiency. Thus, my flying for the Coast Guard was ended.

I should give more details about that flight having to do with the boat. Shortly before I left Miami, there had been a hurricane scare, and I moved my boat from home to the air station, where I could put it into a warehouse. While the boat was there, the C-130 came in from Elizabeth City with a boat in it that belonged to my relief. He had seen an opportunity when a C-130 went from San Francisco to Elizabeth City to move his boat at least to the East Coast, and now it was in Miami. I seized the opportunity, and put my boat aboard to get it closer to Washington, at least, on the return flight. I didn't ask anyone, I just loaded it on.

Now when I flew to Elizabeth City, my friend and classmate in flight training, Bill Brinkmeyer, was a commanding officer. I said, "When you have a flight going to the Washington area, there is space, you can send my boat up. I know now where to park it," (Fort Belvoir.) The following weekend, the duty officer at Coast Guard Headquarters called and told me "There is a C–130 coming to Dulles, and they asked that you be notified." I hardly had time to get to the airport when here is the big plane, and it pulled up in the non-scheduled plane parking area. I drove out on the ramp, backed my car up, and hitched the boat to the car. I spent very little time thanking the crew, I just wanted to get away from the field!

The courses of the National War College started with the elements of national power. Then we looked at how our government was organized to do all the things we need, and then we examined the parts of the world where we had an interest. One of the talks I remember well is when the secretary of education for the state of California spoke to us and his point was very strong, the only way you can succeed in education is to emphasize reading, writing, and arithmetic. It was very persuasive and as we left the auditorium, questioning our own attitudes towards education. A short time in individual discussion groups brought us back to reality, where the subjects are important, but not the only concerns.

We had the director of the Budget Bureau, now the Office of Management and Budget, and he told us he was one of the few people who, when he said, " .9" it meant $900,000. Former President Eisenhower came at one time, and regarding the Korean War, he told us how close he came to authorizing an atomic bomb on China. All the Service Chiefs came and told us what they saw as the challenges for their respective services.

When we studied the problem-solving possibility of the UN, we finished with a trip to New York, with wives, to meet some people involved with the UN, and see the facilities. We were briefed by various people who regularly advised our delegation, and one was the head of the military representation at the US mission Admiral John McCain, the father of the now senator from Arizona. (At one time, the son was a prisoner in Vietnam.) After he finished his presentation, in the question period, I asked, "What does the Coast Guard representative do here and how does he fit in to your mission?"

I had forgotten to give my service (we were all in civilian clothes) for this visit and he replied, "I wish I knew!" Later I found out that my classmate from the Academy, Bob Norris, was working directly for the UN ambassador, and didn't work through the military mission.

We studied the major areas of the world where the United States has interests, and then in the spring, we made three-week trips to those areas. The student body was divided into five parts, and one went to each of the areas we studied: one to Europe, one to the Middle East, one to Asia, one to Africa, and one to South America. I had been busy writing a research paper on South America and I chose to go there. I got my choice and had a very interesting trip.

The group that went to the Middle East was in Greece when a revolution started, and there were tanks rumbling up the street just outside the hotel. They were told to stay in the hotel, and had little to do. One army officer, Al Escola, was pictured on the front of Life magazine, sunbathing next to the pool, as the war went on just outside.

Our group went first to Panama, where the Minister of Foreign Affairs told us they would like to have the (Panama) Canal, but they realized that there was little hope for that, because the US had built it and wanted to keep control. We went to Lima, Peru, and saw some of the ancient ruins, near the shore of the Pacific. I had an opportunity to use my fractured Spanish with a Peruvian Air Force officer, when Tom Hayward, my roommate on this trip, wanted to ask him a question and couldn't phrase it.

The question was "Knowing that Che Guevera is in Bolivia (and Peru and Bolivia had not been on very good terms for decades), if a communist group started an uprising in Bolivia, and they asked for your (Peruvian) help, would you give it to them?"

The answer was a good example of how they think of each

other. He replied, "Of course. But they will never ask."

We flew in the C–141 assigned to us from there to Buenos Aires where we had another interesting exposure to the Latin minds. We were briefed by personnel from the Foreign Affairs Office of Argentina, and the briefer said, "We have no problems of interracial conflicts here, because this country is like a piece of Europe that was moved to this hemisphere. We sometimes wish we had more Negroes here, because we could use them for torment and elevator operators." We had a State Department man of African-American origin, who was later the Ambassador to Botswana and Lesotho, then Assistant Secretary of State for African Affairs and then Ambassador to East Germany. I fully expected him to jump all over this briefer, but he was the real diplomat, and didn't comment at all.

Our next stop was in Brazil, Rio de Janeiro. We knew that they were planning to move the capital to the new location, in Brazilia, but they had not done it yet. We were able to see some of the construction of government buildings from the plane as we flew over, but they were a long way from being ready to govern from there at the time. We saw enough only to whet our appetites to see more of this country. We again had interesting briefings, in a room that was completely protected from bugging, by metal framework inside the normal room.

We went on to Santiago, Chile, where we were briefed as soon as we arrived, because we had to get in a bus over the mountains to Vina Del Mar to stay. Chile, which had the smallest population per square mile of any country in South America, was hosting a conference on population control, under the auspices of the UN, in the city of Santiago, and hotel accommodations were tight in the city. We stayed at a hotel on the beach, but the beach was not warm enough to enjoy, since this was late in the fall for this location.

We went to the Army Navy country club for lunch the following day on Saturday, and had a lovely visit to the club, and a delightful meal. The club was just a club in the country, no golf course or tennis courts. My lunch partner was ahead of the department of Littoral for Peru – their Coast Guard equivalent, even though part of the Navy.

On Sunday, a group of us went to the horse races. We were told that we would be admitted free, if we had identified ourselves as members of the National War College group. Of course, we had to do this in Spanish. I managed to do it, but I never was sure what I was telling the challengers. During the afternoon, a man, apparently a worker around the stables, came to me, and told me that he would let me know which horse was going to win next, if I would share the winnings with him. I accepted, and made a small wager on his choice. He was angry that I had bet only a small amount, but I had to determine if he was good in his choices. From then on, I bet on his horses, and won all afternoon. After splitting with him, I didn't have any great winnings to carry away.

We made a brief visit to Venezuela, which was one of most expensive countries in South America at that time, and went on to Guatemala for the weekend. We were briefed as usual, but since it was the weekend, and there was little doing on Sunday, but we became a tourist group for the day. Everyone in Guatemala City for a weekend goes to Chichicastenango where there was an old church, where the natives have offerings to their gods or saints, just like burnt offerings to their special gods years ago. There is also a market a small distance away, and then the tour usually goes to Lake Atitian, where you can have lunch overlooking the lake. This was our schedule also.

To get to Chichicastenango, the road goes down a valley with a steep road, and many sharp cutbacks. The driver brought along a friend, who was equipped with wheel chokes to prevent rollback at the turn was too difficult. He had no trouble with that, just went slowly, down the hill and back up the other side.

We saw the old church with its burnt offerings, went through the market, but didn't buy much of anything, and boarded the bus again to reverse our path. After we regained the main road, we started down the grade to Lake Atitlan. As we made one sharp turn, I happened to be watching the driver, as he realized that the brakes were not working. He tried to have his helper jump out through the wheel chocks under the wheels to stop the bus, but the helper refused – we were going too fast.

The driver made that turn with little trouble, but then the bus started gaining speed, he knew that the next turn was sharper in the alternative was not the cornfield that he could've gone into as he first realized that he had a problem, now the alternative straight ahead was a drop of at least 1000 feet. He knew he had to stop the bus, now!

He drove across the oncoming lane of the highway, and drove intentionally into the bank cut out for the road. The bus careened over at least what seemed like a 45° bank – it must've been near 30°, and then it slipped back on the road. We gained some more speed, and once more he tried to steer into the bank. This time, almost all the passengers were wide awake. They had not been the first time, but had been snoozing or reading in many cases. Now as the bus hit the bank, Doc Blanchard, better known for his football at West Point than his officer career, push the driver's helper out of the way, and he leaped out the front door.

Others were trying to open the back emergency door. I stood up my seat, several rows back, and tried to compensate for the bank. As the front wheels of the bus hit the bank, the entire wheel came off, and when the rear wheel came off, the bus came to a very sudden stop. One of the passengers who was trying to open the back door, Dave Bolen, was thrown backward – toward the front of the bus– over a seat back. He wrenched his back badly, but got out on his own power. Doc skinned his knee, but nothing more. We all got out and walked toward the lake, downhill but about two miles away. Cars coming by picked some up, then came back and picked up more, and we were soon were all together for lunch.

The group jabbered away at high speed when we first sat down for lunch – and a drink. Then as the initial shock wore off, we all realized how close we were to disaster, and we all agreed that we would not communicate this incident to wives until we were home, to avoid speculation that someone was really injured worse than we were telling. A different bus came out to pick us up that evening and we returned to the hotel.

Our next stop was Mexico City, where one of the class had been just before assignment to the War College. They greeted him as a long-lost friend, and we reflected in his light. Shopping in Mexico has always been good, and I found a screen which is still in our living room.

When we returned to Washington, we were given an opportunity, by teams to let the others know what we had learned about our regions of the world. It is all enjoyable, but yet it took some serious work to portray what we had seen, been told, and experienced. Fortunately, the War College had a very good visual arts department, which could whip out cartoons, maps, and slides for projection in a short period. All the groups gave interesting presentations.

On June 9, 1967, I received my certificate of completion of the course of the National War College. General Lyman Lemnitzer, was the graduation speaker and his son Bill Lemnitzer was in our class. It was the end of a valuable and interesting year, and I was given orders to move across town to Coast Guard headquarters, and I would be the Chief of the Administrative Management Division. I had hoped to be given a little more time to complete a master's degree from George Washington University; as all of the students from the other military services were, but the Coast Guard said they needed me without completing the degree. I attended night school for the next year to complete my degree.

Return to Headquarters

In June 1967, as expected all along, but not confirmed by the powers at Headquarters, I was ordered back into the building I had left in 1959. This time I was supposed to be the Chief of the Administrative Management Division. If I wanted to finish my master's degree program at George Washington University, I could do that on my own time, and Headquarters would pay for my fees.

Administrative management was a fairly small division, but it had some important responsibilities. We looked at every directive before it was sent to printing, for form, consistency with other directives, and while we didn't do the printing, we had close liaison with the printers. I was included in many conferences to make sure that the organization proposed in any new plan was consistent, and if not, if it made sense.

This timing of assignment to Headquarters, and to the Management Division, was important because on April 1st of this year, the Department of Transportation had been formed, with the Coast Guard as the second largest portion of the department. Coast Guard people had been involved in the initial planning for the department, and were being used in several sections of the Secretary's staff. There were still several positions of the department which did not seem complete, and we poured over government organization books to try to determine if there was some other part that should be in the department, or even in the Coast Guard. There were Coast Guard people assigned on permanent assignment to Highways, Highway Traffic Safety Administration, FAA, and to studies involving all sorts of transportation.

We did one informal study of where the Coast Guard and Geodetic Survey would fit, if we brought it into the Coast Guard. There was a lot of talk about whether there should be a Department of the Oceans. The bill to actually form this latter, did not get put into the hopper for consideration until several years later, but this was a time to think reorganization. President Nixon, at the first of his presidency, considered a reorganization that would have formed the Department of Economic Development, or some such title, and the Coast Guard was dumped into this, after merging with the Department of Defense was vetoed.

My division was closely involved with the plan to standardize the signs, and identification of Coast Guard units. The most important portion of this over the years has been the diagonal slash on the bows of the ships. The concepts were developed by the Loewy organization that had first developed the Studebaker auto that looked as if it might be going backwards. They proposed a Coast Guard sign that looked as if it marked the interstate highways. They also proposed signs that only said "San Diego Air Station", instead of saying "Coast Guard Air Station San Diego. They slipped that one through, and I tried to change it years later, without spending a lot of money, and I am not sure if it's ever been gotten corrected. The slash was so successful that it was used for Coast Guards in Germany, Denmark, and Sweden, at least. Some countries don't want to use it because they don't really have any navy, and they want to intermingle the functions of their navy (if any), and the Coast Guard.

All the "super grades" in the civilian organizations of the various portions of the new DOT, brought us to looking at where the Coast Guard could justify higher ranks or civilian super grades. A working group looked at all of the commands of the Coast Guard and we tried labeling them as Rear Admiral positions or Commodore positions. This was before the Navy went back to the single strip for the Commodores, and now Rear Admiral, Lower Half. We downgraded some of the positions that we had been considering just as Rear Admiral billets, but we added several new Commodore positions. Nothing came of this study, except as you will see later, it was thought that the Navy would go to more commodores, and this study would help us to be ready to that way.

Another study we did had to do with the functions of the Chief of Staff of the Coast Guard. Everything that the commandant was going to act on went through the Chief of Staff's office, he also acted as a commanding officer of the Headquarter staff, and there were still other activities that he was involved with. The office was a bottleneck in the flow of much of the important business of the Coast Guard. We took a look at how the work of the Chief of Staff could be alleviated. The ultimate result of the study, which had been going on before I arrived, but was completed while I was there, was that the Deputy Chief of Staff was to split into two Assistant Chief of Staffs, and much of the material which been going to the Chief of Staff himself, would be completed by one of the assistants.

One of the Assistants, was given all the responsibility

for the development of the planning, programming, and budgeting of the Coast Guard. The other Assistant would have Headquarters building personnel staff administration, the management responsibilities, now relabeled, as Management Analysis including some oversight of position control, and the computer responsibilities of the Coast Guard. (The position control is an important function in Washington, because there are strong beliefs that only by reducing the number of positions in government can the cost of government be reduced. The ultimate is to do away with all the people in Washington, and the government cost nothing!)

We completed our study, believed that it would save the Chief of Staff considerable time, and presented it to him. He approved, and wanted it presented to the Commandant. I made the presentation, which didn't have to be in any great detail, since Admiral Smith, had once held my division chief office, and had a good knowledge of the situation. He approved the new organization, and said, "If we get some commodore billets, each of the Assistant Chief of Staff should be commodores." I drew in stars beside the organizational chart.

The next step was to implement the new organization was to fill the blanks with names. The deputy chief at the time was a relatively senior captain, and he had been doing the supervision of planning programming and budgeting anyway, so he was an obvious choice. There was not such an easy choice for the other. Personnel sent in a list of suggested candidates to the Chief of Staff, and he sent it back. Of course these were relatively senior captains (they were filling possible commodore billets). The chief of staff said, "I want Siler to be in that position." I was assigned as the Assistant Chief of Staff for Management!

Once I took this new position, moved into a newly outfitted office, and tried to do the things it appeared to require, I found how hard it is to work with someone who believes he is several layers up in the organization. I dealt more often with the deputy office chiefs than the office chief. But if I had something that required action of the chief, I wanted to see him! I didn't always get in to see some of the people involved without delays. I don't think most of the delays were unacceptable. I had developed a plan for shore maintenance of the ocean station vessels that we were operating then, in order to make sure that the seagoing crews had some liberty when they came in.

This required some small reductions of the sailing crew to make a specialized group available to greet the ship when it returned to its home port, and to do maintenance. These groups were on shore duty, but with expert knowledge of the operating ship. The seagoing crew was able to take liberty, and still have the ship in the condition that it should be. I wanted the Chief of Operations to sign a directive that said that the crew should have a certain amount of liberty if these maintenance groups were available to work on the ships. He didn't want to talk to me – it wasn't like that when he went to sea! That one took a little longer, and some assistance from his deputy. We did put out the instruction finally, and set some maintenance teams in several ports,. The concept is rather broadly used today.

Soon after the Department was formed, the Assistant Secretary for Administration, Alan Dean, made a real point of the fact that the Department should be together. The FAA was not going to move – they had their own building – but the rest should be together, preferably in one building. He found a building being built in Southwest Washington, with no renter yet, and made arrangements to get this.

It was decided, first of all how much space each administration needed, and after filling the top of the building with the Secretary and his staff, the rest were filled in. The Coast Guard was given the sixth, seventh and eighth floors. The top was to be the commandant, but we had to designate space for each office, division, and section in our organization. I had a capable man as Chief of the Headquarters Administrative Division, a Captain Jack Forrester, who was senior to me, but worked very well with me.

The special assistant for the Commandant, Captain Jay Kobler, and I often had lunch together. Now, we contemplated the location of the new office of the commandant. We remembered all the times when air conditioning failed in the building we were in on Pennsylvania Avenue, and felt we would be safer on the cooler side of the building for the big boss, and besides, you could see the Washington Monument, and the Capital if you wanted to get out of your seat and crane your neck. We forgot that the train ran right by at the base of the building comment and might disrupt meetings and conferences, but we felt we would be somewhat soundproofed anyway. The view of the Potomac River and National Airport was much better on the other side of the building, but we passed that up for the Capital. (In my later years in the building, I didn't remember a single time we didn't have air conditioning!)

The rest of the building was cut up for the divisions involved, partitions were located, phones installed, and the move was made in a relatively short time period, after the building was finally completed. The only real loophole, were the spaces for classified documents, and the security of the operation center dragged on for several months without adequate construction, in the watch standards had to stay in the old building, as the only occupants other than rats!

I had a lovely office with attractive paneling and new furniture in this new building, and my divisions also had good space, and equipment. The computer division had a relatively new computer, that had taken a long time to contract for and convert to. Now the Department said they could do all the Department's computer work, and we would not need it after all. We didn't agree that they could to it all, and some computer work was still done in the Coast Guard, on our own computer.

Before we moved to the new building, the Chief of Staff had been relieved of Mark Whalen, the earlier Chief, who went to San Francisco. Rear Admiral Tom Sargent came in as Chief of Staff, and the work level changed, because of styles in the office. I found that I wasn't nearly as busy as I had been, with some exceptions.

I went to the other Assistant Chief of Staff and asked him how busy he was. He, too, felt that he was not as busy as he could be, and we agreed that we would go to the present Chief of Staff, and suggest that we revert to the former organization. Tom Sargent had no object to our changing the organization again and while it made no sense to do this until Bill Riddell retired, on the 1st of July of 1969, the organization changed back to only a Deputy Chief of Staff, and no assistants. I therefore became the Deputy Chief of Staff of the Coast Guard at that time.

Equal opportunity and affirmative action, and how you were

to implement these programs, were always hot questions in Washington, simply because there were such high percentages of black and minority populations in the city. Many were very well-educated, and wanted to better themselves. The Coast Guard had a directive out saying that we would have these programs, and we had staff who worked on the problems that arose.

There were two vacancies for well-qualified supervisory computer personnel in our computer division, and there were two black men who met the requirements. There were others who met the requirements – Caucasians, whom the division chief preferred, because he felt he could work better with them. When Luke Pharris, the division chief, made me aware of the choice problem, I referred him to the directives, and told him to give it some consideration. He spent some time with his people, and came back to let me know that the entire division was having divisive reactions to the questions and the discussions.

I had Lou get his entire divisions together in a conference room and talk to them about affirmative action particularly. I pointed out that there had been a period of about 200 years plus, when the blacks had been discriminated against, and told them, "This is an attempt to rectify some of the past discrimination. We can help to improve the situation somewhat by leaning over backwards a little when we consider selections now. The important thing is that we cannot, and must not, lean so for that we fall over backwards!" The eventual solution was that the black men were given the promotions, but I believe that at least one of them left the Coast Guard's employ shortly afterwards.

DOT required that each administration have a Civil Rights Office, a Civil Rights Counselor, who could meet with people outside of the formal complaint process and an officer who could confer with the counselor to determine whether the Office needed to be alerted to a specific problem. We built a team in the Office, by bringing one of the DOT personnel in to head the office. He had his staff, and one of the black women who worked with me earlier, when I had the Administrative Management Division, was a natural for the counselor position. She had educated herself within the government system, going so for as a master's degree, often on her own time. She was a warm person, who could often help individuals, just by talking. She did need a civil rights officer for Headquarters, however, because every problem doesn't solve itself without some pressure.

She came to me to see who could be appointed as the civil rights officer for the building, and the Headquarters organization. I looked at rosters, and conferred with my boss, now Rear Admiral Bob (Skeeter) Goring, and we couldn't put our finger on the one we felt would do good a job, and who was available without the restrictions of being "be not in personnel, and not in the normal civil rights jobs." When I met with our counselor the next time, I told her we were still working on it, but a solution yet. She responded, "Why don't you take it? You are doing the work of it anyway." As I thought about it, I realized that I was in effect the civil rights officer at that time, and so after taking talking to Goehring one more time, I became the official civil rights officer.

It was now 1970, and when flag officer selections were scheduled, some people thought I was in the running. One such board had been scheduled earlier that year, I knew that Skeeter Goring was on the board. Since he and I work closely together, some people thought it was a good chance for me to be selected, probably ahead of several of my class.

We went to a cocktail party one Saturday evening, just after the board had completed its work, a Coast Guard wife was talking to me about the selection system. She said, "Surely, you must've made it this time!" I had a little difficulty answering her, because I saw that Skeeter was in earshot, and I had not been told that I had been selected. She went on about the system did not recognize good officers, much to the embarrassment of my boss.

The law governing retirements from the service at that time said that a captain must retire when he had 30 years of service, and a flag officer must retire when he had 35 years or seven years as a flag officer. This, in effect, said that and a captain who was selected with less than 20 years of service, because of outstanding performance, but had to retire earlier than classmates were not selected until they had the their 28 years.

There was one officer up to this time, Bill Ray, who had been selected for rear admiral before he had 28 years, and that is the result of the head of the board which was considering him and others, feeling that it was time to move ahead with the early selection of outstanding officers. The law was changed shortly after I made rear admiral to say nothing about a number of years as a flag officer. This allowed selection of outstanding officers to flag when the board believed they were the best qualified. In any case, I was not selected until I had my 20 years, and I look forward to a normal seven years as a flag officer.

In the early spring of 1971, another board was convened to look at captains. Since my office was near the Commandant's, I knew rather well what the progress of the board was. I also knew that the year before, when Al Heckman was selected, the Commandant, Willard Smith, had told him within minutes of the time that he had signed approval of the board to send it on to the Secretary and the White House for transmittal to the Senate for confirmation, that Al had been selected. This time, since my position in the chain of command was so close, I thought I might have known early as well.

One evening, when I felt certain that the board had finished its deliberations, and as Betty and I sat at home in front of a fire, we discussed the future. I told her there was a good chance that I had not been selected, and we considered whether our options might be. The phone rang, I got up to answer it. When I got to the phone, it was dead. "If a man answers, hang up." I said facetiously, and we resumed our conversation. Some time later, the doorbell rang, and we went up from our basement rec room to see what it could be. It was Tom Sargentg, now Assistant Commandant, his wife Lucy, and Ed Perry who is now my boss as Chief of Staff, and Dotty his wife. They came with a bottle of champagne to test the fact that I was now to be a rear admiral! It was to be kept secret until the president sent the nomination to the Senate for confirmation, but the real waiting was over. The earlier phone call had been them, making sure we were at home, before they drove over from where they both lived in Maryland.

The selection process is still a big question mark in the careers of most officers. Some of my classmates, I thought would make flag, and didn't. Joe Steele, who made it at the same time as I, was brilliant, and it wasn't hard to anticipate. We were the only ones of our class to make it at that time, and then Mike Benkert made it a few months later, when another vacancy became available. Mike had built a reputation for pollution control expertise, and Merchant Marine knowledge and contacts, which helped him. Still, it seemed odd that some people did not make flag!

Shortly after announcing that I would be making rear admiral on 1 July, I was given something to indicate my choices for assignment. What can one say when he has just made the ultimate? I said I was available for any assignment that Admiral Bender wanted to send me to. I hoped it would not be Alaska, but other than that, I couldn't complain much about any assignment. When I looked at the assignments of most of the others who were new, they were usually kept at Headquarters for the first assignment, and I really expected that to be true, even though I had been in Washington now for five years. It wasn't long before Chet Bender sent for me and told me that I would go to St. Louis, where I would learn a new responsibility for me, the rivers of the United States.

New Admiral in St. Louis

Bette and I went to St. Louis once before 1 July, with Vice Admiral Tom Sargent, who was to make a speech. We stayed with the district commander I was to relieve, Rear Admiral Russ Waesche. If the name sounds somehow familiar, Russ was the administrative aide when I served as Admiral Richmond's personal aide. This was to be Russ' final assignment before he retired, and it was my first as an admiral.

We arrived to relieve, after driving from Washington, to start our house hunting, late in June. It was hot, as most of the Midwest is at that time. Joe Steele, who was leaving his post as a new admiral, gave us some advice about house hunting, but he left almost as we drove into town. We had sold our house in Virginia, because we knew that we would have to buy again in Missouri, and we needed that money for a down payment.

We covered a lot of city and all of the surrounding cities, before we had found a home we believed would serve our needs. It was in the little city of Warson Woods, not far from the routes that led to the airport, and also not for from the routes to downtown. It was much closer to the city of St. Louis in the district office where the operating base for the buoy tender stationed there, then where Russell had lived. It was a homey little city, just adjacent to an area where really wealthy homes spread over the hills, not far from the Warson Country club, where the Ryder Cup matches were played a couple of years later.

We developed the habit of calling the police when we were going out of town, and they would watch our home while we were away. Once, we returned, and had not had a chance to call the police headquarters, when a policeman came to the door to check on the house, because he saw that the lights were not on the regular time lights. The police would always salute when I drove by on the way to work in the morning, if we happened to meet.

When I reported in, I was given several briefings and what went on in this district. We had no ocean problems, like those I had experienced before, and the terminology was different. We used miles and miles per hour, not nautical miles and knots. The vessels were mainly tow boots, not tugs, with "knees" protruding from the forward edge, where they secured the barges, and pushed them over the river. When a towboat makes a turn in the river, especially downstream, it "flanks" around the turn, using the rudders that are mounted ahead – forward – of the propellers. The propellers are usually mounted in hoods to force the water through at high pressure. They are then "Kort nozzles."

The buoys used in the river are replaced with a much greater frequency than the ones in the ocean, because the current in the rivers change the channel in some areas, and the tows often run over the buoys, and drag them to a new location. The weights to hold buoys are huge concrete blocks, except for where the bottom is mud. Then, by putting a metal cone on water hoses with a nozzle on it, it is possible to place the cone, with buoy anchor line attached, into the mud, and when the hose is removed, the mud fills in to hold the cone in place, forming a very strong anchor – at very little cost. This is called "jetting" the anchor into the mud.

There is very little search and rescue for the Coast Guard in this district. Most of what there is, is either done by buoy tender which happens upon the situation, or by the Coast Guard Auxiliary. The Auxiliary is formed of recreational boaters, and in the 22 states involved, they were very active. They establish their own radio stations, organize search teams, fly airplanes over the cases where a plane can be used, and establish some very useful groups.

It was suggested by my staff that are ride on towboats for a couple of days, through the locks, and with tow out in front, would probably be very useful, to be able to discuss the problems of the rivermen. So, Betty, Marsha, and I went to Davenport, Iowa to meet the tow that was returning to St. Louis. It was the Emma Bordner, owned by Mid-America Transportation Company, which was run by a man who was a Naval Academy graduate from the same year group as I, Bill Fouts.

We had the estimated time of arrival of the toe at the locks in Davenport, and headed for a rendezvous at the lock. The tow was ahead of schedule, a very unusual circumstance, and we could see it just downstream when we arrived at the lock. We thought we would have to drive to the next lock downstream, but the lock master had a faster solution. He was locking through a pleasure boat of rather good size, and he asked if that boat would take the three of us and our luggage down to the tow. The boat's owner agreed, and we had the luggage lowered on lines, and we crawled down the ladder in the side of the lock to the deck of the boat. Then we were off to catch the tow, much slower than a pleasure boat, and transferred to our home for the next three days.

I spent much of my time in the pilot house, watching how the man at the controls did his job. They rarely have wheels to steer with. There are levels that move the rudders, and when the lever is moved to one side, the rudder moves. When it is brought back to the center the rudder stops, but does not necessarily move back to the center position – the lever has to be moved to the other side, and the indicator will tell where the rudder is.

From this position in the pilot house, I could also watch the deck crew in their work to make sure that the face wires (which attach the barges to the forward end of the tow boat) have the proper tension, or how they dropped off a barge along the way at a mooring facility. Since we were going downstream in the Mississippi, we did flank around some of the bends, and this was new to me.

That night, after a supper served after the regular crew's mealtime, Betty and I went to bed in a stateroom that was not quite as nice as a motel, but not bad at all. I went to sleep with no difficulty after the long hours I had spent in the pilothouse, but woke with a start when I realize that the engines were backing. When I had been at sea, backing engines usually meant we were coming to anchor, or to a dock, or in an emergency situation. I wondered which it was, until I realized that we were simply flanking around a bend, and the engines were backing to move the aft end of the tow to the desired side of the river. It was still hard to sleep through the vibrations of backing engines!

We experienced the locks in several locations. Most of the locks in the Mississippi are large enough to take three barges and a tow boat in length, and three barges abeam, but we had a total of 13. There were four tiers of three abreast, with a barge on one side of the tow boat itself. When we came to a lock, the master or pilot (they would take turns for six hours each) would move the forward end of the tow into the lock, and the deck crew would uncouple the lines holding the forward half of the tow to the after half. Then the tow boat would back out with the after half, and wait for the other part of the tow to be lowered to the level of the river downstream. Next the lock would be refilled after the barges were moved out and tied to moorings just downstream. When the lock water was up to that level of the upstream river, the rest of the tow would go in with the tow boat, and the locking operation was repeated until the whole tow could be put together just downstream. Then the tow would move on down the river to the next lock.

Shortly after I arrived in St. Louis there were two laws passed affected the river operations directly. The Port and Waterways Law affected who had the authority to do some things to control the river operations, and the Towing Vessel Operator Licensing Act required everyone in the pilothouse operating the tow boat to be licensed. Both laws required more action of our district personnel.

The operator license didn't really mean much, except that the person operating knew the rules knew the rules of the road. In the spring of 1972, we found out how little that really meant. The water level was high on the Ohio River, and currents could be strong in spots. In the city of Louisville, there was a bridge that had to be opened before a tow could go through. The channel went to the right just downstream, and the rest of the water went down stream to McAlpine Dam, where there was a powerhouse, and several spillways. The amount of water going over the spillways rather than through the powerhouse or simply down the natural river, was controlled by the Corps of Engineers, but opening more gates in the spillways.

On a spring night, with rather high water levels in the river, whether the bridge control man heard whistle signal or heard the radio calls from the tow is unknown, but the tow did not stop to wait for the bridge to open; the current was too strong. It went instead into the channel towards a powerhouse and the dam. One of his barges was loaded with sulfuric acid, and the other was loaded 1600 tons of liquid chlorine. The tow broke into separate barges, when it hit the powerhouse and the dam. Some of the barges went through the dam, and some stayed in the pool above the dam. The acid barge ended across the inlets to the powerhouse, and chlorine barge went halfway through the dam. It hung on the top of the dam, with the lower part of the barge against the huge concrete blocks built into the spillway to prevent the force of the water from eroding away the lower part of the riverbed.

Removing the parts was a joint operation of the Coast Guard, the Corps of Engineers, and several state and federal organizations. The Coast Guard officer in Louisville, the Captain of the Port, realized the political nature of this joint operation, and asked for assistance from the district office. I went over and tried to coordinate the efforts of all the organizations. It took several days, we even went to the extent of suggesting to the mayors of cities on each side of the river that they should evacuate the areas close to the river when we tried to move in to stabilize the barge in the dam. There was considerable danger of breaking the barge in half at that point, and if the chlorine tanks spilled out of the protection of the barge, and the tanks broke, the chlorine would be released to the atmosphere. We had an army officer from Fort Knox, a chemical corps officer, compute how the chlorine from one of the four tanks in the barge would spread if the tank were ruptured. His figures for one tank were so shocking that we never had him look at two or more tanks.

The salvage company which was contracted for, had two PC type vessels connected together by movable lattice work that would extend or reduce the space between the hulls of the original vessels. This entire contraption was maneuvered over the barge and attached to the barge. This stabilized the barge, and the Corps controlled the water level to maintain the same pressure on the bottom of the barge.

Next the chlorine was removed. Since the barge was on an angle, the center valves allowed the chlorine above the valves to flow out with no trouble. The same was true of some of the chlorine in tanks down below the center of the barge, until the angle that the barge was held in, in the dam, no longer allowed gravity to force the chlorine out. At that point, the chlorine was allowed to warm, expand and boil out as a gas, through a chemical mixture to neutralize the chlorine. In effect, the latter portion of the cargo was made into Clorox, and put into the river.

The EPA representatives on scene made many trips into the river below the dam to sample the water, to make sure no chlorine was escaping into the river. After most of the chlorine was gone, and the boiling office was begun, the EPA boat was even more active, since they wanted to assure themselves that the Clorox did not affect the river. I always believed that the amount of chlorine in that huge river, probably made it the purest it had been in centuries.

At one point in the operation, it became necessary to lift a large and heavy object to the top of the lock control structure, to get it to the barge. (I don't remember what it was at this time.) No one could figure out how to get it there without disturbing the stability of the barge in the lock/dam. I called Headquarters, and asked for and got an H3 helicopter from St. Petersburg to come up and hoist the item. It was one more time when I wished we had air units in the district.

One of the effects of the Ports and Water Safety Act was to make it possible for the Coast Guard to control movement of traffic on the rivers. Since this incident in the Ohio River was at least partially caused by strong currents in a full river, I made a recommendation that the Coast Guard establish a control site at this location, to be activated only when the river was at or above a designated height on the depth scale. That traffic system had been in place ever since, when the water is high, and I don't believe there have been any more such incidents.

There was one other result of this incident in my own life. I was awarded the Meritorious Service Medal for my work in coordinating the efforts in Louisville. I certainly did not do all the work by any means, and I hope I gave credit to all the people along the way who pulled together in the operations.

The district was huge in area, and it was difficult to even visit every unit, to show an interest. I wish to times that I had an airplane at my disposal, to fly to various locations. I had an inspiration one day. The Army had a command just a couple of blocks away, and I went to their officer's mess rather often. It was the Army Aviation Systems Command, and they had a few airplanes that their flying officers use to move maintain proficiency. I decided to ask the commanding general, whom I knew well, if it might be possible for them to do their proficiency flying in the direction of a Coast Guard unit that I wanted to visit. He agreed that this made sense, and from then on, until the real oil crunch in 1973, I would call and ask the Army for a plane if I needed to visit a unit. They rarely put a proficiency pilot in the plane, but assigned a safety pilot, regularly assigned to their air unit, to me and I flew the plane. I flew either a Beechcraft Baron or the Beechcraft Queen Air, the U-8. At times we encountered instrument conditions that made the flight quite interesting. Once we had near tornadoes in the vicinity of St. Louis when we returned, and once going back to Louisville, the overcast was at a minimum when we arrived.

By using this mode of transportation, I went to several places in a single day, when it would have taken much longer using the conventional modes. I went to Vicksburg and Natchez in one day, and returned that evening. I went to Louisville, Owensboro, and Paducah, and visited seven Coast Guard units or command in one day, and was on the same evening.

One day I was in the office when Jim Durfee, who was the Chief of Public Affairs in Coast Guard Headquarters, called. He asked if I could go to go to Odebolt, Iowa to represent the Coast Guard in a patriotic observance, where all services would be represented. I replied, "The date you asked about looks okay, but where is Odebolt?" He said, "It is just a short distance from Idagrove." I responded, "All right, where is Idagrove?" He laughed and said "I expected that." Then he told me it was between Iowa City and Fort Dodge. I located it on the map, and once again asked the Army for assistance in getting there.

We flew into Idagrove, where I was met with sideboys from the American Legion, and was driven into Odebolt, where one of the very earliest corn silos was for Cracker Jack. There must have been marching units from all over the state, because there was quite a parade. There were representatives from all the services, some reserves and some only captain or colonel, but we were all there, again in my case, thanks to the Army. I was only one to fly that close – the rest usually drove from Chicago or Des Moines. Even when the congressman from the district arrived by charter plane, he didn't have sideboys to greet him.

I didn't always use the Army planes, at least once I used a Coast Guard helicopter from the Chicago air unit. It picked me up in Indiana, after I had gotten to Dana, where we had a loran station by car. From there, I flew along the river, seeing the condition of the locks, and the traffic, so we would arrive at a city where we had either a GUI tender or Marine safety office. That I would get out, have a car from the Coast Guard unit take me to the unit, and see the problems they might have. Some of the units in West Virginia, seem to vary greatly from what the Coast Guard usually does, but Huntington, West Virginia is one of the river's largest oil ports, there was a GUI tender just downstream from Pittsburgh, as well as a Marine safety office in the city there. It's hard to believe that Pittsburgh is one of the country's busiest ports also.

Transportation seems to be at the root of several of my problems. I had a sedan assigned to me as the district commander, and a driver. He would pick me up at the house in the morning, take me to the office, and from there to other locations in the day, if it was necessary. Senator Proxmire from Wisconsin was waging a campaign against the use of government vehicles when private vehicles could be used.

An admirer of Senator Proxmire in St. Louis, took the same route to work every morning, as we did and he often saw me a black sedan. He wrote to Proxmire saying that I rode in the back seat and read the newspaper. "I never did!" Proxmire wrote to the Coast Guard, and I was asked to justify why I used a government car. I replied that I felt this was my mobile command and control unit, and we didn't hear any more of the complaint at that time. It did come up again later!

I was invited to speak at a Memorial Day observance of Decatur, Illinois in the spring of 1972. There was to be boat races on Lake Decatur, and a short ceremony at 11 AM. I accepted, and Bette and I drove up to Decatur that day. We found that the platform for the speakers was a farm wagon draped appropriately with bunting, with a microphone at the front of the stand – actually the side of the wagon. No one had bothered to tell the boat operators to stop testing their highly supercharged engines at the ceremonies, and when the man who was to introduce me stepped up to the mic to speak to the dozen or so the spectators immediately the front of the stand, I realized that the public address system was working!

I stepped up to the my comment figured I could yell loudly enough that's first crowd could hear me off I went. After a short period of time, between and over the worst of engines, I realize that the peace system was returning my shouts. Attempt at my delivery, and suddenly he was dead again. I said it again, and of course, it returned to service, I lowered my voice. I'm not sure how many times cycle is repeated, but friends told me later that the radio broadcasts version worked well.

The sponsors of the event felt so badly about how the arrangements had worked, that the invite me back a year later. I think they wanted to find out I said the first time, believed I would repeat myself. We went back, the day went well, the boat operator stop testing for the speeches, I can't remember anything more about the day. You remember the anti-interesting ones later. I was often called to represent the Coast Guard and the many state.. Once or twice the national Association of State safe boating law administrators men in the district, because of the tremendous interest in voting in the states. Once we met in Iowa, lots were there was a large lake nearby. We went cruising on the lake one evening, and then everything was designated an admiral of the Iowa Navy. Another time it was held in Arkansas, we went out to a park along the Arkansas River and had catfish barbecued. Betty saidShe ever had eaten. I'm not much of a judge of the epic epicurean value fish, especially captives.

When the conference was the Hot Springs Arkansas we hadn't opportunity to see what a resort. That is. Their hot bath springs everywhere, and auction houses along the streets. They auctioned off an amazing assortment of items, many of, I was sure. Yes the oddest thing to me was that the best of the variety of valuable stones that have been found in the states, and there were few jewelry stores – or at least I didn't see them.

I spoke of catfish, there were two events that particularly come back to mine. Jesse Brent was the owner Brent towing, in Greenville Mississippi, made it a practice to his meeting of the area section of the American waterways operators, every other year. He held a Fish fry in the yard of his beautiful home, and they must've had barrels of catfish. In the first time we went there, I guess Betty and I drove down, and stated motel in town. That evening at Brents was the highlight of the stay, and he gave voice of new glasses at the big beyond them which we had for years afterwards.

Second time, there had been extremely low waters in Mississippi for some time, and the markings are a problem for buoy tenders. I'd never been on the section the Mississippi where there were no locks or dams, so I looked for a way to get to Greenville by topo. We spent some time searching out a toga that would arrive in Greenville at about the correct time for the meeting, before he found out that through sports line would have one that generally met her schedule. Earl and Joe Rose on this line, and have built it from a very lowly start to being one of the best firms on the rivers. Every Tobit was named after type of rose, and we were going in the Crimson glory, starting in Cairo Illinois, where they would make their toe, going downstream to Greenville. The process of making up the tow in a quote fleeting unquote area, where the barges are kept until they are moved into a toe, was interesting, also. With a two was made up we had 16 barges. This is smaller than the usual number because of the shallow water downstream

the trip started as a routine voyage, although there was much flanking now. Unfortunately, we arrived at a very shallow area where the Corps of Engineers was conducting dredging, behind some other toes. There were also two toes hoping to go upstream, and they were waiting on the other side of the restricted area. The master of our toe tied up to some trees on the bank, and volunteered user topo to assist another toe of the Rose company. He would help tape some barges from the toe through. Only about two barges at a time could go through the shallow area, because the dredge was working to widen and deepen the workable channel. After the first trip downstream with a couple of barges, the master thought he knew of a channel that he could go back upstream, without waiting his turn, and it was so narrow that only a single Tobit make it. At three went some distance, he discovered that had gotten still shall overcome and the topo could make it. We went aground, working ourselves free, and went back to way to turn. We finally went through the dredged area, but they were considerable difficulties.

As a footnote to the Rose barges line story, the Rose decided to sell the company to a huge agricultural combine just about the time we left St. Louis. When they sold, the each became millionaires, and the two of them each bottom Mercedes convertible – to look like millionaires. Earl bought a huge farm several miles out into the illicit misery countryside, that he previously been owned by a senator long from Missouri. They owned another farm adjacent for some time, but it was too much for them to manage well Earl died a few years later. They did develop a fine herd of cattle on the farm, and I believe there some cures for for it while he develops another waterway oriented firm in Illinois.

In November 1972, Betty and I decided to take a short leave, and trade military airlift command space available travel. At that time, flag or general officer could write ahead, and asked be put on the waiting list, and you could work your way up the list without being there. That has now changed, you must be there in person, at least to put on the list. You can work your way up the list and am state abstention still. I really had, we flew to Charleston South Carolina to depart for South America on the trip that goes to the capitals of the countries in the southern hemisphere.

We arrived a little early for the flight, knowing which day of the week they departed, and so little of Charleston. Then early one morning, we departed for the South. We flew to Howard Air Force Base in the vicinity of Panama City, but made only quick stop there. We ended that first day in Lima Peru.

We stayed in the hotel's with the aircraft cruise when we could, because I thought they would note the most desirable for the cost. It turned out here they stayed in the same hotel where I had stayed when I was on the national war College trip a few years earlier. I introduce Betty to peace Gus hours, and she enjoyed them as much is Tom Hayward and I had before.

There have been a few the national war College group who would eat at a restaurant that they raved about, called last-place when needles or 313 coins or the 13 coins, so that he and I decided to try that. We waited until after 8 PM, took a cab to the restaurant. Let us in, that the to serve food until after nine. They suggested that we use the bar while we waited, we had another piece go sour. When we look at the menu for food, finally!, I saw they served oysters on the half shell. We had recently been at a Fouts residence in East St. Louis and has enjoyed oysters there, as well as oysters Rockefeller and shrimp, and shrimp in steak all that same evening. I thought we would try to oysters here in Peru, I said to the waiter, quote we will each have a half dozen oysters on the half shell." He replied, quote I don't think you want that. Just a moment. Quotation he went to the kitchen, came back with an oyster shell to demonstrate why we would only want a single oyster. It was at least 6 inches long, and several inches wide. We had a single oyster each. Betty thought it would be funny to take the shells back to show Audrey Fouts what real oysters look like, but the next morning base they were to do for us to take anywhere. I certainly didn't want them in my luggage!

The next evening we stopped in Mendoza Argentina, just because it was to fork to go on to other capitals. Weekend stayed in the hotel with the crew, and they told us were good restaurant was nearby. We went there, and they specialized in Argentine beef, and had a side of beef hanging in the dining room, where they would cut off your piece, and throw it on the grill which was in sight of the diners. I enjoyed my beef, but Betty didn't think much of the presentation.

The next day we flew to Montevideo, Uruguay, where we were herded into a hangar waiting room while the plane was service. The military had a sales room persuade jackets there in the waiting area, Betty bought a check. They didn't have anything that need properly. I left a card with the US military contact there, because I knew had I had were college classmate, Frank Ortiz, they are on duty with the embassy. I thought he was a chief of staff but it turned out he was a charge to fear.

Our next step is when his areas, where the pilot had received a message that we were not to land, if there was any doubt in his mind about whether he would have to remain on the ground. The US Embassy wanted no US planes in the ground anywhere on the airport when one Perrone return to the country a few days later. Again, we were heard herded into a small waiting room, the weather about 4 cups of strong coffee for the approximate lead 20 passengers, we were held there until the plane was serviced and we reported. So much for Argentina, but the airport was miles out in the country and there was nothing to be seen there as far as we could tell.

The end of our travel for the day was Rio de Janeiro. There most of us were waiting the point leaving the plane, and the first thing that happened was a long briefing about how to behave. It seemed to me that the person giving the lecture was trying to impress someone with the importance of his lecture. We finally went into town to the Copacabana beach area, and the first hotel couldn't take the four of us who came in together. We went to the hotel next door and were accepted, we found out the next day that the crew was there also.

We've been told by one of her fellow passengers who had been Brazilian, and married a service man. About a very good restaurant which looked in our maps of the service section, as if it should be close. We started walking with several of her fellow passengers and walked and walked. Finally found the street, but found that the number should have been back the way we came. When we found the never, and the name of the restaurant, it was closed – not just the night, but permanently. We went back to the beach hotels eat some delicious rice and black beans of the hotel next door Dars, after probably walking a mile looking.

One of the highlights of our stay in Rio is eating at a restaurant called quote on the rocks." We had the and address for it and knew it was on the roof, so we took a cat there. When we took the elevator to the roof there was nothing here but assign with an arrow. We went down the hall and then up another elevator, and we run a beer roof, which looked like a construction area, again with the sign. We follow the area. Arrows, and finally found a lovely cocktail area, with a view of Ipanema beach that couldn't have been improved. He went down one level, on another elevator, where we were served a delicious dinner again with the view that couldn't be improved, as it grew dark. We flew commercial from Rio to put it to allegro, San Pablo, and Montevideo. We stayed in love Leo hotel in Montevideo and I remember he particularly with delicious chocolate tort they had for dessert. The Met other memorable thing about the hotel was the toilet tissue they provided! It could've passed for cornmeal chips if it'd been cut into smaller sizes. I called Frank Ortiz from the hotel, and the fighters out to their apartment. They had had to move to a more secure apartment when he became the church the affair because Uruguay had had so much trouble with the two UPA MAR O Ter. He said he would send a car for us so we wouldn't have to take a cab. Yet that the car came, there was a second man in the cart, drove long enough, it felt as if we should've arrived in another country. I was nervous, but try not to let Betty know, we finally arrived at the apartment. We had a very pleasant visit, and Frank's wife Dolores had several coats that were gathered for an embassy auction scheduled the next days. Betty bought one of the sheer lame jackets that Dolores had a real bargain price. Betty still has it but doesn't wear it often in savanna. The next paragraph the next day we took the bus to colonial, where we could board a hydrofoil for Buenos Aires. Writing a bus was throw, because the driver drove as if

There couldn't be anyone else on the road. When he would pass a horse cart on a hill, when he couldn't see over the next rise in the road, so we shall cross her fingers for them.

The hydrofoil ride was very pleasant, and a new experience. Here under ways for about an hour across the Rio de la Platt, and then we arrived in Buenos Aires. I found the embassy and asked to for assistance in finding hotel, and the use my Spanish to tilt caps and tell cabs where we wanted to try and get a hotel room. I felt rather proud that Betty was pleased with the outcome.

Our return trip, back the way we came, was not particular he memorable, except for a couple of fence. We left Buenos Aires very early one morning, and went to San Diego Chile where we had breakfast in the airport terminal. Betty had eggs, and the weight of the ambassador from Lima, he was on the plane, told her that she had probably the last two eggs in Chile. The country was going through one of their bad times! When we left Lima headed for Charleston it was Thanksgiving day. We stopped again in Panama, and we were to have enough time in the ground that we could eat. I tried the officer's club, but it was close. There was nothing to eat in the terminal, we finally found this civilian employee's cafeteria was open. A group of us turkey dinner they are common before we started, we thought everyone someone should say grace. One service man, who had been raised in South America, and had taken his wife to see his relatives in Argentina, was an elder in the Mormon church, Nikkei thinks of the group us. Another couple of the table, said Lieut. Col. from Fort Leonard Wood, and his wife, who was Vietnamese. As an interesting group to be together on Thanksgiving in Panama

In the spring of 1973 brought floods to Midwest. The Coast Guard was busy, now with pretenders and workers along the river as usual, but trying to help people affected by the high water. We needed additional people, but the reserve units had enough people, that it seemed no problem. They reported for duty voluntarily, and spent about two weeks doing what they would've done that summer in their active duty for training. This time it was not just training, was meaningful.

The water receded, we went back to put buoys in place. Then, the floods returned, and they were even higher than before. This time, when we contacted the reservists, the let us know that they were willing, that they were afraid for their normal employment. There Belmar passionately before, allowing the Coast Guard to recall the service for a period of up to six months in cases of natural or man-made disasters, without their concurrence. It gave them drop protection if this occurred. Was exactly what does the reservists needed, where we had never done it. This time, asked for authority to call them under this provision, and the secretary Kurt dissection like most others giving the Coast Guard authority to to fix, designate the secretary the department in which the Coast Guard is serving, to take an action. In almost every case, it is then delegated to the comment and reports perform the actual act. I believe in this case, it was not delegated, and the secretary himself had to take the action. We recalled we service involuntarily for the first time in history.

Water was so high that I asked for helicopter from Chicago to come down and operate with us during the flood. I asked for the communication V and it was available for emergency operations, and it was for him via C-130. The water was so high at the confluence of the misery, the Ohio, and the Mississippi, that miles of farmland was underwater. Farm animals try to find high spot stood fluently, not knowing what to do or where to go. Crops were washed out of the land washed out or the land was so wet that there could be no planting. In many acres of land that had been in Connor tobacco shifted to soybeans because they could be planted later in the spring.

Much later in the spring, the floodwaters moved downstream. Betty and I went down the river to Memphis and Greenville Mississippi driving our car. There are still many places where the water was high, and all too often, we you would see a lovely home with the water as high as the windowsills. I'm sure most of the occupants return, believe that there would never be a flood of that magnitude it happened, almost exactly 20 years later.

As the year went along, I knew I would be moved to other duty with the next shifts of Coast Guard admirals. I tried to think of what I would like to do, but I enjoyed what I was doing, and didn't know of any locations that I really would enjoy more, and would be more challenging. I thought of the Chief of Staff's drop, but I didn't really think I want to go back again to Washington. So I let things go on, not knowing what the future might bring.

Marsh was at the University of Florida and we request leaf close to Christmas so we can go to the beach at Hillsboro Inlet where there is a Coast Guard house available uses a recreation home. We could pick marsh up in Gainesville, or the University of Florida is, and drive to Hillsboro, just north of Pompano Beach. We went to the beach, which we always enjoyed, even when we're living in Florida, we ought also play tennis while we were there. The Hillsboro club is immediately adjacent to the Coast Guard property, and they allow visitors to the Coast Guard quarters to use club when it's open, during its brief seasons. Betty took a tennis lesson from Doris Hart, the former tennis Creek and Wimbledon champion, and I found some club members alike play doubles with. After week there, we drove on home at the expiration of the leaf. Marsha

Marsha told us we picked her up that she just had her wisdom teeth pulled but it wasn't painting her and she had been told to wash it frequently mouthwash. She been given a syringe by the Dennis to support the fluid into the proper place. When we returned Marsha to Gainesville, and we drove up the highway for some time to get a start on the trip home to St. Louis. As we unpacked the car, we found Marsha had not taken her train case with her cosmetics and small toiletries. We opened it to determine whether there's anything she needed immediately or whether she could wait while we send it back instead of driving back. We found, among other things, syringe and in those days of young people trying all sorts of drugs, we really he nearly went wild, while we try to get marsh on the phone. She gonna to dinner, and we had no answer. We went back to the train case, to look one more time, to see if there could be any drugs, and suddenly I smelled mouthwash. I knew then why the syringe, he left at each other, and cried a little out of the disparate daughter. We spoke to Marshall little later, and she simply laughed at us.

When we arrived at our home, the next morning Chip Bender, the common day, call test me to come in to be interviewed to be the calm down. I have covered that earlier, walk over it again. I knew I was not the only one who was called in, but I never knew who else was, except I was sure that Joe McClelland was, and I later made him if I settle, and the Pacific area commander. Even when I was told I was to be the next commentator, was not through the process. I had to be confirmed by the Senate.

Ed Perry, who was to be the vice, Dan, and I appeared both for the Senate commerce committee for a hearing, and it was not like those acrimonious hearings that make the news. Most of the time, the Senators were friendly, and answer easy questions. Sen. Magnuson was the chairman at that time, and he was police of my resume said I had been born in Seattle Washington as he was a Washingtonian. I never told him that my parents took me out of state when I was six months old. Sen. Long, from Louisiana, asked questions about a deep water port and supertankers which I did not answer very well, but I guess he figured that I would get more expertise on the subjects later. I had appeared for the same committee early when I was first nominated for rear Adm. common at that time, I don't believe they asked any questions – I was simply introduced. I hope all confirmations hearings report that committee go as easily. Back in the second District, I went on with business as usual, with many Coast Guard auxiliary,, princes, as happened every year. This time, they made a big deal of fact that I was going to Washington and be permitted. I believe he thought they were gaining something, by having a district commander from their going on to greater things. We received many lovely going away gifts from the auxiliary risk, one of the most interesting trips was to Charleston West Virginia to an Eastern regional conference.

We had to schedule a flight through Chicago, changing planes there. The weather was bad and we were held over in Chicago for a long time. I wasn't concerned most of the time – we had an hour between planes. But we held for more most of the hour, when we landed, our ongoing plane should've been boarding. I rushed down the aisle of the terminal to find any American airlines test to see if we could sell guitar playing. It happened at the First American counter I reach was our flight. I asked about the flight, and the counter man replied," are you ready to board?" Betty had stepped stopped at a restaurant, and I had to say, quote not yet, but I will be in just a moment.""" Another man came up to ask, he was talking, Betty arrives to the American clerk told us to come with him.

The regular boarding passage have been moved away from our plane, and the engines were running, so the escrowed had us go down the stairway to the level of the field. As we stepped on the ground, it was wet with the rain that it held this in the air, and there was a small step down to the pavement. The American airlines man turned me and I think said, quote watch your step." But the jet engine so close I couldn't hear him, and I turn closer to him and didn't watch my step stumble.

I always wore my uniform on trips and on this trip I was wearing the new uniform the chip Bender headed hit upon. In the new trial material, polyester double net. As I stumbled in the symbol to the pavement, my Came off, and rolled across a couple of puddles. Had a briefcase in one hand, my raincoat or my arm, so I went down all the way catch myself my elbow. I hit on one knee, there was a hole all the way through the double net when I stood up. The goal parade on my sleeve was badly worn, and the Needed some work. Fortunately was one of the Plaskett plastic Brady, and could be wiped off.

American Airlines told me that they would have my uniform cleaned when I quote got off at Cincinnati" but of course, I wasn't getting off in Cincinnati. They never mention doing anything in Charleston!

That evening Betty and I exist without our luggage – it had made the transfer in Chicago – we went as we were. There was a country or hillbilly party – seems natural for West Virginia – but her casual clothing was somewhere in the position of the airlines, couldn't hear anything but my uniform and that he's traveling close. I put some black tape on inside of the whole of my trouser knee, and it wasn't too obvious. The auxiliary gave me appear fake shoulder boards they were each a foot long with four stars on them, and so it wasn't too bad that I had to be in somewhat of uniform. We had a good time with the auxiliary risk, and the mishap of the ramp at Chicago make good conversation subjects.

Check bank Bender was so anxious to have the top people in the new uniform, that the uniform people sent me had another double net uniform to replace the damage one, as soon as he heard about the damage. I tried to double net, but never looked as smart as other materials, and I'm glad they feasted out.

When the change of command to turn the district over to Pat Pursley came, in early June, Pat agreed to rent our house. He had house that he kept in the Washington area, and his children were off at school so it worked out well for him, at the change command, I was presented with the Legion of merit metal, for the performance of duty in the district, we were on our way.

When we arrived in Washington, of course, Chet was still in the quarters at the Coast Guard on. I had had a series of briefings earlier, but there was a some short overlap, and we had to find somewhere to live. I could probably have lived in Fort Myers, or bowling Air Force Base, but Lieut. Cmdr. John Finkel, who was a cadet at the cabbie when I was flying the comment that that there often, offered his parents home to us for the interim period. His father, a retired Navy, have frequently flown with us to the Academy in those days, and he spent his summers at Rehobeth Beach, so the house was empty. It provided to us with a very comfortable residence for the period before he was relieved. John later bought the house from his father, and the parents built a new home next door, where we stayed for a month after I retired from the Coast Guard. It was from this house at the first pick this up to go to the change of command where I relief Chet on 30 June 1974. New page, Dan middle of the page

The change of command was to be on the deck of the Eagle which was brought into the Navy yard in Washington for the ceremony. This required some careful maneuvering, since master so high that it was difficult to get under some bridges, and the depth of the water in Washington was so shallow, that the vessel had arrived at high tide. It did come in, and a few days before the change of command, was given a Bicentennial banner to carry until the observances in 1976. Betty and I were on the Eagle for that ceremony, and happily so, because the weather didn't cooperate.

The morning of the change of command on rainy and threatening. Fortunately there was a fallback location, still of the Navy yard remove the change of me and into the Navy seal off, which was prepared for such things. As a matter fact, change of command of the Navy chaplains, which was held about a month later, was also held inside, and the sale off.

We hope the change of command, and then went to the officers club for a reception. Chetna had a small disagreement about this, because he wanted to hear at the receiving line. I pointed out that this reception, I would be commenting, and the common 10K the perception after the change. He wrecked reluctantly agreed, and I believe he and Molly actually had more time with the guests they had the new dam near the end of the line. After there is

After the reception, Betty and I went home to the contents quarters and can one. Chet Molly had had the last of their things moved out while we were at the change in the reception, so is now ours. In the next few days we had all our things moved and commented some renovation. The lower floors of the house needed freshening, and we had new wallpaper put in several rooms. Unfortunately, the government way of taking the lowest bid, didn't work as well as my have, and there were spaces between the strip wallpaper. Had to be done again.

One of the things that was pending, and continue to pen for a long time thereafter, was replacement for the Grumman albatross airplanes that the Coast Guard had been flying since the early 1950s. When the plane was modified in the late 1950 – 1960., It had been noted that there was corrosion in the main strength area. There been additional corrosion there been additional testing done, and the set number of hours of flight time had been arrived at as a time to retire the albatross. Chet believe that we can save a huge amount of maintenance time by using a jet plane instead of a propeller driven one, because propeller maintenance take so much of the maintenance effort, at least a couple planes to try the concept.

The planes leased for the Cessna citation in these really West Wing, although letter was first looked at as the jet version of the Aero Cmdr., the plane seals rates were sold to Israeli aircraft in the middle of the test. Most of the concept look very favorable, but the planes were too small. Equipment that we use for rescue, and they didn't have any draw patches to get things out to people in the water, so we knew there had to be modifications to some planes.

A thought at this time, when I arrived, was that we would buy a few free limited initially, of the T – 39, which was being flown by the Air Force and the Navy as an executive transport, was about the size we wanted. Unfortunately had engines for only high-altitude work, when we did something that would give their efficiency at an altitude where we could see the water fairly well. We believe there were engines that could be replaced, and served her purpose will.

This time Congressman John Murphy of North Carolina was the head of the Coast Guard subcommittee, and the next year became chairman of the entire oversight committee. Since this from New York, he had a Pan American Airways is one of his constituents, and Pan-American had a subzero city rebased in Teterboro Northern New Jersey, which marketed different

French falcon aircraft. Murphy started pushing us very hard toward the falcon. Our first look at planes of this type had examined the falcon 10, with a size about the same as the ones we had leased. There were eliminated for size, and then we found the T – 39 and stopped her looking. Murphy wanted us to look at the falcon 20, which is much closer to what we needed. It was being flown by the Federal Express in the earlier days, and had a lot more space than the falcon 10.

Eventually we used a two-step procurement process, which would allow any plane to be bought, but this was far more complicated than the way we had wanted to buy the T – 39, through the military process. We would simply have told the Navy that we wanted two or three of them at one time, and they would have attacked them onto their purchase order. There we were going to do it ourselves, all the way.

In the two-step process, we had three planes that sit submitted proposals. The falcon, with a different engine, the Lockheed for jet executive plane, which had a be modified to only two engines, it made it more stable, major engineering effort and the German talker, which is much larger with. We would've been delighted to have the Fokker but it was probably going to be much more expensive for such a large plane, unless the German government subsidized it – and I hope they would.

He finally determined that these three planes, with modifications of the proposed, would meet all of our requirements. The T – 39 made no proposals, probably because they didn't have any arrangements to replace the engines, and they had a government contractor ready for the existing plane. It would not meet our specifications without known modifications. The second step in the process as was test the price for these planes would be. We proceeded, and the only one to respond in a second step was falcon. They were planning to test the planes in France with French engines on them. Then they would remove wings and engines, and ship them in a Pan Am plane to Little Rock Arkansas with a written mount the American engines, cut holes for draw patches and search windows, and install American electronics. When all this was done, the planes became American products, is more than half American including all the necessary labor, and there was no problem with quote by American" for an American service.

We progressed down this path for some time, falcon made us another offer. They'd apparently examine the costs again, and said that they could save themselves and us money if instead of removing the wings in France, they simply flew the planes met early configuration to Little Rock. Then they would make the modifications. This, of course, change the figures regarding the American products significantly and we in the department went back to figuring.

This procedure stretched over. Of that two years, before we finally were able to sign a contract. There is a very complicated review by the procurement experts of the department, as well as the Coast Guard zone, and after TS ARC transportation systems acquisition review Council finally approved, I was to sign a contract. The president of falcon Chet USA, the vice president of Garrett engines company, and a vice president of Collins electronics are brought in to sign with me, and they were assembled outside my office. I cleaned out my desk, told Agnes, my secretary to have them come in.

Just say started in the door, the direct line telephone from the secretary of transportation himself rang, and I picked up the phone. Quote sigh," he said, quote is there anything more that we don't know about that plane?" Quote no sir," I replied, not that I'm aware of." Quote well then, go ahead and sign the contract, quote the secretary answered.

I send a contract, and gave each of the executives append that had signed a part of the contract. They still had the biggest one. The contract is for 41 jet airplanes, there was something we didn't know. The engine was the power plant for a drone airplane, and we had said in the contract that the plane must be able to be certified by the FAA or foreign equivalent like the French. The engine had never been certified to carry people, and that includes the ability to ingest either one or two birds and still keep running. It was more than a couple of years after he retired for the engine could pass the bird test. Better known as a chicken test because these chickens of the correct size and weight to actually make the test.

Congressman Murphy had forced her hand in this procurement was not invited to the contract signing, because I believe he was either in jail or indicted at that time for the app scammed the fears. He spent some time in jail at some time. He accuse some of the Coast Guard personnel of being crooks when they were hard at work trying to get the best deal for the government, but we found the creek really was.

While the airplane problem went on for a period of several years, the one of the first things I became involved with was merchant vessel safety concerns of the Coast Guard. Since at that time I have been flying at Richmond to New York, data, and the end of the Coast Guard was a member of the board of the American Bureau of shipping. Now I was flying to New York for this meetings. Ill Ray who was a vice Adm. in New York, was a member of the technical committee and was able to guide me through the first several meetings.

Next came the meeting of the Council of I am CEO, the governmental maritime consultant of organization. The name was changed and simplified after he retired to the international Maritime organization. Often in the past, the comment and had led the delegation to this meeting, although the State Department is officially the representative for meetings where there is to be international negotiation. I was gonna go to the meeting in November, 1974 but this extraordinary session to modify the charter the charter of the organization. There are designated number of members of the Council, made up of states who were ships, states to you shipping, and estates it has an interest. The US had originally been the first group, easily, but was scrapping of ships over the years, it had become questionable. US really didn't have that many ships anymore. They could still easily qualify for the second group, and all the other group was made up of Liberia in any other country which had a real interest.

Systems stay wanted to have it on his, and work towards designation finally told that I went to London, and the meetings were held in the building is really too small for the whole meeting. Delegate from Tanzania was right next to me, because he heads formal state delegate designation of United something, and we talk several times.

This meeting had to do with extending the membership of the

Council to include six more members, and the only problem was who should make Those members. They were going to be in the quote all other" group, that was decided early, but how to choose the was at the crux of the question. The lesser developed nations wanted to have those memberships reserved for lesser developed countries, and some of us could see that they should at times include other nations. The man from Tanzania said it one time, quote what do you have against us?" And I had to try to explain that it wasn't that there was anything against them, but beliefs that there should not be a prohibition of some other states other nations.

We were very concerned about the change of the fisheries limit from the 12 mile offshore, as determined by the Bartlett back to the 1960s and that was to be asked dented to 200 miles offshore by proposal of Sen. Magnuson, my friend from Washington state. There were talks about establishing a perimeter blockade all around the US, and rejection, because it was so impractical. We pointed out that we knew rather well where there were fish, and where fishing vessels wanted to work. We would concentrator Coast Guard efforts in these areas. Were really talking about a large effort on the Alaskan waters off the east coast of the grand Banks.

We realize soon additional long-range aircraft, as we had seen when we were to keep track of all the Russian vessels at the time the Cuban missile crisis, when I was sent to Kodiak. We also believe that we would need additional vessels to determine what the foreigners were doing when they were cited. The Office of Management and Budget, and the wisdom of this pencil pushers, decided that we could do the whole job with one additional ship, we were allowed to bring one of the ships that had once been it's time on Ocean station duty, back in the commission we were allowed enough money to buy some C-130s and put them in Alaska. We didn't get enough support from the district commander in Alaska to justify the memberships we both believe you would need. He became the next, and then it started yelling for more ships!

The act is passed, on the day when into effect, I went to New York, was interviewed on the deck one of our cutters with the skyline of New York in the background I Tom broke all of the today show. That afternoon, we went to Boston, with the then chairman of our house of representatives committee, and whole group of newsmen flew with us in a C-130, to see what foreign vessels were out there. There were only a few Russians, but several American fishing vessels, all of the new identification numbers now painted on the sides.

During the first two years of my term, the present and the secretary had changed. On the day that Gerald Ford was to be sworn in at the White House, is scheduled to go to Cheboygan Michigan to attend the observance of the 25th anniversary of Mackinac, the big Great Lakes icebreaker, being in that port. I attended the ceremonies at the White House, and then went to Michigan.

I went to the White House with Betty, we were seated with Jim Holloway, the chief of Naval operations, as to service chiefs together, but there were Nazis designated for service chiefs, simply an area. Afterwhile, Asher, a young military officer came to me and said quote general, were going to have to move you to a different area." I started to get up believing that the Asher must know what he was doing, when Jim Holloway said quote do you know if you're speaking to? This is the commenting of the Coast Guard!" The Asher apologized and withdrew we stay where we were.

I realize the young officer had wanted us to move didn't recognize because card uniform and certainly not the seagoing aspect of this uniform. I promptly ordered that white shirts would be worn with the uniform at evening, and more formal events. Chet had put into effect the Royal uniform, and it was known as Bender blue, but now it was with the Siler shirt for medical appearance.

The secretary changed about this time, although the deputy did not. The new secretary was Bill Coleman, very capable black attorney, who had once served as a law clerk for Supreme Court Justice Felix frankfurter. Coleman like to document his more formal decisions with determinations, just like a decision of the courts. You knew what he was deciding, and why he reach that decision.

He had a Coast Guard officer as a military a common used them constantly. I never had any trouble getting to see the secretary when he was here, and I perhaps went directly to the secretary more than the deputy, because I knew I could get the decisions I needed promptly that we.

We had some concerns that maritime matters were not given the attention that they needed, we didn't want to be overshadowed by the Nash national oceanographic and atmospheric agency, no. Somehow we came up with a proposal for White House decision to form federal maritime counsel, like the Council of economic advisers, and some of the others in the White House organization. We staff to thoroughly in the Coast Guard and the department, and finally, the secretary made an appointment with Sec. of commerce Ellie Richardson to discuss it. Commerce was where the NOAA organization was, and we believe with both it and at the time, the MA there, that it made sense for the chairmanship of this proposed counsel to be alternated between the two department secretaries.

The group that the meeting consisted of secretary Coleman, Sec. Richardson, myself, Ted Leyland, the secretary's military eight, and the commerce assistant secretary for plans and programs. Bill Coleman told Richardson what we had in mind, and how we were proposing to organize it. All the time he spoke, Richardson had a notepad in front of him, and he never made a note – just doodle. It is really frustrating when someone just doodles when you believe what you're saying is important. When Coleman finish, Richardson turned to us as assistant secretary, and said quote where is our proposal on this?" We realize than the commerce had had somewhat the same idea but they were going to impose it on the Coast Guard, the Navy, and any others would be members of the Council without conferring ahead of time, when the assistant said, quote it's gone to the White House."

I don't believe that Bill Coleman could turn white with rage, but he wasn't happy about this development. We drew withdrew from the commerce spaces with very little more said, and when we were in the car, the secretary told Ted, his aide to get one of the White House people in the car phone as soon as he could. Bill Coleman told the White House man not to let Ford to sign a determination establishing this counsel, until Coleman could speak to White House personnel. That was the last I ever heard of maritime counsel. It was dropped, never came up again.

The year 1976 is a big year for All-America come the Coast Guard had an important part of the celebration. The pork eagle was scheduled to take part in some of the quote racing" from one port to another, and then let leave the tall ships in the New York Harbor on July 4. The eagle was in the Coast Guard. That spring, undergoing routine maintenance, and was to be repainted, to make its white stripe really clean. It. Came into my office one afternoon, and pointed out the eagle was at that time the only Coast Guard vessel without the distinguishing stripe, and in was now being painted. He asked what we should do about putting the stripe on her.

It didn't take long to say, but quote put the stripes on her." The started an avalanche of letters from residents of New England, including Congressman from the area. They said, quote we recognize the eagle without the stripe is a Coast Guard ship." Is sacrilegious to put a stripe on the side of the pristine sailing vessel. I stuck to my guns, and the equal sealed with the stripe.

, The tall ships went from Bermuda to Newport Rhode Island in anger there for a couple of days before the final trip to Sandy Hook, New Jersey and then into the New York Harbor. It was foggy in Newport, and suddenly the only tall ship that could easily be seen which was eagle. Several people told me that they only wanted to find a specific vessel the, the standard beginning was, quote see the eagle, with the stripe, the vessel you are interested in his fourth to the left, quote or some such approach.

When we flew to New York to take part in the observance of the fourth, we flew over Sandy Hook, where all the big tall ships are at anchor. Just seeing them in anger was a throw. We landed at laborious seal, and saw more, smaller, sailing vessel sailing down the East River. In the next day, we went out on at the C tender to the cutter Morgenthaler, with our guests who had phone up with us. It was hazy, when the tall ships came into view to the case, with the equal leading the way, all the spareby cadets, to air you broke cheers. That night was a fireworks display in the harbor, with music coordinated on the radio. It was truly stirring of it. Really made one proud to be an American

The next day, and new, Bill Ray and I were invited to lunch on the square rake ship, Denmark Denmark. I have been a cadet on the damar, and remember the trips around Long Island sound with a great deal of nostalgia. Danish Amb. was up from washing, then, as was the Naval attaché. The captain was named Hansen, the same as when I have been a cadet, but it wasn't the same man – that is just very common name for Danes. We were given much aggravated to consume, and then we left to recover. The Danes had Marcus coming, and they must have had all the liquor they could stand!

That evening, Betty and I were invited to a dinner party given on for the flagship of the British represent representation for the Naval rebuke given in can junction with a tall ships review. The British investors was there, and for the first Sea Lord in the first Sea Lord of the British Navy. What's more, a really memorable evening.

I made only after events New York, I have been invited to a naval seminar Newport, Rhode Island, the Naval war College. It was for all the Naval chiefs of native South American other countries such as the SE ATO nations of the Pacific. It was good attendance by all countries. The countries were split into discussion areas, and I was assigned to the group the South American and Central American countries, as if I were the head of a small Navy. I was elected as chairman of her group, and try to lead the discussions on the subject suggested. I received an interesting and attractive name from the head of the Bolivian Navy – the only water they have is part of Lake Titicaca, shared by Peru, and some of the headwaters of the Amazon. I believe the only boats they have on the lake! Close, thanking me for my services head of the Western Hemisphere group. Of course, it wasn't Spanish but I had no difficulty reading it,.

There was one session where the subject of enforcement of fishing limits further and see was a primary concern. I pointed out that enforcement by white vessels made it clear that it was enforcement and not able challenge. The British naval officer on the panel pointed out that there Coast Guard vessels, painted white which they were not, would be agreed would be spread so thinly that they would not to adequate job of enforcement, they needed to use their naval vessels as well. Obtaining the Coast Guard vessels and naval vessels all the same a foreign fishing vessel made saw no difference. It made eminently good sense, and I was sorry I had not realized sooner. Had said something to the Norwegians when I had been over there, their response is not so well reasoned as the British now.

Just before I became common to the search is minute for two Norwegian coal colliers and it sailed from Norfolk, disappeared. The Coast Guard conducted a long search for the vessels, without result. A year later, another Norwegian vessel, and the South Pacific, disappeared. This latter vessel had always used the Coast Guard automated merchant vessel reporting system

Amber, to report positions which is used in case of trouble or medical emergency. On this trip they did not have a radio operator and he omitted the reports, but they did some reports to AMB ER. Those reports are the only way to determine where the ship had been and what happened, until two crewmen were found afloat a small hatch cover.

The vessel has had an explicit scene had gone down very quickly with only these two men, who had been working forward in a separate compartment, as survivors. The Norwegians appreciated have a Coast Guard was able to assist in locating the ships, and wanted to wreck as a service in some way.

The method that the Norwegian used to honor the Coast Guard was to give me, the commentary, the declaration of the order of St. Olaf, which is a very large, prestigious, pretty metal. It was presented to me at the Norwegian Embassy, and followed by a lovely dinner at the embassy. We became quite friendly with the investor's wife, and sell them rather often after that, even when he left the service of his country and simply was a resident of Washington.

Suggested after that it would be appropriate for me to call on the King of Norway when I was in Europe. It went on the agenda for the next trip to your, which was finally set for the summer of 1976. I visited never countries to present prevent award presented awards to the captains of vessels that participated in the automatic vessel reporting system, and we were in Athens run Paris Copenhagen pay Stockholm and finally Oslo when we were there, we stayed with the American ambassador, we had met when he was appointed in Washington, it was a thrill, just to meet him since he was an astronaut before – – Bill Anders.

When we were at the embassy, hit many of his accommodations regarding his moonwalk out where they could be easily seen, and he was cited by many governments around the world.

When bidding I were told that we would be seeing the King, we are also tool would be appropriate to present something to him we whacked her brains to something we could present the king, and finally came up with the idea of presenting him with the print of snowboards maritime heritage of America, and shows the print of New Orleans, with a petal steam we weave a paddlewheel steamer, sailing vessel and in the distance the dome was St. Louis Cathedral, Scylla landmark in the city. We arrived at the castle, and have been told that we were expected to spend about 20 minutes Olaf

We met him, their only the three of us. I admitted before it can earn Washington warehouse, but I hadn't spent any great amount of time speaking to them. I found that he had a way of sort of giggling as he spoke, he had one Betty that he did this. It was a good thing, because he did it with almost every statement, and it was slightly unnerving.

We overstate or 20 minutes by about twice that amount. He enjoyed seeing the print we had brought comments that he had visited New Orleans and his family had been in the states during the war. We talked sailing quite a lot. And I knew that he was planning to go sailing that afternoon. The weather was lovely for sailing if there was enough when, and you certainly didn't have to worry about rain that summer; it was one of those rote summers where everything Europe was much too dry and hot. At the American Embassy, the trees returning Brown in July.

Who went through London our return trip to come home,

thereto, the weather was too hot. The grass in Hyde Park was brown, you really need in an umbrella, not Paris but to seek shade.

Early in 1976, the chief of personal had come to me and told me that he was receiving applications and inquiries about female cadets at the Academy. Think that that time there was no good reason, no economical way to use Academy trained officers. We had been training a number of officers at OCS, and some of them were very well-qualified for the duties we assign, but if an officer went to the Academy, was commissioned, what damage which you have over that OCS graduate?

Prolonging heart consideration we decided that it would there was no good reason to deny the opportunity of being a Academy graduate to woman, we declare that we would open the Academy to female cadets. The tablet comfort this action. There are many questions that needed answering, such as has have we provide for head facilities in the barracks? Should the women be segregated restricted to only a single section of the barracks? The real question which needed answering, but not immediate with the was weird he was side these well-qualified women to utilize their education?

The immediate question was resolved by the superintendent, the Academy itself. The women were spread throughout the building, and some Heather at adequate facilities made available. The stories I heard years later from the then superintendent, made me realize there were still many reasons why they should not have been integrated into the Cadet Corps as just so many more cadets. I spoke to the Cadet Corps every year about what was expected of them, and what the service is going to be doing, and I could not give a good answer to the question of where the women would be assigned when they graduate.

As 1976 came to an end, the elections that year told us there would be changed. I believe that Sec. Coleman was convinced that the Coast Guard personnel was so well-qualified, that it would make sense to have a deputy secretary for policy was a Coast Guard officer. There have been devoid of maritime matters in transportation and in other affairs, and I had been suggesting this is a solution. Of course the election made it clear that it would not happen with this administration, we look forward to a number new Democratic administration.

Brock Adamson's secretary designate, came to came in to meet me wait shortly after the first of the year. He told me, first that he would not want to military aid during the inaugural ceremonies. All the cabinet level officers are assigned during the inauguration, and Adams was coming in as the head of the department that included a military summer service, and he wanted no aide!

This is a real shock that he went on to say that he wanted no real military aide in his office after the games into serve. I didn't know I had a successor, but he never used Aden in all the time he was secretary. It made things much more difficult for the Coast Guard but some other administration may have said it made things smoother for them.

Just around the first of the year, also, there was a maritime casualty when the tank Argo Merchant when went aground on the Nantucket Island. It started spilling oil almost immediately, and the war the water was so cold that it came from the ship like chocolate mousse. The Coast Guard had developed the public system with huge river bladders to put the oil in, for situations just like this. The only problem knows how to get the pumps onto the ship – we did it but helicopters, – but even more, how can you heat the oil to a temperature sufficiently high to make pumping even hot possible.

He found an immersion heater some type, and arrange to have it put on the ship's deck by helicopter, but then the ship started to break up, we knew that the time to decently about the oil was limited. The great concern about the oil was it was drifting in the direction of Georges Bank, one of the richest fishing grounds near the American coast, it was shared by Canadian-American fishing vessels. Oil that stayed on the surface went on, all the way toward Iceland and would become before you reached your, but some of it probably sank into the water column around Georges Bank and this concerns. We lost the ship to the sea eventually, and found no result from the oil.

The equipment that was usable for navigating on the ship showed us once more how important it was for us to look at ships that wanted to come into an American port. We listed some required equipment, and some standards for meaning, and the ship's officers, and increase the rate of inspection of all foreign vessels and report, by shifting personnel around in the Coast Guard. I flew to Nantucket with the secretary on the plane while the ship still aground so we knew quite a bit about what had occurred.

As happen so often, politics got into the picture in the Senate decided to hold hearings regarding the Coast Guard's inspection of foreign vessels take her specifically. The secretary was asked to be the lead witness, followed by me, and in the chief of Marine safety, Mike bent Kurt. The secretary was given a prepared statement and then Sen. Magnuson and Sen. Hollings, staunch Democrats, started questioning him. I really thought at one point that Bill Coleman would be the seat go up to confront Magnuson personally, the discussion became so heated. Finally the hearing broke for lunch, and I was expected I expected I would be the next witness, but my statement.

That afternoon, took my seat is the witness, when Sen. Magnuson the chairman of the hearing said, quote we have a witness who cannot stay, so we would like to have him before your period appearance, Adm. Do you mind? New pair 'of course, you step back and let the committee order its own witnesses. I was back waiting for other witnesses for two days, while each of these labor and union witnesses said that the ship designed to be different inspection standards should be tightened.

We had maintained for some time that double bottoms and takers were not as viable as protective spaces and void areas near the bow, which would've been used to put quotes lops quote into, or left empty. The Exxon Valdez grounding force the hand of the Coast Guard in later years, but I still believe that the use of other protective spaces is better than just having a double bottom. A great far greater number of spills are caused by collisions between ships that are caused by groundings. Of course, there are ships which can be filled in only half the space because so much is reserved for protection and that's not very economical. Some of the witnesses said they believed that double bottoms were desirable, although their reasoning for these presentations was faulty. Magnuson let Mike and me set through all these long discussions, just cool your heels.

Finally, on the lunch break of the third day, I went to the chairman Magnuson and told him, and if you're not going to call me this afternoon, if's mother matters that must take care. I won't be here." He replied U quote do you mean this isn't the most important thing for you to do?" I respond, quote it is important, but not the only important thing I missed you. Quote any said quote we will call you this afternoon." He have one other witness to see how porch out the Coast Guard had been any cold me and I had Mike beside me for presentation.

We had owns the same conditions as the secretary, I'm not sure whether Mike had to call me down, but there were moments when I reached out to Mike to try to smooth feathers and slow down the flow of words. It was just a political show, it was kind of thing makes Congress less respected. Nothing came of the hearings, they just wanted to show their interest!

It was to short time after this when the new administration was to come in, and secretary Coleman. He wanted to make some presentations to his people before he left, and improve reparation, the question was asked of me weather it. I would rather have military decorations are the secretary of transportation metals. We thought about it, and have difficult society time deciding whether would mean more to us to have military metal more tour secretary we he appreciated so much to give us the transportation metals. We finally said the military ones.

On the data presentations are broader wives in, and metals were given to several of the staff, and then if I were presented not only the Coast Guard distinguished service medals, but the secretary of the transportation guild medal for outstanding achievement. It made a great ending to working with outstanding secretary. Sorry to see him go INSERT information about dad's retirement

US Coast Guard text only

01W Siler 1974 through 1978

Owen Wesley Siler was born on January 10, 1922, in Seattle, Washington. He was graduated from Santa Maria, California in 1938 and received an associate of arts degree from Santa Maria Junior College in 1940. Appointed the cadet in 19 July 19, he graduated from the US Coast Guard Academy, New London Connecticut with a bachelor of science degree in engineering and the commission's ensign on 9 June 1943 the usual for your quick curriculum having been short because of World War II.

From the Academy he was ordered to combat duty in the Pacific. On board the assault troop transport USS Hunter legate he took part in the invasion of Bougainville 1943 and other Pacific landings. During his two years of duty in that transport, he served as in various pellets including that of gunnery officer, assisted navigator, and deck watch officer. He was then transferred to the assault troop transport port USS Bayfield in July 1945. While on board to participate in the occupation of northern Honshu Japan, following the sort there of the Japanese.

On returning to the United States in April 1946, he served as personnel officer in the Manning section of Alameda training station, Californian insert for the remainder of the year as Navigator for the US for the cutter detainee out of Alameda. Bite January 1947 he was stationed his communications officer at the 11th Coast Guard District office at Long Beach California.

Assigned is a student aviator in June 1947 he took his flight training at the Naval air training bases at Corpus Christi Texas and Pensacola Florida. Yes served as next tour of duty at Coast Guard headquarters, Washington DC is a to the common tent, as well as administrative pilot from August 1954 to July 1959. During the following three years he's commanded the Coast Guard air Station at Corpus Christi Texas.

From August 1962 to August 1961, he served as chief, search and rescue branch, at the 17th Coast Guard District office in Juneau Alaska. From there he transferred to the Coast Guard air Station, Miami Florida where he's first served as executive officer for year and then his commanding officer for year. Under his command that station received a Coast Guard unit commendation for the Cuban Exodus operations during October and November 1965. During this period the air station was involved in 85 assistance cases and, with other Coast Guard units, help deliver 8100 refugees to Key West. Care paragraph after year of student work at the national war College from August 1966 to June 1967, he began his second tour of duty at US at Coast Guard headquarters in the post of chief, administrative management division. In February 1968 he was named assistant chief of staff or management, and one July 1969, soon the post of Deputy Chief of Staff. Meanwhile, he earned an MS degree in international affairs from George Washington University in 1968.

By nomination of the president in January 1971, and the approval of the Senate, then Capt. Siler was appointed to rank as permanent rear Adm. from one July 1971. Subsequently, he began his first assignment as flag officer in the post of commander, second Coast Guard District, St. Louis Missouri. For his service during that tour of duty, he received a meritorious service medal in 1972 for directing successful efforts to avert a potential major disaster near Louisville Kentucky were a barge filled with deadly chlorine had smashed into a dam. In May 1974 a week received the Legion of merit for his overall performance a second district enter.

Following his nomination by Pres. Ford in February 1974, where most ever succeeded retiring Adm. Chester R Bender, US CG, to the post accommodated the US Coast Guard with a rank. For for storage Adm., effective on June 1, 1974. He accomplished many significant things during his tenure's comedy. The first month this term solve the end of the 34 year old ocean station program. He instituted a minority recruiting program that substantially increase the representation of minorities in the service. Moreover, the distinctly unique new Coast Guard uniform made its appearance under him. Also, he was instrumental in arranging to have women cadet submitted to the Coast Guard Academy in the first female officer sent to flight training. Adm. Siler also prepared his service for its new responsibilities of congresses passage of the fisheries conservation and management act of 1976, which increase the Coast Guard serious jurisdiction to jurisdiction along the nation's coastline to over 2,000,000 mi.².

Enough significant occurrences to start December 1975, the processing of applications for the construction of deepwater ports in the Gulf of Mexico, which would give deep draft tankers access to the United States and help reduce the nation's fuel bills. In the fall of 1975, the Coast Guard again demonstrated its polar expertise, when three Coast Guard cutters and their helicopters escorted 15 barges around point Barrow to the North Slope region with more than five mill $500 million worth of equipment, including assembled seven-story modular buildings. Then in January 1976, the new polar ice breaker, US Coast Guard Cutter polar star was commissioned. 1975 strike team members at the request of the government of Japan, flew to Singapore to help stem the flow of wealth from the ground to take a Tinker show a barroom. A year earlier, in August 1974, the Chilean government heaters utilize similar assistance when the tanker my tool of when it the ground in the Strait of Magellan. Strike team members also assisted in the February 1976 cleanup operation falling at 250,000 gallon oil spill in Chesapeake Bay. Described as the worst of base history, it occurred when the store patrolling company barge ran aground in rough weather.

Early 1975, through chemical analysis or quote oil fingerprinting" of samples from 34 ships that were tested at the Coast Guard research and development Center at Groton Connecticut, because God was able to identify the polluter responsible for dumping 40,000 gallons of oil in the Florida Keys. This resulted in the rest the rest of the master of the Liberian flag tampered Corbis. In November 1974 the Coast Guard but pleaded 275 miles of Florida's East Coast as a means of curbing drug smuggling, this is the first time in American waters have been blockaded since prohibition. Before July 1976, Coast Guard Cutter Eagle probably lived worlds tall ships in a bicentennial salute to America New York as part of operation sale. Strong emphasis on the Coast Guard's Marine environmental protection – MEP – program during the 70s, much of it during Adm. Siler's tenures, Dan. A plethora of will take her mishaps during the winter of 1976 – 1977 brought the effectiveness of the MEP program under close scrutiny of the concerned media and the public. Although the grounding of the Argo merchant – a Liberian taker that spilled some 7.5 million gallons of oil off into island – forced new attention to the MEP program and sparked presidential initiatives for pollution prevention, much of had already been accomplishing the groundwork for implementing the president's policy already existed. Oil fingerprinting to identify polluters in airborne surveillance method had been developed. These is highly skilled in specialty trained Coast Guard personnel, ready to respond to pollution incidents – strike teams – also greatly expanded. In fact the strike teams have an international reputation. Responding to requests from the governments of Norway, Chile, Japan, Colombia, and Ecuador, they fought pollution in the North Sea, streets Magellan and Malachi and the Pacific Ocean.

Following the Carter initiated in March 1977, new regulations were present would require, for certain vessels, double bottoms, segregated ballasts, improved emergency steering systems, inert gas systems, and backup radar and collision avoidance equipment. At the February 1978 international convention on tanker safety and pollution prevention in London, the only deviation from the Coast Guard proposals agreed to assist substitution of crude oil washing systems and protectively located six gated ballast tanks. This was instead of double bottoms for new tankers in the exemption of small product curious from the segregated ballast requirements. The Masters agreed the measures agreed to at the conference were contained in new protocols, one of which supplemented the 1974 safety of life at Sea convention in a second which incorporated a modified in 1973 Marine pollution convention.

The pollution the prevention aspect of environmental concerns also have their effect on the Coast Guard commercial vessel safety import safety programs during the four years. Increased emphasis on pollution prevention greatly expanded workloads in this field. In addition to the proposed regulations already mentioned in legislation enacted prior to the Argo merchant's grounding, facial vessel traffic services to reduce the risk of collisions, groundings, and Ramming's became operational in Puget Sound, Prince William sound in Alaska, San Francisco, Houston – Galveston, Burwood Bay, New Orleans. These increased demands required the Coast Guard, not only assume greater workloads for personnel, but also to identify more efficient ways of using these personnel and their equipment. An excellent example of this was the combining of nearly 40 captains of the port in Marine inspection offices into the new Marine safety offices that were better able to meet the related needs of environmental protection maritime safety.

All public awareness of the Coast Guard and its missions are greatly enhanced during the Siler air, one of the major challenges faced by the service provided the best vessel for image enhancement. The preparation for and implementation of the new 200 mile fishery conservation zone created by fisheries conservation and management act of 1976 – F CMA – not only placed increased demands on personnel and equipment, and also press the Coast Guard into the national media spotlight. Despite some pre—FC M a phobia concerning potential potential confrontations over fishing on the high seas within the zone and some skepticism of the Coast Guard's ability to do the job, implementation of the act went smoothly. During the first year of enforcement, approximately 2400 boardings of foreign and domestic vessels were conducted more than 500 citations for minor violations were issued in 250 civil penalty actions were initiated in case of more serious infractions. During the early months of enforcement, three foreign vessels receives results resulting in the assessment of criminal and civil fines totaling $580,000. In the edition in addition, in February 1978, Japanese fish this fishing vessel was saved for deliberately trolling in a closed area. 16 tenet of illicit catch from another foreign vessel were also seized in early 1977.

Perhaps the most apparent result of the US fisheries management rose must decline in observed foreign fishing activities. The foreign fishing effort was down to a 12 nation operation with five fewer countries and 35% fewer vessels involved since the FCM A went into effect. Overall, the attitude of foreign fishermen toward the regulations was excellent and it was apparent that they're trying to comply with F CMA and cooperate with enforcement personnel. During March/ April 1977, the first two months of enforcement, violations were detected on 50% of the foreign fishing vessels boarded. This percentage decreased only 13%, and those these were only minor infractions of the regulations, in July and August. Thus with fewer infractions the trend in conformity with the law continue

Yet another challenging expansive expansion of its responsibilities three missile years with the Coast Guard's growing involvement in drug interdiction activities. Although anti-smuggling efforts were historical Coast Guard role, there had been little modern activity in this area until 1976. This is when increased cooperation with the Drug Enforcement Administration the US customs service so Coast Guard interdiction efforts rise significantly. In the three years preceding 1976 Coast Guard efforts resulted in the seizure of 24 vessels and narcotics valued at $72 million. But in 1976 alone, 20 $630 million worth of narcotics seas. The services renewed emphasis on drug interdiction operations continued throughout 1977 and by years end, Coast Guard units cease to participate in the seizure 52 Vestal vessels and the legal drugs of the street value of over $400 million.

In a related area test group for the prosecution of vessel hijackings were formed in October 1977. This group develop procedures for the identification and prosecution of vessel hijacking cases and problem promulgate periodic advisory suggesting procedures that got yachtsmen could take to minimize sustainability to hijacking. Although the actual number of concern hijackings is low, Adm. Siler had stated quote any incident involving the taking and controlling of the vessel and personnel aboard by force or threat of force is a serious metaphor concerning action." In addition to creating the task force he issued new guidelines intended to make the Coast Guard more responsive to vessel theft victims and the service now will provide, within its jurisdictional authority and resource capability, as much assistance in stolen vessel cases as possible

The shift in emphasis among Coast Guard programs was visible in a you quite the way and the aids to navigation program. Maintenance and operation of aids to navigation traditionally has been a manual operation. For many decades, the men lighthouse or lightship was the major component of the a time program. This function, however, had been undergoing a continuous monitoring modernization process and became highly automated with most lighthouses mean and mean to miss lightship's being replaced by large navigation GUIs are up offshore light structures. In addition the role of radio aids rapidly extend. This automation process enable the redistribution of personnel to more critical areas. In 1974 Lori – see was designated as a government – provided primary Marine navigation system for use in the coastal confluence zone CCC of the United States in the Great Lakes. The Coast Guard move steadily toward completion of the Lori – see system in the CCC and the Great Lakes through the Lori – see national implementation plan. This plan was part of the Department of Transportation's national plan for navigation. New paragraph the chain serving the unites states West Coast, Canadian West Coast, the Gulf of Alaska were completed, and in operation. These for the firm first the ran chains constructed specifically for civil use. The Canadian Coast Guard constructed a Lori – see station at Williams Lake, British Columbia. The station operated with two United States stations to form the Canadian West Coast ran – see chain and represented the first time in which another country, at its own initiative and express expense, joined the United States in providing ran – see service. There are several ran see stations established on foreign soil to meet Department of Defense requirements, however, the stations were operated at the expense of the United States.

When he became, Dan, one of the aims of Adm. Siler was to revitalize a Coast Guard aging capital plan. 3303 Thomasville Road, Suite 201 these became increasingly difficult to manage and costly to maintain. Six of the high endurance cutters had been built in 1936 and five medium interns cutters have been around since the mid-1940s. Most of the medium – range aircraft were nearing the end of their operational effectiveness. His efforts revitalize the fleet in reverse the trend were successfully. What strong efforts were made to reduce federal expenditures. The urgency of the Coast Guard's need web needs was presented so the Department of Transportation, the Office of Management and Budget, and Congress clearly recognized. This resulted in the commencement of historic replacement program. This included two new 399 – put polar ice breakers in the construction of a new hundred and 40 foot tugs with domestic icebreaking capabilities. In addition a new class of hundred and 60 foot construction tenders were built. These tenders were nearly 70% faster, had a smaller crew, require 10% less maintenance than the tenders they replace. Contracts for four new 27 270 foot medium endurance cutters were awarded. New 41 motor 41 foot motor boat motor lifeboats and 32 foot ports and waterways boats were also brought into the inventory. In addition the service refurbish the hundred and 80 foot buoy tenders in the 90 foot patrol boats. Search and rescue stations at Rock Island Maine, Mena mesh Massachusetts; Fort Myers Florida in Bayfield Wisconsin were renovated while a new station was constructed in Provincetown, Massachusetts. The same the stations it seemed indigos on Chesapeake Bay and, Destin, and Fort Lauderdale also became operational. These latter improvements resulted from Adm. Siler's feeling that quote the time had come when we must address the shore plan. Continued deterioration in these. In this area forces expenditure of funds on inefficient patchwork repairs, detracts from operational efficiency, and forces or personnel to continue to live and work in an unsatisfactory, and wholesome, and often unsafe environment." The role of women in the Coast Guard also expanded dramatically during Apple Silas four years is, Dan. Under his direction the Coast Guard get away with many of the old. As to the career fields women could counter. The Coast Guard Academy in New London Connecticut was the first the military service academies to announce acceptance of women cadets. In January 1976 the first female Coast Guard flight student reported for training and earned her wings in early 1977. The second woman pilot completed her from flight training later that year.

A significant development in the role during the Siler years was to decide to assign women officers and enlisted personnel to both seek seagoing and isolated bullets. Four officers and 20 enlisted men served aboard this 378 foot high endurance cutters Gala Tyne and Morgan Ball. Many shore stations also had mixed gender crews.

There are numerous other accomplishments during this either command and see. These included the licensing of deepwater ports off Louisiana and Texas; the development, 1976, the most comprehensive precatory package of safety standards ever devised for recreational boats; the expanded use of the Coast Guard auxiliary's for search and rescue and ricotta patrols; enlightened deployment of reservationist to augment regular forces and normal missions in emergencies; an ever increasing role in international affairs, including negotiations on the law the seam partition dissipation in IMC oh, the intergovernmental Marine consultant tip organization, which is the maritime branch of the United Nations; and the day-to-day struggle to remain quote always ready quote whatever the mission.

The traditionally the Coast Guard is simply the quote humanitarian service," the waterborne rescue agency of the federal government, did not disappear during the Siler years, but it was altered. All the search and rescue are still the quote bread-and-butter" mission of the Coast Guard, legislators and the general public obtained a broader perspective as a service. It can be recognized as a leader in marine environmental protection, law enforcement agency with which to be reckoned, conservation conscious protector of our maritime resource are Marine resources of the major force doesn't other roles at the public thereto for unaware.

On the 30 May 30, 1978, Admiral Owen W Siler closed 35 years 35 Coast Guard career retired. One of the characteristics of the Coast Guard was a Coast Guard's rapid growth responsibilities and resulted shift in program emphasis. While experiencing only modest growth in personnel, service under Adm. Siler's leadership, with successful meetings expanding missions by redirecting resources, improving techniques and making maximum use of personnel and equipment. Over

Overall, the Siler years were four years of change in expansion, challenging growth, marked by active accomplishment. Adm. Owen Wesley Siler is the Coast Guard a legacy of inspired leadership in which he was justifiably proud. The following is a resume of Apple Silas appointments and rank: Cadet, July 19, 1940; Ensign,, July 9, 1943; Lieut. JG, April 1, 1944; Lieut., November 1, 1945; Lieut. Cmdr., August 26, 1952; Cmdr., July 1, 1959; Capt., July 1, 1965; rear Adm., July 1, 1971; Adm., June 1, 1974. Furthermore Adm. Siler's metals and awards included,: Coast Guard distinguished service medal 1977; Sec. of transportation award for outstanding achievement – 1977;

Legion of merit – 1974; meritorious service medal – 1972; Coast Guard unit commendation – 1965; Norwegian order of St. Olaf, commission commanders rank – 1976; World War II campaign service medal and ribbons – American defense service; American area; Asiatic Pacific; World War II victory; nasally occupation service – Asia; also the national defense services mental Korea Korean and Vietnam. Compiled March 2000.